Telecommunications, Transportation, and Location

TRANSPORT ECONOMICS, MANAGEMENT AND POLICY

Series Editor: Kenneth Button, *Professor of Public Policy, School of Public Policy, George Mason University, USA*

Transport is a critical input for economic development and for optimizing social and political interaction. Recent years have seen significant new developments in the way that transport is perceived by private industry and governments, and in the way academics look at it.

The aim of this series is to provide original material and up-to-date synthesis of the state of modern transport analysis. The coverage embraces all conventional modes of transport but also includes contributions from important related fields such as urban and regional planning and telecommunications where they interface with transport. The books draw from many disciplines and some cross disciplinary boundaries. They are concerned with economics, planning, sociology, geography, management science, psychology and public policy. They are intended to help improve the understanding of transport, the policy needs of the most economically advanced countries and the problems of resource-poor developing economies. The authors come from around the world and represent some of the outstanding young scholars as well as established names.

Titles in the series include:

European Union Port Policy
The Movement Towards a Long-Term Strategy
Constantinos I. Chlomoudis and Athanasios A. Pallis

Structural Change in Transportation and Communications in the Knowledge Society
Edited by Kiyoshi Kobayashi, T.R. Lakshmanan and William P. Anderson

Globalisation, Policy and Shipping
Fordism, Post-Fordism and the European Union Maritime Sector
Evangelia Selkou and Michael Roe

Cost–Benefit Analysis and Evolutionary Computing
Optimal Scheduling of Interactive Road Projects
John H.E. Taplin, Min Qiu, Vivian K. Salim and Renlong Han

The Future of Automated Freight Transport
Concepts, Design and Implementation
Edited by Rob Konings, Hugo Priemus and Peter Nijkamp

Telecommunications, Transportation and Location
Kenneth Button and Roger Stough with Michelle Bragg and Samantha Taylor

Competition in the Railway Industry
An International Comparative Analysis
Edited by José A. Gómez-Ibáñez and Ginés de Rus

Telecommunications, Transportation, and Location

Kenneth Button
University Professor of Public Policy
George Mason University, Fairfax, USA

Roger Stough
NOVA Chair of Public Policy
George Mason University, Fairfax, USA

with

Michelle Bragg
Wellesley College, Wellesley, USA

Samantha Taylor
Victoria State Government, Melbourne, Australia

TRANSPORT ECONOMICS, MANAGEMENT AND POLICY

Edward Elgar
Cheltenham, UK • Northampton, MA, USA

Published by
Edward Elgar Publishing Limited
Glensanda House
Montpellier Parade
Cheltenham
Glos GL50 1UA
UK

Edward Elgar Publishing, Inc.
136 West Street
Suite 202
Northampton
Massachusetts 01060
USA

A catalogue record for this book
is available from the British Library

ISBN-13: 978 1 84064 846 1
ISBN-10: 1 84064 846 5

Printed and bound in Great Britain by MPG Books Ltd, Bodmin, Cornwall

Contents

List of Figures   vi
List of Tables   viii
Preface   ix

1   Introduction   1
2   Social Change and Mobility   16
3   Some Basic Economic Considerations   41
4   Telecommunications and Travel Behavior   60
5   Videoconferencing and Work Travel   90
6   The Business of E-commerce   112
7   Telecommunications and Intelligent Transportation Systems   137
8   Telecommunications and the 'New Geography'   155

References   173
Index   183

List of Figures

2.1	US national economic and transport trends	22
2.2	The notion of the value chain	34
3.1	Williamson's characterization of where institutions become important	43
3.2	Connectivity and interconnectivity	46
3.3	Optimal networks	49
3.4	Positive network externalities	50
3.5	Pre-deregulation airline route structure	52
3.6	Post-US deregulation hub-and-spoke airline route structure	53
3.7	Decreasing costs and the empty core problem	57
4.1	Substitution, enhancement, and synergies	64
4.2	The constrained interaction curve and telecommunications	67
4.3	Potential savings to employers from teleworking	86
5.1	Various workplace communications interfaces	94
5.2	Work induced interactions	96
5.3	The costs of videoconferencing	97
5.4	Telecommunications–travel cost trade-offs	99
5.5	The classic product life-cycle	101
5.6	Videoconferencing in Switzerland (public studios, 1989/90 in minutes per year)	102
5.7	Videoconferencing by large Swiss chemical firms (hours per month, 1991)	102
5.8	Examples of organizational structures	107
6.1	Typology of electronic commerce definitions	115
6.2	Structure of the transportation chain	122
6.3	Traditional and emergent distribution systems	124
6.4	Outsourced logistics in the US by revenue	126
6.5	Warehousing and warehouse and trucking/courier in the Washington–Baltimore consolidated MSA	129
6.6	Warehouse and trucking/courier locations in the Baltimore MSA	129
6.7	Warehouse locations, and warehouse and trucking/courier locations in the Detroit MSA	130
6.8	Warehouse and trucking/courier locations in core area of Detroit	130
6.9	Optimal security expenditure	133
8.1	The 'concentric' pattern of urban land use	161
8.2	The 'axial' pattern of urban land use	162

| 8.3 | Simple representation of the edge city concept | 164 |
| 8.3 | The space–time prism concept | 167 |

List of Tables

2.1   US passenger miles (millions)   17
2.2   US Gross Domestic Product attributable to transportation
      final demand (chained 1996 $billions)   18
2.3   Retail new car sales in the US (thousands)   21
2.4   Average length of haul – domestic US freight and passenger
      in miles   23
2.5   Principal means of transportation to work (percent by mode)   24
2.6   Penetration levels of teleworking   33
2.7   US federal, state, and local government transportation-related
      revenues and expenditures (fiscal years $million chained
      to 1996 prices)   39
4.1   Comparison of traditional and boundary less careers   65
4.2   Teleworking in EU countries   71
4.3   Types of technology advances and their areas of impact   76
4.4   The nature of the potential costs and benefits of telework   77
4.5   Stated preferences for telecommuting program (percentage
      of responses)   82
4.6   The most congested US urban areas   87
5.1   Elements of the long-run average total costs of meetings
      by videoconference and through travel   97
5.2   Factors likely to influence the future use of videoconferencing   100
5.3   Uses made of videoconferencing in the UK   105
5.4   Users of videoconferencing in Switzerland   106
6.1   Major legal changes to US transport regulations 1976–89   113
6.2   Shifts in the business model from physical to electronic markets   117

Preface

The last decades of the twentieth century saw a considerable change in the way people lived and worked, and how industry provided goods and services. The rapid and wide-ranging changes that had been taking place in telecommunication technology began to have a profound effect in all types of society. This book was motivated by a feeling that the implications of these changes for transportation are still not fully understood but are inevitably going to have on-going consequences for the way we live and work.

The subject matter of the book is also a reflection the more general interest within the School of Public Policy at George Mason University in the ways in which society is changing, the ways in which technology is being transferred and used, and in the appropriate public policy responses to these changes. There is also an interest not only in the way public policy may evolve, but also in the ways in which it may be implemented. Indeed the School has within it's Center for Transportation Policy, Operations and Logistics, the US Center of Excellence for the Implementation of Intelligent Transportation Systems that has a strong focus on the institutional aspects of transportation policy and the role of ITS within the larger transportation framework.

The book initially grew out of one element of the Center of Excellence's work on transportation – the part that has focused on role that communications has in influencing transportation demand and travel behavior. The primary interest being stimulated by the mounting traffic congestion problems that have emerged as the Northern Virginian economy has grown. The proximity to Washington, coupled with a very vibrant high-technology economy has led to the region's population expanding rapidly but with only limited new transportation infrastructure becoming available. Congestion has thus become a serious practical and political issue.

As one of its activities, the Center has been active in looking at the role that telecommunications can play in both managing this traffic growth and also seeking ways of ensuring the region can enjoy its full, economic potential without much more traffic growth. The book is not a case study of this work, but rather the Northern Virginia experience provides a stimulus for the effort that has gone into it.

The book has taken several years to surface. During that time the work has benefited from the input of several people and we would particularly like to acknowledge the contribution of Samantha Taylor whilst she was a Visiting

Fellow at George Mason and of Michelle Bragg who worked on a number of key related projects.

Kenneth Button
Roger Stough

1 INTRODUCTION

1.1 INTRODUCTION

The world is in a state of continual change. Part of this is due to the natural elements. Climatic variations, both in the short and long term have always existed, and over time the movements of the planet's tectonic plates have created continents and forged landscapes. Mankind has only been around for a fraction of the earth's existence but he has been responsible for significant physical changes affecting the biodiversity of the planet, and, to some extent, the Earth's geography. But this has also been responsible for altering the way that he lives.

While part of this latter impact has been accidental, or perhaps subconscious, other elements have been more deliberate. They have been the product of the vast range of institutions that mankind has developed to facilitate his existence and forge his current dominance. Therefore, many changes have been unlike changes linked to other animal species. Society has more generally as a result of this, evolved over time in response to an interaction of institutional and technical change, as well as external natural forces.

There is something of a popular belief that the twentieth century saw the most rapid changes to date, and that the twenty-first century will see an acceleration of this process. There may be some truth in this, but what is often neglected are the profound shifts that have occurred in the past due to military conquest or technology changes that altered the way large parts of mankind lived. Printing led to tremendous changes in communications and was instrumental in the fragmentation of the Christian Church in Western Europe, whilst the earlier Roman conquests in Europe and the Mongol campaigns in Asia brought massive social changes within very short periods – indeed, these were times of the first globalizations. It also seems unlikely that large parts of the world could currently be populated without the advent of air conditioning.

The objective of this book is to examine some of the changes that are taking place during the early part of the twenty-first century. Some see this period as potentially being a time of radical social upheaval, at least as significant as the Renaissance and the Industrial Revolution, that will have impacts into the foreseeable future. Following this line, we are moving into the 'Information Age', and are perhaps already part way through it. Others take the view that all this is part of a continual Darwinian evolution that has its own nuances and peculiarities but that its genesis can be traced to an ongoing process of change.[1]

We are less concerned with the 'big picture', although it is certainly germane to our discussions. Our focus is more limited in this book. The technological changes, and their associated social effects, that are taking place may well be wide ranging and permeating many aspects of life. The interest here is centered on the changes that are taking place with regard to telecommunications and the way that it is affecting transportation and travel behavior, and, together with this, its longer term implications for land use and location choices.

It is not concerned with technology *per se* but rather the ramifications of technological change and, to a somewhat lesser degree, the forces that forge it.[2] Also while it is intellectually interesting to look at the big picture, the issue of whether we are currently in a social and technological revolution or merely a phase of something that is more of an ongoing phenomenon is not at the core of the book. From the contemporary documentation of the time it does not seem that those engaged in the Renaissance, the Industrial Revolution or other eras of sea changes that were isolated by later historians were actually cognizant of the importance of what was happening around them. Contemporary views, it transpires, often deviate from retrospective historical interpretations.

The remainder of the chapter concerns itself with offering some contextual background to the book and placing it in a larger setting. It is important to appreciate that the material discussed in the volume is only looking at a part, albeit possibly a very important part, of the ways in which developments in telecommunications and transportation are affecting people's lives. It looks at the more direct links but in doing so, it is a clear simplification of what may be more profound causal effects.

1.2 THE CONTEXT

1.2.1 The emerging information world

Advanced communications technologies are growing and evolving at a very rapid rate. Penetration rates of mobile phones are expanding around the world while household Internet access in the US is at about 70% of all homes. Links in the workplace appear almost ubiquitous. Globally, the number of people with access

---

[1]   Memmot (1963) was one of the first to examine the substitutability of telecommunications for transport. Brög (1984) offers some early insights into some of the intellectual and empirical difficulties of studying this dynamic process. A useful set of papers is to be found in Stough et al. (2003).

[2]   Garrison and Deakin (1988) and Banister and Stead (2004) offer brief overviews of some of these linkages.

to the Internet and Worldwide Web is growing and, if the stock market is a reflection of future expectations, is still seen as the world's most dynamic sector.

The take-off of the Internet was relatively rapid. Even in 1999 some 17% of US homes used the Internet for purchasing goods and services (although over half spent more than $500), and online and business-to-consumer (B-to-C) transactions were worth about $20 billion. This compared with 10% in the UK, 9% in Canada, and 2% in Italy. Some 2% of the US travel transactions were done over the Internet in 1999, and that figure has grown considerably. In terms of physical movements a study by Forrester Research shows that 20% of package traffic in the US is by electronic retailers (Gardiner, 2000). There has been significant growth since then. For example, in 2003 over 64% of Canadian households were using the Internet regularly from home, school, work, library or another location. At the same time 50% of Europeans used the Internet that year, with more than 82% of these connecting to the Web weekly and nearly 40% of users making purchases on-line (excluding banking transactions) annually, and over 45% for making travel arrangements.

Although Internet commerce is still relatively limited, it is clearly growing rapidly, and Internet commerce is having a significant impact on the supply chain – one US organization suggested growth in consumer purchases over the Internet of 2500%, between 1997 and 2001, albeit from a very low base (Konezny and Beskow, 1999). The most popular purchases over the Internet are books, CDs, electrical components and those goods perceived as having a known quality.

The phenomenon is also certainly not purely American. As early as 1994 1.2 million French were buying over the Web compared to 0.8 million in the US at the same time. Now, although the US has pulled away from Europe, retails over the World-wide Web in Europe amount to well over $3.6 billion (Peet, 1999).

The largest growth though is in business-to-business (B-to-B) transactions that now amount to well over $114 billion annually in the US or about 80% of total Internet transactions (Cohn and Brady, 2000). Ford, DaimlerChrysler, and General Motors, for example, have transferred all their purchases to the Web via a single e-hub exchange for auto parts and General Electric has been rapidly moving in that direction. Internationally, Sears, Roebuck and Carrefour have moved to an Internet retail exchange to handle the $80 billion they spend annually with suppliers.

One explanation for these developments is that B-to-B transactions are purely commercial in their orientation, there is no utility involved in the act of shopping *per se*, and because of their frequency of purchase, buying generally involves a known quality. They effectively cut transactions and search costs. In contrast, consumers often enjoy the act of shopping and require non-quantitative information about products. That is largely why, although as many as 40% of car buyers consulted the Internet at some point, only 2.7% of new car sales in the US in 1999 took place on-line.

Simultaneously, as Internet use has risen physical traffic volumes are also constantly growing; congestion and environmental issues are causing major political and social concerns in the US and Europe (UK Royal Commission on Environmental Pollution, 1994). Road traffic has grown in all countries. With the widespread growth of urban sprawl, however, public transit is seldom a viable alternative for the car and with limited scope for additional road building in most cities, alternative transportation solutions are being sought. Further, while much of the local pollution associated with the automobile has been considerably reduced through the adoption of new technologies, it has not been eliminated and the problem of greenhouse gas emissions remains.

In response to these concerns, public authorities in countries like Australia, the UK and the US have launched travel awareness initiatives, predominantly aimed at increasing individuals' and firms' 'susceptibility to change'; in other words encouragements to change their travel patterns. Alternatives may take the form of teleworking, transit, non-motorized transport or car-pooling. The European Union (EU) has wider initiatives aimed at fostering a system of what it considers 'sustainable transport' (Commission of the European Communities, 1992). This seeks to establish policy packages of sticks and carrots that would stimulate the use of alternatives to the automobile. A large part of the effort is the correction of transportation prices and taxes to reflect externality costs.

In the US there is a greater overt, as well as a popular, interest in the ability for advanced technology to contribute to alleviating traffic congestion. This includes intelligent transportation systems but also the use of technological alternatives to travel. Inherently, the American culture is proudly car dependent and the US urban form is very different to many European cities. There are fewer desirable alternatives available so a slightly different emphasis to that in Europe is required. This is not to say that the results from Europe and the UK are not relevant to the US, but rather, they are not always entirely portable across the Atlantic.

1.2.2 Predicting change

The literature on the 'information age' is large and, like the universe seems to be ever growing. The origins of the 'Big Bang' in information systems are equally as contentious as those of its mega counterpart. Despite increasing interest in the notion of an information and knowledge age, we really still have little by way of a comprehensive picture of what is actually happening, or of the exact nature of the underlying causal links that have stimulated the changes that we see around us.

That technology is exerting a powerful influence we witness everyday as meetings are interrupted by the sharp ring (or the less than melodic sound of an electronic tune) of cell phones, as we dash to see what e-mails have arrived, or as our cars grind to a halt because one of its myriad of engine control microchips has failed. But putting hard numbers on how these changes have, for example, affected national income has proved elusive even for Alan Greenspan at the US Federal Reserve.

This is perhaps not all that surprising. Most academic work is very good at explaining, or perhaps 'interpreting' would be a better word, what has occurred in the past, albeit often after some time has elapsed. But it is far less good at identifying what is happening now and even worse at predicting future turning points. The best statistical bet on any stock exchange, for example, still seems to be to assume tomorrow will be like today.

Also much of the effort at exploring events has been driven more by concerns about the technology involved than with the role of economics, and the implications of social and psychological factors.

Indeed, there was a period quite recently when it was fashionable to dismiss conventional economic thinking as dated and inappropriate for the 'New Age'. Technological advances and the information society had, so it was argued, made traditional economic concerns with business cycles obsolete, and expanding output into the future would mean no more concerns about such things as national budget deficits.

Subsequent events, and in particular the sudden slowing of the US economy in 2000 and the dramatic fall in the value of high-technology companies (the 'Dot-com' companies), sent the newspapers pundits, government advisors, management science gurus, and industry wisely reconsidering the situation. Traditional economists were proven right and they had lived up to their reputation of being 'dismal scientists'.

As Robert Rubin (2003), the former US Treasury Secretary, recently argued more generically, there is no certainty in the world and the wisest actions are based on accepting that outcomes are inevitably unknown in advance. There may be changes in situations but the world is complex and this makes for inevitable uncertainty. This poses problems not only of how to prepare for suddenly changes, but also what sort of approach should be adopted towards remedial action once any unforeseen event has taken place.

There remains the fundament question of whether there has been a genuine information revolution in either the cultural sense of the Italian Renaissance of the fifteenth century, or of an economic kind generally associated with such structural changes as the UK's Industrial Revolution of the late eighteenth century. How a revolution is defined poses problems in its own right. While political revolutions can be quite rapid and transparent – the French demonstrated that rather well in 1789, and the Russians in 1917 – economic and social revolutions are generally longer term, sometimes extending into centuries, and are more difficult to discern by those involved.

Short-term factors can often be mistaken for structural shifts and history is full of 'bubbles' that have been hailed by gurus as fundamental changes only to burst and later to be seen as nothing but hot air. Even when the changes have been fundamental, such as those associated with the UK 'Railway Mania' in the mid nineteenth century, the public reaction may be overblown and excesses result. That there is still debate, and learned books periodically published, about when (and by some, 'if') the Industrial Revolution took place simply highlights the challenge. In contrast, Americans seem to have no trouble in defining when and, albeit perhaps to a slightly lesser degree, what their political revolution was in the eighteen century.

1.2.3 The information revolution

The notion of an information revolution is widely held, and not only in the popular press that inevitably seeks simple classifications. It is seen to be a special period in history because of a number of factors.

There has been a rapid and widespread adoption of computer technology; changes in the nature of employment for many people and, in particular, a significant expansion of the service sector; an enhanced range of personal and business communications technologies; and a widening of geographical markets with fuller economic participation. Concomitant to this, most would agree that these changes have largely been beneficial, albeit not to everyone. These are certainly discernable features but do they constitute a revolution akin to that of the Industrial Revolution, or are they simply a phase, perhaps an accelerated phase, of a longer-term process?

We take it as axiomatic that some changes are taking place in the way that information is now made available, that there is now more information in the public and private domain, and that information is now handled differently. But one may also look at this from a slightly different perspective. Developments regarding information may themselves only be part, and even an outcome, of wider social shifts and only attract immediate attention because of immediate visibility. There are also ongoing, and major geopolitical shifts occurring as capitalism has emerged as the major political and economic structure over large parts of the globe. The information effect may in this way be seen as an outcome of another revolution rather than being a driver of change.

There are many ways one could argue this. For example, the freer markets, and the need to more fully exploit the economic resources that are accompanying this, could be seen as permitting and stimulating the information age. There are important social changes taking place, for example, in terms of the role of women. The growth of female participation in political processes and their expanded activity rates in the formal economy could be seen as necessitating complementary shifts in information systems.

One could also argue that more effective ways of handling information are necessary as the global population expands and other resources become scarcer. A natural market reaction to this inevitably more complex situation is to improve the coordination of the ways in which production is carried out. This requires more and better information.

The book does not dwell at any length on these interesting macro/macro topics but focuses on the narrower, meso-matter of the direct effect of improved information systems on transportation and, through this, on to land use and locations patterns. The factors driving the information age are essentially treated as exogenous in the discussions that follow.

In doing this, however, it needs to be fully appreciated that things are currently far from being in long-term equilibrium, if indeed long-term equilibriums exist. Many of the newest innovations and applications of telecommunications, and *ipso facto* their potential implications for transportation and land use, are likely to be transient as the market adjusts. Some products will be driven from the market, others will metamorphose, and new ones will be born. Isolating the longer-term implications is not easy in this type of situation.

1.2.4 Computer technology

That there have been major changes in the efficiency of computers is unquestionable. How this can be measured in purely technical terms is less simple but worth briefly commenting on. Computer power (in economic terms this may be seen as the price of computing) can be measured either in terms of performance in carrying out a given task, or as the prices of inputs or components of a computer. Economists often focus on the later – e.g., on the cost of semi-conductors – using hedonic prices frameworks. But this really misses the point that output is almost always the best performance guide.

The underlying problem with looking at performance in computing is that computers are now capable of performing many more tasks than previously. Simply using a Laspeyres's type of index comparing say how fast a set of calculations could be completed 10 years ago to the time it takes now does not really say much about genuine performance. It is simply not a comparison of like with like. Not only can a more modern machine do basic tasks faster it can do many more tasks and, important from an economic assessment, perspective it is being asked to actually do more tasks.

In an effort to come to grips with these complexities, Nordhaus (2002) assessed a benchmark minimum performance indicator that shows performance of computers in constant dollar terms improved by a factor in the order of 1 to 5 trillion in the twentieth century – a compound growth rate of 30% to 35% per annum. Much of the growth in performance of computers came after 1940 at a compound rate of some 50% a year.

Of course not all of this performance increase has been exploited, and exploitation has varied across activities and sectors. In terms of our interests, what has occurred in recent years is that the Internet, and other developments in the collection and dissemination of information, has reduced the costs of many market type interactions. History tells us that the immediate effects of such developments are largely incremental. Basically it is much easier and cheaper to do the things that we are already doing. New technologies are risky and we are reluctant to change because of the uncertainties involved.

Change also generally involves incurring stranded costs as technically functional technologies are replaced by new, more cost effective technologies. In practice, being rational economists, and accepting the notion that bygones should be treated as bygones, is often not easy. It is also often different groups that benefit from the new technologies and others that are left with the stranded costs.

This raises distributional questions in some cases and, perhaps more often, leads to the latter seeking restitution or a more gradual path of change.

In the case of communications there are also important network economies involved – for example, others need a telephone before it is worth me getting one – and these take time to emerge and for society to develop institutional forms that allow for their exploitation. But over time, and despite these challenges, there are important income and substitution effects that affect the entire way that things are done, the choice set that is available, and the overall level of activities that are possible.[3]

There are also a variety of feedback loops, often of a more macro nature to consider. These can include such things as enhanced productivity and the ability to exploit new management techniques that push up the entire level of activity in an economy. Basically there are perpetuity effects that accompany significant structure changes that are difficult to quantify but perhaps are the factors that actually identify a genuine 'Revolution'. In traditional economic terms, they result in a shift in the production possibility frontier rather than just movements around an existing frontier.

While the chapters that follow put some flesh on the complexities of these various stages in terms of telecommunications interaction with transportation, some brief introductory comments on the topic are justified at this point. The

---

[3]   The introduction of the motor car into a family's choice set provides a fairly standard illustration of the implications of a new technology in the short to medium term. In the very basic model set out below, the total utility of a household at a fixed location without a car (e.g., before cars were invented) can be denoted as U_0 and that of a household at the same location that owns a car as U_1. Their respective utility functions can be described as:

$$U_0 = U(y, T - \sum_{k \in D_0} r_{ik}X_{ik}, X_{ik}) \text{ and } U_1 = U(y - p, \sum_{k \in D_1} T - s_{ik}Z_{ik}, Z_{ik})$$

where, y is the total disposable income of the household, p is the annual cost of owning and operating a car (assumed independent of the number of trips), r_k and s_k are travel times from location i to location k, without and with a car respectively (money costs of travel being disregarded), T is the available household leisure time, X_k is the number of trips the household makes to location k by 'alternative mode', Z_k is the number of trips the household makes to location k using the car, and D_0 and D_1 are the sets of, locations accessible by the household using 'alternative mode' and car, respectively. This very simple short-term framework does not even allow for the possibility that changes in income (y) will occur as the result of a car becoming available. But it does reflect effects on disposable income after travel, the number of trips that are made, the range of destinations that can be accessed, and the net leisure time available. In the longer term location patterns make the structure even more complex.

effects come on both the demand and the supply sides, and they are often interactive.

1.2.5 Computers and transport

Improved telecommunications has undoubtedly reduced the costs of producing the hardware of the transportation system.[4] A visit to a modern car production plant reveals a mass of robotics and computer control systems. Actual people are thin on the ground, which largely explains the steady decline in manufacturing employment in many countries. Much of the recent growth in electronic commerce (e-commerce) has involved transactions between companies that, in the transportation context, have permitted the more efficient production of vehicles, aeroplanes, ships, trucks, trains, and automobiles that move people and goods. It has fostered the adoption of management production techniques that minimize inventory holding, both within production and within retailing, and so reduced production costs.[5]

The introduction of what is often called intelligent transportation systems (ITS) – e.g., computerized traffic signals, route guidance systems electronic toll collection, and electronic incident reporting on roads – has lowered the generalized costs for users of transportation, and in particular the costs of using transportation infrastructure. It has done this by reducing travel times within a given context, and by offering more and better information about options in terms of routes and schedules. Telecommunications has also changed the way many modes of public transportation are provided, and the ease with which users can make use of it (e.g., real time arrivals information and electronic ticketing).

On the demand side, e-commerce offers individuals a wider choice of shopping options, including through such providers as eBay, the possibility of genuine auction systems.[6] On-line services such as travel agencies, banking, investing,

---

[4]   Linked to this, there has been some discussion that it may be possible because of the information revolution for some of the poorer countries in the world to 'leap-over' the traditional industrial stages of development by avoiding the need to build large amounts of physical transportation and communications infrastructure. This has yet to be fully explored.

[5]   In fact electronic coordination of information did exist prior to the creation of the World-wide Web. Electronic systems such as electronic data interchange (EDI) have been available for some time but the Web is easier to use, more flexible, and a richer medium. EDI involves point-to-point communications done over proprietary networks. The US Department of Commerce (Phillips and Mecker, 2000) estimated in 2000 that there were 250,000 companies in the US that used EDI and that they processed about $3 (US) trillion in transactions.

[6]   What innovations such as the Internet actually do is to expand the range of possible alternatives when the cost of moving physical goods is low. They allow potential buyers to search across many markets, to the extent of exploring global sources on occasions, and for sellers to advertise their wares to millions of potential

child-care advice and education are part of this realm of activities that may influence domestic travel demand. In some cases they may influence demands for international travel by offering information that would formerly have been difficult to access, as well as simple booking services. In many countries there has been a very rapid decline in the number of travel agents as these on-line services have become available (National Commission to Ensure Consumer Information and Choice in the Airline Industry, 2002).

Teleworking (telecommuting), and activities such as telephone and video conferencing, may affect travel-to-work patterns, and the ways in which certain types of business are conducted. The actual situation still seems very fluid, and it is unlikely that the full potential for teleworking has yet been realized. As we see later in the book, the exact implications of all this are also still far from clear. Teleworking, for instance, by removing the commute may free up time for activities involving other forms of travel, or may simply lead to new route patterns emerging as people engage in more complex travel patterns.

Both the potential supply-side and demand-side effects of telecommunications on transportation have potential longer-term effects on location and land-use patterns, as well as for medium-term car ownership levels and shorter-term travel behavior effects (Sullivan et al, 1993). At the global level, telecommunications can influence the nature of the supply-chain by facilitating easier and cheaper shipments of goods. This affects the comparative advantages of nations and ultimately their import and export patterns. This in turn determines the types of industry they support and where that industry is located within their borders. At the other extreme, measures such as electronic road pricing, designed to contain urban traffic congestion, can push up the costs of commuting and lead to more spatially concentrated urban areas.

One of the problems in assessing the linkages between telecommunications, travel behavior, and location is that we still do not actually understand travel patterns and logistics behavior very well. This is despite considerable efforts from the early 1960s to develop integrated land-use transportation models (see papers in Hensher and Button, 2000). Such models are now highly sophisticated, generally involving complex mathematical simulations and make use of carefully collected data.

While one may criticize early models for being excessively engineering driven, treating humans as simple flows though systems, in recent years there have been significant inputs from economists and other social scientists to reflect the behavioral aspects of transportation decision-making. This has certainly made

customers. The increased reach makes markets for goods more efficient by improving the number of matches between buyers and sellers.

the models more efficient in terms of their data needs and more intellectually defensible. Nevertheless, they are still not renowned for their forecasting accuracy.[7]

This makes quantitative assessments difficult even when considering conventional transportation matters such as building a new road, changing a flight schedule, or initiating public transit subsidies.

The problems are compounded when dealing with changes in telecommunications that have a variety of entirely new effects that, as we have seen, affect both the supply and demand for transportation services. Much of the work in the field has, therefore, tended to be highly controversial or, at the other extreme, limited in what it can show. Aggregate studies, for example, looking at simple correlations at a national or regional level tell us little about causality. At the other extreme, there are very local, micro studies that often fail to encapsulate full system effects.

Some work is also colored by the preconceived policy agendas of politicians; for example, politicians have long sought 'painless' ways of containing urban traffic congestion, and some have seen aspects of telecommunications provision as a way of doing this. The fact that the only major urban areas where traffic congestion has actually decreased – Singapore and London – came as the result of the stick of economic road pricing seems to be absent from the political mind in many places.

The longer-term linkages between transportation and land-use are perhaps even less understood. One reason for this is that land-use change takes so long to occur and linking change to any particular stimuli is thus extraordinarily difficult. Land-use is also very heavily regulated making the separation from the impacts of any market or technology change difficult to isolate from regulations and controls. But there are new ideas about how land-use patterns can be influenced by communications and transportation and there are new quantitative techniques emerging to provide more substance to what has often been an impressionist series of debates.

1.3 THE BOOK

This book is aimed at those with an interest in the interactions of technology, economics, and social forces. It emphasizes, one could perhaps say excessively, the economic aspects of the interactions between telecommunications,

---

[7]   In his Nobel Lecture, the economist Daniel McFadden (2001) talks of his forecasting work on the BART transit system for San Francisco. He indicates that short-term traffic forecasts based upon standard, essentially aggregate gravity models, modeling suggested that 15% of commuters would use the system, whereas his random utility maximization model forecast 6.3%, which was much closer to the 6.2% that materialized. As he admits, however, 'We were lucky to be so accurate, given the standard errors of the forecasts.'

transportation and land-use. But economics links are important. The book is also designed to be as accessible as possible to those without any prior knowledge of economics, or indeed transportation or communications. This does not mean that there is no technical material – some of the footnotes have already contained equations. But the more technical content is largely reserved for footnotes and Chapter 3.

The contents are almost exclusively concerned with the situation in the wealthier countries of the world. This is a pragmatic limitation imposed by the information and facts that are available. It should not be construed from this emphasis that the changes taking place in telecommunications have not been impacting on developing countries. Indeed, in a relative sense the impacts in some developing countries are likely to have been greater. Transportation infrastructure is often inadequate and transportation costs are generally high. The advent of the wireless telephone often provides a cheaper alternative to physical movement.

The book is also fairly heavily referenced. This is a deliberate policy and not one designed to give confidence to the reader that the authors are familiar with all the literature! Writings on various aspects of telecommunications and transportation linkages are copious and are growing in volume. It is also scattered widely across various forms of publications and there is an extensive 'gray' literature to be found in students' theses, official studies, and consultant's reports. It is also to be found in publications from a wide range of disciplines. The objective is, therefore, to add utility by bringing some of these key references together.

The book begins by looking at some of the recent social changes that are taking place and, in particular, with regard to developments in mobility and transportation. This is intended to help put the information revolution in a much larger context.

There have been many periods when sea changes have been highlighted in the path of history. Many of these have been military or political in nature. Others have been pinpointed by cultural shifts – the oncoming of the Dark Ages and the Renaissance. Economic and technical changes are also important – the Industrial Revolution and the advent of Fordism. But none of these were uni-dimensional and their implications were complex; not linear nor simple.

As we have argued, whether the so-called information revolution will hold up to scrutiny as a sea-change only history will tell. But what is important about all these previous changes is that while a core shift is emphasized there were also background developments that fed into the larger process. The First World War would have been impossible to sustain for over four years without the developments that had taken place in transportation, communications and production in the preceding 50 years. The Industrial Revolution needed major improvements in agriculture and demographic changes as a prerequisite. The same seems likely of the latter part of the twentieth century into the twenty-first. Technology changes have run in parallel with social stability, changing family structures and demographic changes. It is this wider context that is treated in the following chapter.

Chapter 3 is concerned with the basic microeconomics of telecommunications and transportation. The coverage is not intended to be highly theoretical but argues that there is nothing really specially in an economic sense about these sectors and their interactions. The theory just needs a little tweaking. There are certainly features of telecommunications and transportation that direct the analyst to specific elements of microeconomics.

There are also some tools that are particularly germane to the study of telecommunications, transportation, and land-use but this is true of any specific industry or sector. International trade analysts and financial economists, for example, have some specific tools to help in their work, but they still rely on a core set of analytical instruments. The underlying issues that we are concerned with in this book are far from exclusively economic in their nature, but standard microeconomics does provide a powerful set of tools and concepts for analyzing them. There is no need to reinvent the economic wheel to understand their interactions.

There has been a tendency in some of the literature towards the end of the twentieth century to dismiss economics as incapable of explaining any of the major shifts that are taking place in society. This, however, would seem premature. Much of the argument seeking to undermine standard economics has been at the macro level. It has rested on the very rapid growth of the US economy, and the seemingly unstoppable rise in share prices in the late 1990s that seemed to run counter to standard economic theory.[8] The subsequent slowing down of the growth rate and the notable slippage in share prices, especially of high-technology companies, from 2000 indicates that conventional notions of economic cycles have not yet become obsolete.

Microeconomics is concerned with the way that individuals, including individual firms, behave. Relevant microeconomics is inter-mixed with what is often now distinguished as 'mesoeconomics'. This focuses on the behavior of groups of individuals or firms – i.e., industries or regions – at the sub-national level. It also encompasses such subjects as urban and regional economics and hence embodies the analysis of spatial patterns of economic development. This can be a very useful level of analysis when studying shifts in the economy and for looking at policy options, especially in diversified economies with more decentralized institutional structures.

Much attention has been paid to the possibility that transactions of all kinds could be more efficiently carried out through electronic media rather than through physical meetings. Electronic interactions may be less personal but, it has been argued, this disadvantage may be more than off-set by factors such as their lower

---

[8]   For an analysis of the shifts in the stock market that accompanied what Alan Greenspan called the 'irrational exuberance over the new economy, see Shiller (2000).

cost of providing very detailed information, their ability to offer effective asynchronous communication and their flexibility and search capacity (Borenstein and Saloner, 2001). These are the sorts of issue considered in Chapter 3.

Chapters 4 and 5 of the book are concerned with the issue of the degree to which there is scope for more teleworking, videoconferencing, electronic banking and so on to reduce, in particular, the use of the automobile in cities. The two chapters examine, in this sense, the attractions and attributes of telecommunications as a substitute for travel. Some policy-makers argue that if substitutability is possible then this will reduce strains on physical transportation infrastructure, and would at the same time be environmentally beneficial. Indeed, the US government in 2001 began providing support for a number of states that have initiated teleworking policies for these reasons.

More specifically, Chapter 4 focuses on teleworking (or telecommuting as it is sometimes called) as a substitute for going to and from a remote workplace (most often an office) every day. Teleworking is not seen as a substitution for work travel but rather as a means for influencing where people work and also when they travel to work when this involves visiting a remote work place. Chapter 5 looks at the ability to use such techniques as teleconferencing to reduce travel within the work context. Basically having at least some meetings from the office via a telecommunications link rather than moving to the work place of others.

Chapter 6 moves on to investigate the growing importance of e-commerce, and considers both business-to-consumer (B-to-C) and business-to-business (B-to-B) activities.

The advent of new information systems has affected the ways in which customers and clients can interact. It offers many new opportunities for shoppers, opens up a variety of types of markets, and introduces novel ways of conducting transaction. New information systems also affect the ways in which transportation of goods, and larger aspects of production are undertaken. It has only been possible to deploy efficient modern supply-chain management techniques, such as just-in-time production, because of advances in telecommunication. As a component of this process electronic warehousing not only influences transportation costs, but affects locations of storage and depots. The impact extends beyond local markets and the globalization that has been a feature of the past 20 years, relies heavily on advanced informatics.

These new channels of communication also affect passenger transportation and this is dealt with in Chapter 7. It takes something over 10,000 telephone calls and innumerable digital electronic interchanges to get a commercial passenger Boeing 747 flight into the air. But in addition, airlines use computer reservations systems (CRSs) to determine fares and payloads, and to sell their seats. The push for ITS to improve the efficiency with which public transit and road capacity is used is now an integral part of transportation planning and public policy. This ranges through from on-vehicles technologies designed to help route planning by drivers of trucks and automobiles, to information systems at public transit terminals.

Production and consumption take place in geographical space. The pattern of economic activities has also changed in response to the new information and control systems that have come on-line. The ability to exploit more fully international comparative advantages has led to rapid expansions in international trade in goods and services. At the more local level, just-in-time production has resulted in reductions in warehousing requirements; essentially much warehousing is done in containers on trucks, trains, boats and planes. In the case of some products, such as books, much of the stock is increasingly stored electronically in computers and only translated into physical form as required.

Telecommunications are also changing the comparative advantage of certain types of retailing, and not only in terms of the development of e-commerce. There are economies of scale to be enjoyed in the new information age, and larger retail chains have the scope to exploit these. The advent of the information age has also affected the types of employment that people do and this in turn affects their location decisions. It is this plethora of location considerations that are addressed in Chapter 8.

2   SOCIAL CHANGE AND MOBILITY

2.1 INTRODUCTION

Transportation is an integral part of any modern society. The demand for transportation services in virtually all countries has grown steadily over the years (Table 2.1, for example, offers US data). But this increase has neither been spread evenly across space nor modes. The richer countries of the world have invested in major transportation infrastructure networks that have facilitated traffic growth, whilst the developing countries have lagged seriously behind. But even within the wealthiest countries infrastructure networks are not ubiquitous and travel patterns vary according to geography and local income levels.

The importance of the motor car as a major mover of people and of the truck as a major mover of freight is now almost widespread, although again vehicle ownership various considerably both between and within nations. The growth in transportation has also not been a steady upward movement, but has fluctuated as economic and other conditions have changed. The trend, however, has been irresistibly upwards.

As well as providing the means for mobility, the sectors that provide the hardware for transportation – the car, ship, aircraft manufacturers, the infrastructure construction companies, and the military – are also responsible for a significant part of any county's gross domestic product (GDP), and often contribute a large part of a country's trading activities.

Table 2.2 provides data on the US and indicates that transportation final demand contributes over 10% of total GDP. These industries engage in extensive lobbying to further their interests and are the subject of extensive academic study in their own right. But the interest here is much less in these hardware providers, and much more centered on the role that transportation plays in society.

Transportation provides mobility and access. As such the demand for transportation is usually seen by economists, and by many other social scientists, as derived in its nature. Put simply, people want transportation to move about and reach destinations while companies require it as part of their overall production activities, as part of the supply chain.[1] But there are important differences between mobility and access.

---

[1]   There are a few exceptions to this, notably tourists who drive to see the scenery around them and those who take leisure cruises, but these are relatively small in

Table 2.1 US passenger miles (millions)

	1960	1970	1980	1990	2000
Air	*33,399*	*117,542*	*219,068*	*358,873*	*531,329*
Air carrier, domestic	31,099	108,442	204,368	345,873	516,129
General aviation	2,300	9,100	14,700	13,000	15,200
Highway	*1,272,078*	*2,042,002*	*2,653,510*	*3,561,209*	*4,390,076*
Passenger car	1,144,673	1,750,897	2,011,989	2,281,391	2,544,457
Motorcycle	U	3,277	12,257	12,424	11,516
Other 2-axle 4-tire vehicle	U	225,613	520,774	999,754	1,467,664
Truck, single-unit 2-axle 6-tire or more	98,551	27,081	39,813	51,901	70,500
Truck, combination	28,854	35,134	68,678	94,341	135,020
Bus	U	U	U	121,398	160,919
Transit	*4,197*	*4,592*	*39,854*	*41,143*	*47,666*
Motor bus	U	U	21,790	20,981	21,241
Light rail	U	U	381	571	1,356
Heavy rail	U	U	10,558	11,475	13,844
Trolley bus	U	U	219	193	192
Commuter rail	4,197	4,592	6,516	7,082	9,402
Demand responsive	U	U	N	431	839
Ferry boat	U	U	U	286	330
Other	U	U	390	124	462
Rail					
Intercity/Amtrak	17,064	6,179	4,503	6,057	5,498

Source: US Bureau of Transportation Statistics (various years).

In terms of individuals, mobility is concerned with the general ability of people to move around. It is aspatial in the sense that it is independent of where the travel takes place. Access, in contrast is concerned with the ability of individuals to reach specified destinations, or to undertake certain activities. For example, it may be concerned with access to employment opportunities to shops, or to schools.

The distinction is an important one for policy making, as well as analysis, and has relevance for considering links between telecommunications and transportation futures.

Most public policy has traditionally been aimed at improving accessibility, and this may mean providing options to reach different locations, or meeting a

number and often use specific infrastructure (e.g., parkways). There are also those, such as 'grissers' in the UK with their interest in trains, who gain utility from observing transportation rather than using it for travel.

particular need, rather than improving transportation *per se*. Access can be enhanced by moving the objectives (e.g., jobs or schools), by making it easier to reach the existing ones, or by providing a non-transportation means, such as a telecommunications alternative, of attaining the underlying goal (substitution). It seems to have become the focus of policy because it is easier to articulate arguments for specific policies aimed at enhancing access to jobs or education than it is about a more amorphous improvement in mobility. It also has the useful pragmatic advantage that it is easier to develop quantitative indicators of accessibility than it is for mobility.

Table 2.2 US Gross Domestic Product attributable to transportation final demand (chained 1996 $billions)

	1980	1990	2000	2001
Personal consumption of transportation	*362.3*	*532.6*	*727.1*	*751.8*
Motor vehicles and parts	142.7	246.1	338.4	361.9
Gasoline and oil	94.9	113.1	135.7	138.8
Transport services	124.7	173.4	253.0	251.1
Gross private domestic investment	*84.0*	*91.1*	*191.7*	*168.6*
Transportation structures	6.4	3.7	5.1	5.0
Transportation equipment	77.6	87.4	186.6	163.6
Exports (+)	*76.2*	*123.7*	*169.5*	*161.8*
Civilian aircraft, engines, and parts	26.9	40.9	43.2	44.8
Automotive vehicles, engines, and parts	28.3	39.8	78.5	73.4
Passenger fares	4.5	19.1	19.8	17.0
Other transportation	16.5	23.9	28.0	26.6
Imports (-)	*81.2*	*155.0*	*272.7*	*265.3*
Civilian aircraft, engines, and parts	6.0	13.5	23.9	27.3
Automotive vehicles, engines, and parts	52.5	101.6	192.5	186.7
Passenger fares	5.5	12.7	20.9	17.7
Other transportation	17.2	27.2	35.4	33.6
Net exports of transportation-related goods and services	*–5.0*	*–31.3*	*–103.2*	*–103.5*
Government transportation-related purchases	*96.4*	*127.5*	*162.2*	*167.2*
Federal purchases	13.3	16.1	19.3	20.1
State and local purchases	77.3	101.1	134.2	138.4
Defense-related purchases	5.8	10.3	8.7	8.7
Gross Domestic Product	*4,901*	*6,708*	*9,191*	*9,214*
Total transportation in GDP (%)	*11.0*	*10.7*	*10.6*	*10.7*

Source: US Bureau of Transportation Statistics (various years).

Neither the mobility nor the accessibility concepts are policy neutral. Policies aimed at extending mobility implicitly favor travel over other uses of resources. But it is neutral as to favoring any particular destinations. Mobility may, in this sense, be seen as leaving the potential trip-maker with decisions as to where to go, whereas accessibility has a second inherent bias in policy analysis in that it favors some destinations over others.

Here we are concerned with matters largely to do with mobility and not so much with questions of direction or relocation. To ignore issues of access entirely, however, would be too limiting.

Mobility is not just a matter of where one can travel to but also entails the ease of travel. In many cases it is the quality of travel that is important rather than the simple ability to get somewhere. This raises issues of how transportation networks are used and managed as well as the size and capacity of any network.

Traffic congestion is often a major constraint on mobility and on freight movements over even very large networks where there may be numerous potential routes. The problem often arises simply because the system is poorly managed, information on alternatives is not available, and incentives to use the network efficiently are not in place. In some cases this is the result of poor controls over access and especially inappropriate pricing.

The basic fact is that one individual's mobility is not independent of another's and without an awareness of this, and without measures to force individuals to take account of it in their decision-making, infrastructure simply becomes overloaded. This, for example, is basis of the long-standing economic argument for appropriate infrastructure pricing.

Transportation of goods also often interacts with that of individuals; cars and trucks use streets and passenger and freight trains often share common track. Although not dealt with here in any great depth, social changes inevitably are affecting the types and quantity of goods that are being transported and this, in turn, has indirect effects on the mobility of individuals. The congestion caused by trucks is one factor, but new distribution systems (e.g., large shopping malls) often means that the distinction between person movements and freight distribution merges as people serve to distribute goods to their homes as part of their own travel.

Social change itself is not a simple, nor indeed, a single concept. In a narrow sense social change tends to be seen in terms of sociological change and to focus on how interactions in society take place and how they change over time. For a number of reasons, this has become isolated from a wider definition that embraces economic change although the latter has a long tradition as a premier social science. These economic changes can be in terms of how markets function and how economic institutions change. In this chapter, the broader, much older tradition of including economic changes as part of social change is adopted.[2]

A crucial thing about social change, whichever definition is used, is that it is strictly wrong to try to categorize components of it in the way that is attempted for pedagogic reasons below. The various elements of social change are interactive, and these interactions can vary with time, context and location. This is one of the main factors that make planning future transportation systems so difficult, and that makes forecasting the implications of changing policies with regard to current systems so challenging.

We do make divisions, however, because the human mind finds this a convenient way of trying to come to come to grips with complex phenomena; it may be imperfect but it is practical.

The chapter's coverage of the way social changes affect mobility is not entirely balanced. More weight is devoted to those factors that are becoming increasingly important, rather than to those that have been influential for a longer time. This does not mean the latter have a diminished absolute role. Economic growth, for example, is possibly the greatest single factor affecting the demand for mobility and the ability of public and private agencies to supply it, but of more contemporary interest is the way that the effects of this growth are changing how mobility is viewed and how it is affecting different groups in society.[3]

2.2 ECONOMIC GROWTH AND URBANIZATION

Economic prosperity is not the only goal that society pursues, but if the results of democratic elections are a guide, it is an important one. In many of the poorer countries of the world economic growth is quite literally an imperative for survival. Without it there is starvation, disease and low life expectancy. In more prosperous societies economic growth is often important for the maintenance of political stability and the creation of a socially acceptable income distribution (Hirsch, 1977).

---

[2]   One way of looking at this in terms of economics is that there has recently been a focus on shifts in the demand for mobility. These shifts may reflect changes in what economists refer to as taste changes – and these are often associated with sociological or psychological changes – but they may also reflect changes in economic variables such as income or prices elsewhere in the economy. These latter effects can often be dominating factors.

[3]   An alternative way of thinking of the issues is in terms of continuing trends (which would embody such things as income effects), trend breaks (which may include such things as female participation in the labor force), and new trends (which could include new telecommunications technologies). While this trichotomy has attractions, the divisions are often artificial and open to dispute.

Transportation forecasters have, however, long made use of this relationship between economic growth and transportation in producing their traffic forecasts (see papers in Hensher and Button, 2000). While traffic management involves the control of existing transportation movements and can generally assume a relative fixity in land-use, this is not a realistic assumption when making major infrastructure decisions that can have implications for decades ahead.

Mobility is linked with economic growth both as an input into the process (households need mobility to access employment opportunities and to act as consumers of goods and services) and as an output of the process (wealth stimulates higher levels of car ownership and use, and of travel more generally). The degree of correlation between economic well-being and transportation is not, therefore, a simple one, and it is made more complex as countries become wealthier. The number of cars sold, for example, tends to decline after a point as vehicle ownership moves to a more-or-less replacement level. Some indication of this can be seen in the US (Table 2.3).

Table 2.3 Retail new car sales in the US (thousands)

	1970	1980	1990	1995	2000	2001
Total new passenger car sales	*8,400*	*8,979*	*9,300*	*8,635*	*8,847*	*8,423*
Domestic	*7,119*	*6,581*	*6,897*	*7,129*	*6,831*	*6,325*
Imports	*1,280*	*2,398*	*2,403*	*1,506*	*2,016*	*2,098*
Japan	313	1,906	1,719	982	863	837
Germany	750	305	265	207	517	523
Other	217	187	419	317	637	738

Source: US Bureau of Transportation Statistics (various years).

There is also increased evidence of at least a limited decoupling of income growth and the demands for transportation in the most developed countries. Figure 2.1 provides trend data since 1960 for the US, but also the data on the share of transportation final demand seen in GDP shown in Table 2.2 is of relevance. This does not, of course, mean that the demand for transportation is not still expanding in absolute terms, and that it will not pose serious challenges in the future, but it does suggest that some of the more traditional drivers are becoming less influential.

One issue is the way that economic growth continues to indirectly influence transportation through other markets. Economic growth has also been associated with urbanization. In all societies the employment in agriculture and the importance of agriculture in GDP has declined as affluence has increased. The greater demand for transportation, combined with greater urbanization, produces a major dilemma for mobility policy.

Whether transportation leads economic growth, or whether the effect is the other way round is endlessly disputed. The Industrial Revolution in eighteenth century Britain was only possible, some claim, because of a prior Transportation Revolution that produced canals, seaports, navigable waterways, and turnpike roads. Others maintain that the prosperity resulting from more efficient production generated a social surplus that was invested in the transportation system and added to mobility. Cause and effect have produced a plethora of PhD theses. The main point is, however, whatever the direction of causality, economic growth is inevitably associated more and better transportation.

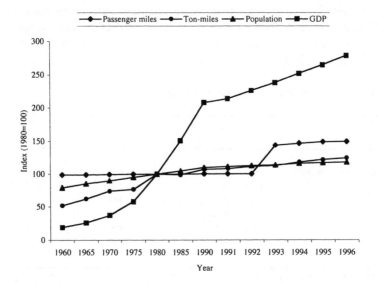

Figure 2.1 US national economic and transport trends

Cities themselves could only grow as transportation allowed supplies to be brought in, and as internal transportation systems permitted their distribution. Trains and canals afforded the former and the bus and the truck the latter. It is no accident that the star-shaped axial urban form emerged as development took place along the rail and road arteries into cities, or that edge cities have become a feature of the twenty-first century America as car ownership has become ubiquitous (Garreau, 1991). As can be seen in the US, one result of this is a continual increase in the average length of trips by virtually all modes for both individuals and for freight (Table 2.4).

There has also been a major mode shift as urbanization has taken place and cities have become more complex places to live and to conduct business – see

Chapter 8. The automobile now dominates urban commuting in many cities, whilst in others it is steadily taking a larger share (Table 2.5).

Table 2.4 Average length of haul – domestic US freight and passenger in miles

	1960	1970	1980	1990	2000	2001
Freight						
Air carrier	953	1,014	1,052	1,389	982	973
Truck	272	263	363	391	473	485
Class I rail	461	515	616	726	843	859
Coastwise (water)	1,496	1,509	1,915	1,604	1,251	1,228
Lakewise (water)	522	506	536	553	506	509
Internal (water)	282	330	405	470	481	476
Intraport (water)	U	U	17	13	16	15
Crude (oil pipeline)	325	300	871	812	U	U
Petroleum products (oil pipeline)	269	357	414	387	U	U
Passenger						
Air carrier, domestic, scheduled	583	678	736	803	833	842
Bus, intercity	79	106	125	141	143	U
Commuter rail	21	22	23	22	23	U
Amtrak	U	U	216	273	244	237

Note: The average length of haul for freight is calculated by dividing ton-miles in the previous table by estimates of tonnage from the various data sources. The calculation of average length of haul for passenger trips varies by mode: for air carrier it is calculated by dividing revenue passenger-miles by revenue passenger enplanements; for commuter rail, intercity bus, and Amtrak it is calculated by dividing passenger-miles by number of passengers
Source: US Bureau of Transportation Statistics (various years)

But the challenges posed are perhaps more acute in poorer nations. The larger mega cities whose populations can be measured in tens of millions that are becoming a feature of many developing economies in Asia and South America pose major challenges for maintaining mobility levels. Congestion is a common feature of these cities and public transportation and goods distribution systems seldom expand at a pace to cope with rising demands.

The problems associated with increased numbers of automobiles in countries that are experiencing economic growth are already serious. An individual sees the automobile in this context as a mechanism for increasing personal mobility, not to say status, but in doing so the vehicle's use slows the travel of others and the movement of goods. In some wealthier countries, such as the US, the absolute number of cars on the roads at any one time is tending to stabilize, although the pattern of use is becoming more problematic. In many poorer countries the issue is one of rapidly rising car owners as incomes increase and people seek greater personal mobility and the status that car ownership confers. The street patterns of many cities in these countries are particularly unsuited to this type of transportation.

Table 2.5 Principal means of transportation to work (percent by mode)

	1985	1989	1993	1997	1999	2001
Automobile, total	86.5	88.1	88.0	87.5	87.7	87.8
Drives self	72.4	76.3	76.6	77.5	78.2	78.2
Carpool, total	14.1	11.8	11.4	10.0	9.4	9.7
2-person	10.4	9.1	8.8	8.0	7.4	7.5
3-person	2.0	1.6	1.6	1.3	1.2	1.4
4+ person	1.6	1.1	1.0	0.8	0.8	0.8
Public transportation[a]	5.1	4.6	4.6	4.6	4.9	4.7
Taxicab	0.1	0.1	0.1	0.1	0.1	0.1
Bicycle or motorcycle	1.0	0.7	0.7	0.6	0.6	0.7
Walks only	4.0	3.4	3.1	3.3	3.1	2.8
Other means[b]	0.3	0.5	0.5	0.7	0.8	0.9
Works at home	3.0	2.6	3.0	3.1	2.8	2.8

Notes: [a]Public transportation refers to bus, streetcar, subway, or elevated trains; [b]other means include ferryboats, surface trains, and van service.
Source: US Bureau of Transportation Statistics (various years).

But as incomes rise, so the social perception of car ownership also tends to change, adding to problems of mobility. The positive, non-transportation effects of automobile travel can be see in terms of its 'club effect'. What a person gains from joining the club are the network externalities, and from car ownership and driving there are parallels with Internet club membership.

Obtaining a driver's license provides an identity card that is a sign of independence and adulthood. Acquiring a vehicle allows a driver to realize freedom and independence, travel at speed and increased accessibility, relative to those who do not have a car. Benefits increase as the number of cars in the fleet increase, e.g., driving a popular car results in accessibility to spare parts, roadside service and after-sales services, that are more difficult to acquire with a unique vehicle. Aggregate experience shows that the more people using the road network the better the quality of road and the denser the traffic network, and the more accessible facilities are relative to those not using the network. The outcome is that while congestion may be a cost of being a member, the overall situation is one of benefit to the car commuter *vis-à-vis* those without access to a car.

City forms are also changing in part as a response to economic growth and the types of activity that underlie it. In the traditionally industrial world, the inner cores of many cities have lost some of their economic vitality and populations have tended to move out as a result of this. Additionally, rising incomes have fostered a desire for more living space – suburbanization is one result, but a return to ruralization may be another. In effect, as people have more income, and as technology allows it, many elect to enjoy the financial returns of an 'urban' job with the lifestyle of the country, and often the climate of specific locations.

These trends are not entirely new but there are three particular elements that would seem relevant to mobility in the longer term.

- First, there is the phenomenon of the edge city (Garreau, 1991) – 'suburban down towns'. These are self-contained spatial economic entities located in areas adjacent to old, traditional urban areas. The number of significant agglomerations of this type may be as high as 18 or more for the largest metropolitan areas in the US. They provide access to a range of employment, social, educational and retail activities for those that live around them.

    This means that those living away from the city core can enjoy a high level of accessibility but, because of high levels of traffic congestion in areas surrounding the edge city, their overall mobility may actually be lower than previous residents enjoyed. The nature of the urban architecture often leads to more complex travel behavior that ultimately can adversely affect mobility.
- Second, there is empirical evidence, supported by emerging economic theories, that rather than urban areas suffering from depopulation and economic decline as congestion grows, there is a sort of cumulative effect with wealthier areas continuing to expand whilst those that are in decline continue their downward path, at least in industrialized countries.

    The 'New Information Age' leads to a greater divergence of economies. The regions or cities that have an initial advantage in information systems will enjoy a variety of benefits that will allow them to develop their advantages further. Their position has been supported by a body of empirical findings showing that regions are not converging significantly in their economic performance and certainly not in a way consistent with traditional neoclassical economic analysis.
- Third, and somewhat linked to the previous point, there has been observed by some (Kotkin, 2000) a change in the type of people that live in many urban areas. They often do not conform to the standard family stereotype of two adults and two children. In many city cores, a large number of units are childless, often with a single dweller, and with significant concentrations of homosexual units. But given the considerable growth in these types of living units, they are leading to a revival of many urban core areas. These types of unit are often very

focused on local activities with limited demands for anything other than local transportation.

2.3 GLOBALIZATION AND INTERNATIONALIZATION

Globalization and internationalization are two major industrial trends of the late twentieth and early twenty-first century. Part of this is reflected in the significant trade growth that has taken place from the early 1990s, with real export growth in the industrialized countries that make up the Organisation for Economic Cooperation and Development (OECD) at over 7% per annum. Comparatively, from 1964 to 1992, first world production was up by 9% per annum, exports by 12%, and cross-border lending by 23%. Equally, there has been a significant rise in foreign ownership of assets that are now estimated to total about $1.7 trillion.[4]

This globalization process has clear implications for the mobility demands on the freight transportation side. There is an ever increasing volume of traditional goods being moved by land and sea across national boundaries with air transportation now playing a significant role (about 40%) in value terms as low weight, low volume high-technology products form a major component of trade. But air transportation is also serving a second mobility role in terms of permitting the personnel involved in this globalization process to move around.

From a straightforward economic perspective, globalization means seeking out the cheapest (in the general sense) sources of supply by buyers and the quest for the most lucrative client in terms of suppliers. This inevitably means more mobility in terms of sales, marketing and purchasing even for traditional sectors. The maritime transportation sector has responded by developing global hub-and-spoke networks of services based upon key regional ports and making use of ever-larger ships (e.g., post-Panamax vessels) for longer ocean legs. The widespread use of containers and the demands for high quality service by consignors, has fostered the growth of both mergers of carriers and the formation of industrial alliances (consortia) amongst them. This in turn has led to the development of specialized information systems for invoicing and tracking of containers.

Modern, new economy sectors such as telecommunications and biotechnology involve even more personnel mobility with the average high-technology employee

---

[4]   A significant part of this growth has resulted from the institutional changes that have gradually removed both tariff and non-tariff barriers to trade. The General Agreement on Tariffs and Trade led the way in terms of commodity flows and the General Agreement on Trade in Services initiated freer trade in services. The emergence of trading blocks such as the European Union, the North America Free Trade Area, and the Asian Pacific Economic Community has led to more international trade within regions.

in the US, for instance, making 60% more trips per annum than his blue-collar counterpart. Much of the increased trade, by value however, is in the service sector and, although a significant part of this can be conducted electronically, this means additional business travel.

As a result of this process, it seems that much of the demand for enhanced international mobility will fall on the air transportation sector. This seems likely to continue expanding into the foreseeable future, albeit at differential rates, in various geographical sub-markets. A number of international agencies, aircraft manufacturers and airlines regularly produce forecasts of aviation traffic. While forecasting remains an art rather than a science, it seems likely that passenger traffic will grow at a rate between 5% and 7% into the foreseeable future, much of it in the Asian–Pacific region (up to 9% a year). Forecasts have also foreseen slower growth in the more mature US and European markets.

In line with other sectors, aviation has experienced significant internal moves towards globalization and internationalization. Indeed, it is the stated objective of the UK carrier, British Airways to become a 'global carrier'. In pursuit of wider market coverage and in an effort to enhance their own internal efficiency, other airlines have followed a similar strategies. The most recent development is the creation of various forms of global strategic airline alliances with carriers coordinating services and customer loyalty schemes such as frequent flier programs. It appears that these strategic alliances are rapidly converging on three – the Star Alliance, OneWorld and Skyteam.

2.4 LEISURE AND AGE DISTRIBUTION

Tourism has become the mainstay of many economies, especially in the developing parts of the world. Indeed, it has been estimated that travel and tourism now accounts for over 11% of the global GDP and make up one of the world's largest economic sectors. The forecasts produced by the World Travel and Tourism Council are that travel and tourism will grow by 4.2% a year between 2000 and 2010. There are a number of reasons for this growth in leisure-based travel and the form that tourism is taking.

Increased income is one obvious factor; travel, tours, hotels and recreation cost money. Leisure travel is a luxury good and, with more disposable income, as the basic necessities of life are met there is scope for spending more on recreation and on visits to friends and relations. The leisure industry is itself responding to this by being increasingly inventive in terms of the types of activities that it offers.

In some countries there is also a trend towards shorter working weeks and earlier retirement. But there is combined with this a gradually changing age distribution in countries that are enjoying much of this increase in disposable income. The populations of these countries are getting older and, indeed, in many the reproduction rate is insufficient to maintain the population levels; Italy, for example, is forecast to have a 30% decline in its population by 2050. This older population has more leisure time as its members reach retirement, is generally fitter and more active than previous generations and these features, combined with greater accumulated wealth, allow for more tourism and other leisure activities. Some of this is quite localized in terms of traveling to eat out or to some local recreational site such as a sports club.

At the other end of the spectrum, in many countries people are marrying later and, this combined with smaller families, affects time allocations. Smaller families mean that parenting is taking up a smaller part of the normal employment phase of life and providing more opportunity for leisure pursuits. When there are children the finances available for leisure travel are spread over fewer family members making more, or at least different, patterns of travel possible.

The nature of leisure travel has also changed. The combination of higher incomes, lower costs of long-distance travel (brought about by both technological and institutional changes), and the seeking of fresh stimuli are increasingly leading to longer trips to places that have not been traditional destinations. The relative costs of many destinations in what were formerly seen as remote and exotic destinations now add to their attractiveness as tourist locations. The greater mobility of workers in seeking employment also means that visits to relations and friends over longer distances are rising. All this has resulted in greater demands for air transport.

2.5 GENDER ISSUES

The role of women in many societies has changed profoundly over the past century and change is likely to continue. These changes have both an immediate effect on travel patterns and a potentially longer-term effect on the ways in which mobility will be viewed (Root, et al., 2000).

The mobility patterns and travel needs of women have several implications for sustainable development. These patterns differ in a number of important ways from that of men. In particular, gender differences arise in the distance traveled, the mode of travel, and the complexity and purpose of trip-making. While there has been some convergence between genders regarding the first two differences, the last difference does not show signs of convergence. Future demographic changes, and in particular those that relate to the population aging, are likely to further these trends, but also create new patterns based on the travel needs and desires of elderly women.

2.5.1 Distance traveled
In western society women have traditionally been less mobile than men, although this situation is changing. In the UK for example, women in all age groups are

increasing the distances that they travel by mechanized transportation and especially as car/van drivers. Over the last several decades, the mobility of women in the US from all age groups has also improved. Between 1969 and 1995, the average annual person trips taken by women increased by 11%. This rate of increase was less for men, despite the fact that the population growth rates of men and women were both about 40% over the same time of period.

Improvements in mobility can be largely attributed to more women becoming licensed drivers. Since 1969, the number of licensed female drivers in the US has increased by 95%, while for men it has only increased by 53%. Furthermore, in the 1980s and 1990s the increase in women drivers exceeded that of new men drivers.

This situation is not unique to the US. In the UK, there was a 90% increase in the proportion of women with driving licenses between the mid-1970s and mid-1990s, but only a 17% increase in the proportion of license-holding men. In 1975/76 women drove 17% of the miles driven by men, but by 1994/96 this proportion had increased to 37%. Further, in 1975/76 almost twice as many men could drive as women, but by 1993/95 the difference had lessened to 81% of men being able to drive and 55% of women.

The situation is similar in Germany, where women aged between 25 and 34 years have the highest levels of vehicle ownership. In addition, the 18 to 40 age group are catching up with men's levels of driving license holding: 80% of women and 90% of men have a full driving license for ages 18 to 40 compared to respective figures of 82% and 52% for all ages.

These trends could reflect the declining quality and availability of public transportation in some countries or more general trends of greater population dispersion as incomes rise, higher labor force participation rates and changes in family structure. A more geographically dispersed population, for instance, requires more complex travel patterns to meet traditional household care-taking and family obligations let alone labor force participation.

2.5.2 Mode of transportation

Despite their increase in automobile use and enhanced mobility, women still travel shorter distances than men and when they do travel, they travel on what are generally considered less prestigious modes of transport. In the US, women drive only 60% to 70% as many miles as men, and on average they travel 27.8 person miles a day, which is considerably less than the 35.2 person miles a day that men travel. In 1994/96, women traveled less far than men in the UK by all modes apart from buses, walking and as passengers in private cars.

Statistics on aircraft, ship and channel tunnel journeys according to gender are not available for the UK, but they would probably tell the same story. In addition, women are passengers for about half of the travel they do, while men are for only one-fourth of the time. In 1975/76 women drove about a fifth of the miles driven by men but by 1994/96 the gap had closed somewhat, and women drove about two-fifths of the miles that men drove.

In Germany, many adult women have less car availability than men and are, therefore, more likely to be captive transit riders. Fewer women than men, irrespective of whether they are employed or not, have a car available. The biggest differences however are between men and women who have a car available to them in the household, but do not have a driving license.

2.5.3 Complexity and purpose of trip-making

Women often seem to have somewhat different reasons for traveling than men. Women's entry into the workplace has created a new set of trips, referred to here as 'knock-on' trips, or trips generated by the substitution of home production for market production. Statistics show that women are more prone than men to make these types of trips. Approximately 50% of all person trips made by women in the US are for family and personal business and two-thirds of the trips women make are to take someone else someplace.

In 1994/96 women in the UK made 28% fewer commuter journeys and 68% fewer trips during their work than men. Evidence in the UK shows that women take a greater share of household responsibilities, and, linked to this, they are making 65% more 'escort education' journeys (taking children to school) and approximately 30% more shopping trips. The same pattern appears across the previous 10 years. Category changes make longer comparisons impossible for the UK.

In the UK, there also appears to be a correlation between the distance traveled by women and the need to tend to child-care, and caring for the elderly and domestic responsibilities. In this sense the pattern has changed little in recent years. Until the age of 20 in 1994/96, women in the UK were typically traveling almost identical distances to men. In 1995/96 between the ages of 26–59, the prime years of domestic caring responsibilities, women's travel dropped to just over half of men's, a pattern that was broadly the same as 20 years earlier. The pattern is not unique to the UK or US.

Complex travel behavior such as trip chaining is also more common for women than men. This is certainly the case in the US even when both males and females are in employment. Women stop more for running household errands than do men on both inward and outward commutes and irrespective of the number of persons in a household or its structure. On average two in three American women make stops on their way home and 25% make more than one stop. The places visited differ with women tending more often to visit schools, day-care centers and shops than men; the latter are twice as likely to go to a restaurant or bar.

The trend for these more complex commuting patterns is upwards. In the US the number of intermediate stops on the way to work has grown by about 50% since 1980 and the number on the way home by about 20%.

2.5.4 Attitudes to transport

Women are generally physically smaller than men and more often travel with vulnerable children. This poses both real fears of attack and affects perceptions of the safety of travel. In the UK 'stranger danger' fears appear to be re-emerging, compared to the middle years of this century. In the late 1980s, between 50% and 70% of women were found to be frightened of going out after dark in cities. In the mid-1990s one in eight women surveyed said that they felt so unsafe on public transportation that they avoided using it. Eleven percent of women interviewed never ventured out after dark. Nevertheless, despite the difficulties of travel, it would appear that women were, in general, less confined to their homes at the end than earlier in the century. This was largely because of car ownership. There is an irony in the fact that fewer men worry about attack, but they are more likely to suffer from it.

Women's experience of traveling at night often makes them feel unsafe when compared to trip making in the day. For example, 10% of women in the UK felt 'unsafe' or 'very unsafe' waiting on a railway platform in the day, but this figure rose to 53% at night. Similarly heightened fears were experienced by women in relation to waiting for underground trains, walking to a car in open or multi-storied car parks etc. More attacks happen during the day, but, due to fewer numbers traveling at night, the probability of attack at night is higher. Thus the common perception of the danger of traveling after dark is grounded in actuality. Women, however, are more often attacked by people they know and in the home than outside by strangers. Yet the fear of public spaces and stranger danger in them dominates particular groups of women's lives, especially middle class and younger women.

Despite these concerns, more women are now traveling at hours later in the evening. Currently, about half of all 'moonlighters' in the US, for example, are women. Furthermore, for many women who work during the day, trips for household and domestic duties must be completed in the evening hours. These trends raise security issues for women, particularly for those who choose to travel by public transit. Security will increasingly be a concern as more women demand transportation. This increase in demand has been and will continue to be precipitated by the new 'post-Fordist' economy.

2.5.5 Future trends

Demographic trends indicate further improvements in mobility for women and continued growth in the number of women drivers on the road. Many of these drivers are likely to fall in the older age cohorts (e.g., 65 years of age). In the US, between 1969 and 1995, the highest rates of growth in population were in these cohorts. In 1995, almost 65% of the 75 year old and over population were female. Currently, elderly women are predominantly not driving license holders and consequently have only limited use of cars as passengers. This picture will change dramatically when the current cohorts of younger and middle-aged women begin to enter the older age categories. A far higher proportion of these women, about one-third from German evidence, will have been car owners for the majority of their lives and will expect to use cars for their mobility in their old age.

As these trends continue, the share of elderly women on roads is likely to increase dramatically. Many of these women will be highly educated, wealthy, licensed to drive, and as a result extremely mobile. Furthermore, life expectancy figures suggest that because women are out-living men, they will wish to be mobile for longer. Women's life expectancy is greater than that of men's in North America and the EU. Additionally, if the whole population ages, the proportion of very elderly women who still have mobility requirements will increase further. These points suggest that as the female population ages, gender differences may be reduced or even disappear. At the same time, they might suggest an increase in leisure-related travel on the part of women.

2.6 THE TELECOMMUNICATIONS REVOLUTION

The world has supposedly moved into the information and knowledge age and this is inevitably having effects on the link between social change and the demand for mobility. Despite the problems of the early 2000s when many telecommunications companies encountered serious financial problems and institutional barriers were still evident in many countries, advanced communications technologies are growing and evolving at a very rapid rate.[5] These trends and their implications are discussed in much more detail in subsequent chapters, here we make just a number of introductory observations.

When discussing telecommunications and transportation, there is increasingly a move to investigate teleworking (or telecommuting) and the like as alternatives to transportation. Teleworking is defined here as any proportion of work done at home, which would traditionally have been done at the workplace. This would include parts of days or weeks working at home. There are difficulties in estimating the current levels of telecommuting. The types of data that have been produced (Table 2.6) indicate that there has to-date been a rather patchy up-take of teleworking in the major economies.

Widespread adoption of activities such as teleworking that the Internet and e-commerce could, however, allow a reduction in the need for interpersonal interactions at work and hence travel. Such a development is attractive politically since it circumvents the generally unpopular idea that traffic should be restrained by measures such as road pricing or traffic controls. In addition, the information

---

[5]   Internet use has not only grown in the 'developed' world but also in Third World nations; indeed the indications are that there is a slowing of growth in Europe (rising 161% between 2000 and 2005) and North America (106.7%) with significant growth in Africa (258.3%) and the Latin America/Caribbean region (277.1%).

technology sector is promoting the introduction of its technologies and services as solutions to a range of business, societal and domestic problems. The idea is also raising expectations in the public at large, *viz*; that information systems may be a panacea to their transportation problems.

Table 2.6 Penetration levels of teleworking

	Penetration level of telework (percent of the workforce)
The European Union (formal and informal arrangements)	3.1
The European Union (formal arrangements)	0.8
Japan (formal arrangements)	1.05
The US (formal and informal arrangements)	10.56

Source: Illegems and Verbeke (2004).

At the macrolevel the development of telecommunications can also influence the global location of production. Globalization and internationalization has seen considerable amounts of outsourcing as work has been redistributed to places where labor is relatively cheap, firms thus reduce their costs and regions exercise comparative advantage. This has implications for trade-flows and ultimately will affect location of individuals and the nature of urbanization (Autor, 2001).

Changes in information systems have also profoundly influenced the way freight is moved, stored, sorted, and distributed. This in turn has implications for personal mobility in terms of where people work and how they collect the final goods that they are to consume. The development of telecommunications has already impacted significantly on the freight transportation sector. It is now an integral part of modern supply chain management, of which transportation is a central component, and is especially relevant for just-in-time management methods.

As each producer and manufacturer strives to gain as much market power as possible, the elasticity of the supply-chain is critical in ensuring quality (e.g., the cold chain requires goods to be maintained at or below a certain temperature and delays can affect quality, cost and the production life-cycle), convenience, and time compression. Customers are increasingly able to shop around at a minimal cost for a product and service that satisfies their individual needs. From a producer's perspective, this equates to the threat of competition and the opportunity for greater market share.

Another way of looking at this is to take Michael Porter's (1985) notion of the value chain. The concept (Figure 2.2) is based on the process view of organizations, the idea of seeing a manufacturing or service organization as a system made up of sub-systems each involving a number of inputs, transformation processes and outputs. The inputs, transformation processes, and outputs involve the acquisition and consumption of resources – money, labor, materials, equipment, management, etc, and how the value chain activities are carried out determines costs and revenues.

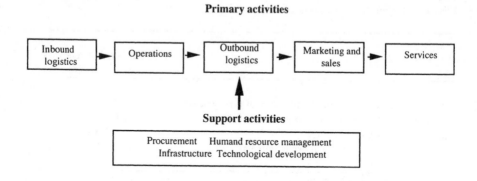

Figure 2.2 The notion of the value chain

The figure indicates how, in the context of a single company, goods are received from suppliers and stored until needed for production (inbound logistics), how these inputs are combined through some operations process to produce a product, and how outbound logistics then send these products along the outbound logistics supply-chain of wholesalers and retailers to be marketed and sold. The services element reflects the need for after sales servicing. The nature and efficiency of the value chain determines final margins. The use of telecommunications can both reduce some of the costs in the chain and improve the integration of elements. In either case, there is potential for increasing profit margins.

2.7 ENVIRONMENTAL AWARENESS

Societal concerns about the impacts that transportation is having on the environment have grown in recent years for a variety of reasons. Increases in income have led those in the wealthier states to look at their physical surroundings and seek cleaner, quieter and more attractive surroundings in which to live and work. Increases in scientific knowledge have shown that many of the environmental implications of transportation are harmful to health. Technology has also advanced to offer ways of lessening the environmental effects of transportation. Overall these developments have brought to the fore notions of sustainable development that transcend the narrow limitations of transportation. These are now in some countries as important in policy considerations as more traditional concerns about the noise, local pollution, and visual intrusion of transportation.

Many of the environmental problems that have become both real and sensitive community issues, stem from the use of transport infrastructure by passenger and freight vehicles. Automobiles, aeroplanes and trucks are major sources of local pollutants, such as lead, carbon monoxide and noise. Traffic congestion exacerbates these problems, and also imposes direct economic and health costs on users and non-users in the form of wasted time and money, stress, and other illnesses. Transport systems also make a significant contribution to global warming through emissions of carbon dioxide and other greenhouse gases.

The main environmental issues associated with the transport sector are air quality, enhanced greenhouse gas emissions (mainly CO_2), noise, impact on biodiversity, and land use (Button, 1993). Emissions from transport – primarily road and air traffic – represent a very high share of the overall emissions: about 90% of all lead emissions, about 50% of all NO_x emissions and about 30% of all volatile organic compound (VOC) emissions. Some 22% of the total CO_2 emissions are from the transport sector. Of this, about 80% of the emissions arise from road transport and more than 55% from the private car alone.

The main components of transport emissions include: carbon dioxide (CO_2), carbon monoxide (CO), hydro carbons (HC), VOCs, (nitrous oxides) NO_x, sulphur dioxide (SO_2), particulate matter (PM), lead and other combustion by-products. Some exhaust emissions from road transport also produce secondary pollution, such as photochemical oxidants. Apart from the resource use and depletion of non-renewable resources as well as the main emissions problem, other environmental issues concerning transportation include operational pollution, land-intrusion, and water pollution.

Land use and biodiversity have recently received major consideration in the sustainable transportation debate. The main problem seems to be landscape fragmentation caused by transport infrastructure. The construction and use of roads, railways and canals creates several negative effects on the biodiversity of land. It has direct effects, such as loss and disturbance of habitats and species, as well as the long-term influence of partitioning and isolating ecosystems and species populations. Transport infrastructure covers an increasing amount of land to the virtual exclusion of other uses, cuts through ecosystems and spoils the view of natural scenery and historic monuments.

2.7.1 Local effects

Transportation has been described as industry on wheels because of the pollution and noise associated with modern transportation systems. Many of the adverse impacts of transportation are immediately perceived by the local communities that are affected – e.g., noise issues and the affects of acid rain – and these have for a long time called forth public reactions. Much of the traditional concerns about transportation have centered on limiting these effects. But in three ways transportation associated environmental effects pose particular challenges.

- First, transportation is responsible for a very wide range of adverse environmental effects the sources of which are interrelated. This makes remedial policy formulation difficult because of the trade-offs that are often involved. For example, nitrogen oxide that is associated with acid rain can be controlled through the fitting of vehicles with catalytic converters but this results in lower fuel efficiency and more carbon dioxide, a greenhouse gas.
- Second, it is extremely difficult to separate transportation from where people live and generally go about their business. There is an expectation that transportation should be available almost instantly on demand. This limits the types of policies that can be applied to combat very localized pollutants and to meet the challenges imposed by noise and visual intrusion of vehicles and transportation infrastructure.
- Third, and almost by definition, transportation is a mobile source of pollution. This poses a range of technical problems, but perhaps more importantly it poses a series of institutional challenges. Legal authority is spatial in its structure – there are local, regional, national, and supra-national forms of government. This poses obvious problems when there are spill-over environmental effects, but there are also difficulties where adverse environmental effects are purely local in their implications. The mobility of transportation vehicles means that compliance with a variety of local laws and regulations can be highly inefficient from an economic perspective.

2.7.2 Sustainability

It is for this reason that notions of 'sustainable transport' or 'sustainable mobility' really have limited meaning other than as guide-posts. The question of developing a transportation strategy that fits within this global framework involves deciding which social and environmental objectives are to be promoted. This task was most famously undertaken in the Brundtland Commission's definition of sustainability as 'ensuring that the needs of the present are met without compromising the ability of future generations to meet their needs'. Although succinct and memorable, it should noted that there this definition confers little actual clarity about how the needs of the present generation are to be balanced with those of future generations.

There is also an ongoing debate about the extent to which sustainability in transportation should involve conserving social goods (e.g., communities or social capital such as trust), or whether it should mean priority being given to protecting or upgrading the physical world. For instance improving air quality, reducing noise, preserving tranquil landscapes. In itself it also says nothing about sustainability in transportation or any other sector. Indeed, it takes little imagination to develop quite plausible scenarios in which the expansion of transportation may be the preferred option from the perspective of sustainable development. Much depends on the way resources are used outside of transportation and the links between transportation and other activities.

Although the process of climate change is complex and the full effects cannot be predicted, there is broad international agreement that anthropogenic change is taking place. Transportation is responsible for some 23% of carbon dioxide, the main 'greenhouse gas' emissions, in OECD countries, up from 19% in 1970. In 1995 transportation was responsible for about two-thirds of nitrogen oxides in the UK which damages forests. At the local level, transportation damages urban environments and rural landscapes, e.g., through ozone smog and physical destruction of landscapes for road building. Many transportation emissions are recognized as toxic and potentially damaging to health.

The importance of these meso and local levels of environmental intrusion, besides their immediate impact, is on the sustainability of socio-political systems. Sustainable development, although couched largely in environmental terms, also implies a sustainable social and political infrastructure if it is to be durable. Environmental spill-over can, for example, lead to international and inter-regional tension. A degraded local or urban environment poses social problems and is a severe handicap for economic development. Simply thinking of sustainability in global warming terms is, therefore, inadequate. It is in this broader sense that, for example, the European Union has attempted to develop an integrated transportation and environmental policy.

2.8 INSTITUTIONAL CHANGE

Social change is reflected in public policy, at least in democratic countries and often with a lag. Governments have always heavily regulated transportation, initially because of its strategic importance. In this traditional context, investment in transportation infrastructure and the way access to it was granted was treated as part of a wider social process with the strict efficiency of the transportation system (and, with it, mobility) given less weight than attaining other objectives. This is the 'Continental System' under which the premise is that government regulates unless the market clearly meets the primary objectives most efficiently. The alternative, the 'Anglo-Saxon' approach treats transportation in its own right and is concerned with internal efficiency within it. Markets systems are normally preferred with regulations only being initiated when there are clear 'market failures'

The past 25 years witnessed major reforms in transportation regulation across a large number of countries reflecting shifts in societies' preferences. While there are marked national differences in the nature and pace of change, this process has, in the case of public transportation modes, been characterized by moves toward more liberal regimes and a withdrawal of government from the ownership of transportation operating companies.

In contrast, there has been an increasing emphasis on the containment and the management of automobile use both on environmental grounds and because of congestion problems.

The generality of the regulatory trends across industrialized countries raises questions concerning the underlying causes of change. Overall, society has shifted its views on regulation as exemplified by Reaganomics in the US, Thatcherism in the UK and the decline of central planning in Eastern and Central Europe. Certainly, in the specific context of transportation one can point to the demonstration effects exerted mainly by the deregulation of US domestic aviation from 1978.

But there also seem to be more fundamental issues in terms of the failure of regulations to achieve their stated objectives, new theories of optimal regulation emerging and a greater understanding of how markets function that have influenced the way society views the regulation of transport, and with it the way mobility is treated.

The resultant changes that have taken place across the world since the mid-1960s have not been uniform either across countries or modes. Part of this stems from the different starting points that existed in the early 1970s. In very general terms, the US led the way in legal change with a rush of liberalizing measures during the 1970s and early 1980s that removed much government control from its domestic transportation system.

Other countries have followed the trend in part because of demonstration effects that indicated significant benefits from change, but in some cases because of the direct impacts of changes in the US – Canada, for example, was so affected. In effect, the systems of Boards and Committees that regulated the industry have gradually had their powers curtailed and transportation industries are increasingly being treated like other commercial undertakings. Where controls remain there has been a shift in their emphasis.

This quest for efficiency has been emulated in the UK as, first, the 1980 Transport Act and then the 1985 Transport Act liberalized bus markets and introduced new financial mechanisms for providing social services. *De facto* reform has been brought about in domestic aviation as the Civil Aviation Authority has adjusted its position on licensing since 1982. Developments within the EU mean that there will be further *de jure* changes as cabotage is phased in within the Community by 1997. Indeed, the creation of a Single European Market means that cabotage rights, albeit initially often in rather limited forms, now extend across all transportation modes within the Union.

Similar changes occurred elsewhere with the domestic Canadian road haulage market, partly as a result of increased competition from the more efficient US carriers, being liberalized in 1987 and its aviation market, after some *de facto* changes in 1984, being legally deregulated in 1988. New Zealand has seen extensive liberalization. Reforms of a similar nature ended Australia's 'two airline' domestic aviation policy in 1990 but liberalization of surface transportation has progressed more slowly. Gradually the effects of reform strategies, especially through the influence of agencies such as the World Bank and Asian Development Bank, are also being felt in developing countries.

The extensive, although decreasing, public ownership of transportation that existed in countries such as Canada, Australia, Japan and most of Europe has meant that reforms there have often also involved elements of privatization. The privatization process, while reducing the direct control of government, has stimulated the creation of new regulations, for example, to limit market power and to meet social objectives. Many of these relate to quality of service, especially safety, and to the nature of ownership (such as governing allowable foreign ownership of shares) but economic regulations have also been imposed. The overall aim is to provide society with greater mobility by removing constraints on transportation supply.

This does not mean that the public authorities do not still regulate and control transportation, nor that they do not have a direct input into the finances of its provision. Economic regulations do remain, albeit often with generic laws on anti-trust and mergers, and there is a growing body of controls aimed at safety, security, and environmental protection. Much infrastructure is still publicly owned and even in such supposedly market oriented economies as the US, federal and state monies going into transportation, and revenues collected from transportation activities are large (Table 2.7). It is rather a shift in focus and emphasis that underlie the way transportation is thought about that has taken place.

Table 2.7 US federal, state, and local government transportation-related revenues and expenditures (fiscal years $million chained to 1996 prices)

	1980	1990	1999	2000
Total government revenues	60,135	82,229	118,888	U
Federal	18,410	26,091	48,928	42,610
State and local	41,725	56,138	69,959	U
Total government expenditures	102,324	117,458	144,745	U
State & local expenditures less federal grants	58,159	79,807	103,365	U
Federal grants	26,033	24,022	26,309	U
Federal expenditures less grants	18,133	13,629	15,071	14,477

Notes: Figures for state and local expenditures, less federal grants, were determined by adding the total number of federal grants and federal expenditures less grants and subtracting the sum from the total government expenditures.
Source: US Bureau of Transportation Statistics (various years).

2.9 CONCLUSIONS

Society is continually changing and with these changes come modifications in the demands for mobility and access. As incomes rise, so this demand increases but there are many other factors that influence the nature of the new demands, and some of these are increasing in their importance. Economists have placed emphasis on the income and price effects of alternative systems, whilst sociologists and psychologists have added important contributions looking at preferences.

In particular, there are issues of urban form that is continually changing interactively with society's perception of mobility, the influence of different gender attitudes and roles and of the demographics of populations. More recently, society has become more environmentally conscious, and this has affected the priority given to mobility and how it is viewed in the longer-term. This is not just a matter of how much travel is undertaken but the form of this travel and where it takes place.

What this contribution has attempted to do is to pinpoint some of these effects but, as emphasized at the outset, social change embodies a whole set of interacting forces, some complementary and some conflicting, and any division into categories is essentially arbitrary. The future, therefore, is not simply a matter of the way in which the individual effects develop, but also how they will play off each other. This possibly makes forecasting transportation and related activities more challenging than it has been in the recent past.

3 SOME BASIC ECONOMIC CONSIDERATIONS

3.1 INTRODUCTION

This chapter is concerned with some features of the Internet and e-commerce, very broadly defined, that raise particular economic questions. Strictly there is no such thing as 'The Economics of the Internet and E-commerce' but it is useful shorthand. What there is, is a set of features associated with the Internet and e-commerce that differentiate them from many other activities and, therefore, require a particular portfolio of economic techniques and theories to understand the nature of their supply and appreciate why they are demanded. They also have characteristics that make it interesting to see how they influence the markets for other goods and services such as transportation and land.

A primary focus here is on the importance of economics in understanding the way in which the spatial use of the Internet and the growth of e-commerce can affect the location of economic activities, either directly or through changes in travel behavior. It looks at the theoretical issues and the implications of public policy interventions in markets. In particular, conventional economic analysis assumes that markets offer optimal solutions, but many of the underlying assumptions of simplistic Marshallian neo-classical economics are not relevant to the Internet, or at least need some finessing to be useful.

The realities of the ecommerce sector could potentially lead to under-supply in certain parts of the market. This is particularly so when, to adopt economic jargon, the core is empty.[1] What this means is that incentives are such that in the long term insufficient companies will enter the market, or those in it will under-supply despite that from an overall economic perspective this is economically inefficient.

There are many good reasons to suppose that the particular structural features of network industries, such as shipping and air transport, make them potentially prone to severe empty core problems and that many of these conditions are common to the supply of ecommerce services. From a geographical perspective, an empty core in one network would seem to imply distortions in linked, competitive and complementary networks, and with this a sub-optimal spatial distribution of land-use may result. Issues then arise as to how public policy

---

[1]   An empty core in economics exists when there is no stable equilibrium. Put another way there is no dominant coalition of interests that can sustain supply.

should be developed to deal with this and how to define the appropriate conditions that ensure workable competition evolves.

The overall topic of the economics of the Internet and e-commerce is a large one and here attention is largely on only two elements. The first is concerned with the implications of the Internet for sales activities and what this in turn may mean for supply, distribution and deliveries. The second is on the links between teleworking and travel demand. As indicated earlier, the notion that teleworking can help alleviate some of the traffic congestion found in many cities is an attractive one, especially for policy-makers unwilling to tackle the problem at its source. It does, however, raise a number of economic issues. Tied to this, although not fully explored here, are the changes in the labor market that a wider adoption of teleworking could induce.

The aim here is not to offer a comprehensive overview of all the relevant economic material that can be useful in studying the interactions between transportation, communications and land-use, but the more limited one of highlighting a few of the more important concepts. We begin by looking at how institutional structures can play an important role in influencing how these interactions occur and the forces that are important in their outcomes.

3.2 INSTITUTIONAL STRUCTURES

The focus of most texts on economics is on the profit motive ('rent seeking') as the main driver behind company decisions, and on utility maximization as the motivation for individual behavior. There are exceptions to this – for example ideas such as 'satisficing' whereby acceptable targets form the basis of decision-making rather than any notion of maximization – but for our purposes, the neo-classical ideal of profit and utility maximization offer a good basis for exposition; some of the other ideas are touched upon later

The ability for any company to maximize its profits stems from both the formal and informal structure in which transactions take place; it is not independent of either socially accepted behavior or legal requirements. Figure 3.1 from Williamson (2000) illustrates the issue.

The figure is largely self-explanatory with the dark arrows showing constraints that come down from higher levels of analysis and the lighter arrows the direction of feedback. There is also information in the boxes on the general frequency in years over which change takes place; but this is only meant to offer a broad indication.

The traditional situation examined by neo-classical economics of supply and demand – the uppermost box – results in market clearing at any point of time; for example a shortage of oil leads to a rise in the price of gasoline that in turn results in less driving and the purchase of more fuel efficient vehicles. Even in the Soviet system where there were no real prices, a shortage led to people forming lines and those willing to spend the most time queuing got the goods. The details and nuances of these types of situation are well explored, and certainly apply to the subject matter of this book.

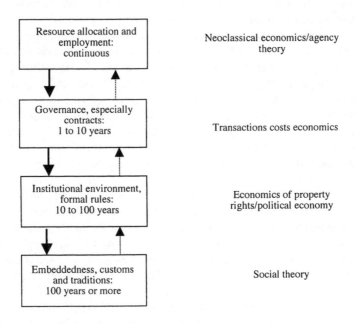

Figure 3.1 Williamson's characterization of where institutions become important

For these market-type structures to work effectively various forms of contracts are needed. In some instances this may involve payment at the time of purchase, but at other times to minimize transactions costs there may need to be periodic payments; e.g., monthly telephone bills or repayment of mortgage loans. Whilst there may some legal controls over these, they are often simply a matter of the nature of the transactions involved and the parties participating. In effect these are the *de facto* operations within any formalized legal institutional structure; they form the governance structure.[2] The nature of these contracts can be quite long-

---

[2]   Within this realm also come changes in ways in which laws and regulations are interpreted by the authorities. For example, the US domestic airline industry was deregulated in 1978 by changing the law (a *de jure* reform), but similar changes in the

term but there are periodic changes in the forms they can take, sometimes influenced by new thinking but also often affected by the types of product that come onto the market. The growth of the service economy, for example, characterized by non-durable products led to some innovative changes in governance structures.

Changes to the legal institutional structure generally take longer to materialize in democratic systems both as an appropriate level of political support is formed and as the new laws are framed. Technically, laws alter 'property rights'. Changing a law affects the rights of various individuals and may re-define existing rights or create new ones over matters previously outside of the market; allocating various wireless frequencies is largely of the latter form; whereas copyright over music rights may fall into the former category. There are generally significant matters of efficiency to consider when the institutional environment changes, but also questions of who wins and who loses become part of the political economy debate.

The ways in which legal structures are determined, and also how governance is practiced, is not fixed. There are long-term forces that influence the overall system and while there may be 'embedded' societal norms these do change over times as society itself changes. Some embedded views take time to change – one may think of the divergence views of Christian and Muslims on interest rates – and only come about after crises or conflict. Others may be a reflection of large scale technology shifts, such as the eighteen to nineteenth century Industrial Revolution in the UK, that change society's views of its internal structure. The interesting question that is garnering attention at the beginning of the twenty-first century is whether the 'Information Revolution' falls into this category.

Our attention here is much more on the short- and medium-term interactions between transportation, telecommunications, and location choices than with debates about whether there have been sea-changes in the underlying nature of society. Consequently, what follows looks at some of the key tools of neo-classical economics that, within particular systems of governance and laws, are influencing these interactions.

3.3 THE CONCEPT OF NETWORKS

From an economic viewpoint, there are many common technical features shared by transportation and telecommunications, and so, for ease of exposition, and to minimize the tedium of repetition, it is helpful to just focus on the former. Transportation is a network industry akin to such other sectors as telecommunications and energy distribution. As such it exhibits a set of economic

UK came about by the regulatory agencies changing the way it implemented laws (a *de facto* change).

characteristics that influence the way it is viewed by economists and the way it has been treated by regulators (Economides, 1996). These in part stem from the potential separation in the supply of the network infrastructure links (roads, rail track, etc.), the hubs and interchange points (stations, ports, airports, etc.) and operations (cars, trucks, trains, ships, etc.). But equally important are the interdependencies that exist between the costs and benefits of providing the various elements in any transportation network.

In some cases the networks are provided by a single mode, but more often transportation is provided by a series of interconnected networks; the road network can be combined with the air transport network to offer door-to-door service. In some instances the networks are combined and provided by a single operator but in others independent actors offer interactive networks of services. Transportation networks also overlap with other complementary and substitute networks. Telecommunications can be both a complement (a large commercial aircraft involves about 10,000 calls before it can provide a commercial flight) but in other cases it may be a substitute and, for instance, a potential replacement for work travel (Button and Taylor, 2001).

Transportation infrastructure can also service a variety of transport networks (e.g., roads cater for passenger and freight trips) but may also meet the needs of other networks (rail rights of way are often employed to carry fiber optic cables).

There are also important links between transportation networks and the spatial economy. The form and technology of a transportation network affects location and production decisions. The pioneering economic analysis of von Thünen and others on spatial economics explained concentric patterns of agriculture around towns largely in terms of transportation economics. The early twentieth century phenomenon of axial cities (i.e., with a broadly star-shaped configuration) was due to the radial development of suburban rail and tramway networks.

3.3.1 Forms of networks
Networks issues can be considered in several ways. The discussion here largely concerns networks involving interconnectivity. Connectivity occurs (Figure 3.2) when there is a connection between two points. Interconnectivity involves at least three nodes. For it to be worthwhile to develop a network of any configuration rather than providing single link services there must exist some form of network economy. Such economies may be on the cost side but they may also reflect the possibility of earning higher revenues on the demand side. On the cost side there may simply be traditional economies of scale linked to having larger operations and the ability to spread fixed costs over a larger number of customers but there may also be additional network benefits associated with particular network configurations.

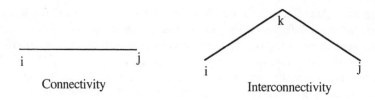

Figure 3.2 Connectivity and interconnectivity

To make effective use of networks there is a need for users to be able to access the entire system and potentially to access competing or complementary networks. To adopt the jargon favored by the European Union (EU), this introduces notions such as interoperability (the ability of transportation systems to offer harmonized interfaces and an acceptable level of service thus giving easy access to users) and interconnectivity (the physical linkages and coordination of transportation systems to facilitate the transfer of freight or passengers between links or networks).

To attain this level of integration across networks there is a need for standardization. In the transportation context the classic issue was that of rail gauges and, more recently, of electrical power sources for rail engines. In the US there were seven different railway gauges in 1860 that impeded internal trade. The problem of different gauges was not unique to the US and it is only comparatively recently that large parts of the Spanish rail network were brought into line with other EU countries.

Lack of technical standardization imposes costs and increases fragmentation if there is a lack of institutional coordination. The UK drives on the left and Continental Europe on the right and this imposes a cost over the EU transportation network. Borders can impose institutional costs if there are different standards on either side, or if legal barriers prevent operating units from one country to use the infrastructure network of another (e.g., as with trucking at the US/Mexico border). This is sometimes referred to as a lack of institutional interoperability.

There are, however, costs in standardization. It may mean adopting what transpires in a technologically dynamic world, a sub-optimal standard. It may mean that potential economics of specialization are lost because a generic standard is adopted that is sub-optimal for parts of the network. There is also the issue of incentives. If a standard is in place then the economic incentives are to optimize within that constraint. This reduces incentives that could improve the efficiency of a network by introducing new standards or removing them. Changes in standards are costly but can prove efficient as seen in Sweden when the country joined the rest of Continental Europe and switched to driving on the right.

The decision to adopt a uniform standard across a transportation network essentially involves employing a cost–benefit calculation. This basically involves trading-off the benefits of optimizing the use of an existing network and its associated technology against the longer gains of developing an optimal network and technology.

3.3.2 Economies of scale, scope, and density

Network suppliers may benefit from a range of cost features. Traditionally, economies of scale have been seen to reflect declining costs of production as, say, an airline's output increases but this concept has been supplemented by notions of economies of scope, networks, and density. Also on the demand side, ideas of economies of market presence have come to the fore in terms of influencing the optimal scale of network activities.

Strictly, economies of scope relate to falling costs of providing services when the range of services offered by a carrier increases while economies of traffic density refer to falling costs as the amount carried increases between any given set of points served. In this sense economies of scale can be seen as a special, single product case of economies of scope. The technical distinction between economies of scale and scope can be seen by referring to equation 3.1,

$$S = \{[C(Q^1) + C(Q^2)] - C(Q^1 + Q^2)\} / \{C(Q^1 + Q^2)\} \qquad (3.1)$$

where $C(Q^1)$ is the cost of producing Q^1 units of output one alone, $C(Q^2)$ is the cost of producing Q^2 of output two alone, and $C(Q^1 + Q^2)$ is the cost of producing Q^1 plus Q^2. Economies of scope exist if $S > 0$. There are said to be economies of scale if C/Q falls as Q expands.

These economies may materialize through natural growth in a network but frequently they involve combining existing networks. Market concentration through mergers is only likely, however, if there is adequate incentive for suppliers to combine. Take the simple network case discussed in Varian (1999). If it is assumed that the benefit v of a network is proportional to the number of users on that network (n) and for simplicity the constant of proportionality is taken as unity, then following Metcalfe's Law the value of the network is n^2. A simple calculation shows that combining two networks (1 and 2) of size n_1 and n_2 yields:

$$\Delta v_1 = n_1(n_1 + n_2) - n_1^2 = n_1 n_2 \qquad (3.2)$$

$$\Delta v_2 = n_2(n_1 + n_2) - n_2^2 = n_1 n_2 \qquad (3.3)$$

Each network gets equal value (v) from the interconnection. Those on the small network (2) each get considerable value from linking with the large number on the other network. The large number of people on the other network (1) each get smaller additional utility but there are a lot of them. This offers scope for reciprocation with the networks having settlement free access to the other network. The problem is that the large supplier may need to keep its market power to allow adequate price discrimination to recover costs and make an acceptable long term return. In this case the larger concern may merge with the smaller and attain twice the value of interconnecting:

$$\Delta v_1 = (n_1 + n_2)^2 - n_1^2 - n_2^2 = 2n_1n_2 \qquad (3.4)$$

Suppliers of network services may also benefit from additional revenues as the number of links in their system grows. These benefits come from economies of market presence. Essentially a supplier of many interconnecting services can meet the needs of a large number of potential customers. For example, a bus company offering a service from A to B via C is effectively meeting the needs of three markets (A->B, A->C, C->B) and can reap revenues from each. If a direct service is offered then only A->B traffic generates revenue. There is a trade-off because indirect services over the longer route are slower but the additional traffic to and from C allows overhead costs to be spread more widely and hence average fares or rates to be lower.

This market pressure for concentration in providing Internet and other network services can also ripple through the economy. An extensive Internet system, for example, has potential implications for those supplying inputs into the process (e.g., transportation) and for users of the services (e.g., in terms of the costs they bear and the services they can receive that can in turn have implications for, among other things, the growth of teleworking). The external effects are effectively across as well as within specific network systems.

3.3.3 User benefits and costs

There are also user benefits that may or may not be exploited by suppliers of transport network services. Larger networks can offer the advantage of access to a much wider range of destinations and generally greater service frequency. This can be important in terms of making efficient use of operating capital. On any single link in a network demand may be asymmetrical. The demand to carry coal from a mine to a steel mill, for instance, is seldom balanced by return loads of any kind. This is the 'back-haul problem'. The existence of a complex network allows scope for a variety of routings that have the potential for minimizing empty running on back-hauls. The developments in information technology and in scheduling algorithms has permitted this exploitation of networks to be refined but even in the days of sailing ships the use of trade winds often involved triangular routings between Europe, the Americas and African to ensure hold capacity was used to the maximum.

Additionally, any individual user helps ensure that this range of options is available to others. What this means in terms of an individual user of an air transport network, for example, is that, by paying the full attributable cost of using the service, the user helps ensure that the service is also available for other potential users as well as benefiting from their support of the network.

The main reason for this is that the costs borne by air travelers extend beyond those of simply the fares being paid for the opportunities that larger networks may offer. In Figure 3.3 it is assumed that the costs, C, of providing networks rise with the size of the network, proxied by passenger numbers, but at a decreasing rate (i.e., some scale benefits are implied but these diminish with the size of the network).

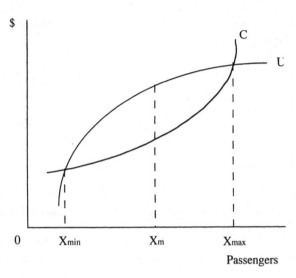

Figure 3.3 Optimal networks

For the user there are increased benefits associated with larger networks (U) but the rate of increase declines with the size of the network. To obtain any passengers there is a minimum size of network (X_{min}) but after X_{max} the additional traffic the transport service supplier will gain from adding links is less than the additional costs and further expansion will not be justified.

From the perspective of passengers the optimum network is at X_m where there is a maximum deviation between the financial costs they must pay to cover airline costs and the network benefits to be enjoyed. Passengers, however, will continue to seek flights up to X_{max} since their marginal benefit exceeds the costs they will be charged.

Another way of looking at this is to take the simple case of a positive externality, as seen in Figure 3.4 Here an individual's or company's demand (marginal benefit) for a transportation service is shown as MB with the marginal costs involved of MC. For simplicity, it is assumed that there are no negative environmental externalities arising due to congestion. The journey made by the individual helps sustain the network for other potential users so that the marginal social benefit curve, where society is deemed in this club good context to embrace other travelers on the same network, is to the right of the MB curve at MB*. It is assumed that in drawing this, the larger the number of trips taken by the individual, the greater the social benefit.

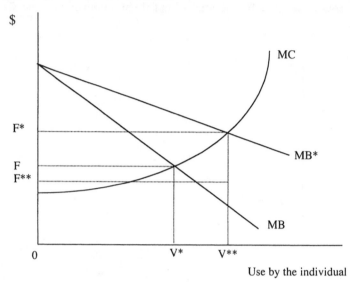

Figure 3.4 Positive network externalities

If no allowance is made for this external effect then the fare is set at level F and the volume of service used is V*. Allowing for the externality pushes the optimum volume of service out to V** and the fare up to F*. There is no incentive for the traveler to move out to V**, however, because he/she does not recognize these benefits. One policy solution is to subsidize fares down to F** which would achieve the optimal volume of traffic. Another approach would be to adopt a form of price differentiation that allows costs to be recovered by airlines at an output of V* by extracting consumers' surplus from intra-marginal users of the network.

In addition to the positive externalities that may be associated with larger networks, there are also issues of possible congestion that can arise on links, but are often a major problem at hubs. There is an optimum level of congestion that that arises simply because there is interaction between those using elements of the network and without this the facility would be under-used in an economic sense. The bigger concern is that of excess congestion when a facility is over-used and the benefits that are being derived from it are not maximized. This normally stems from inappropriate pricing of the facilities involved.

The extent to which congestion is an issue depends to some degree on how much of it is already internalized within the fares paid by passengers and cargo shippers. Unlike externalities such as those associated with noise or air pollution, the inefficiency costs of congestion are borne by the users of network services and those that provide those services.

In situations where there is only one carrier monopolizing an airport, for example, there is thus an incentive for that carrier to make efficient use of facilities and to allow for congestion costs when setting fares and establishing services. This is not the situation on road networks where, without congestion charges, large numbers of uncoordinated users bear the costs implicitly in terms of longer travel times and operating costs but have no incentive to modify their behavior to optimize them.[3]

3.3.4 Hub-and-spoke networks

Transportation networks take a variety of forms. Some of these have been imposed by institutional factors but there are market forces that tend to favor particular configurations of links and hubs in the absence of regulation and extreme geographical features. The radial network is perhaps the most common. In urban transport this is seen in the road and rail networks that serve to carry commuters into and out of cities. Historically they often stem from the days when long-distance transportation systems (canals and railways) were more efficient than local distribution systems (walking and horses). The economies inherent in focusing trunk haul operations on a limited number of nodal points led to cities growing around terminal and interchange points. Local distribution and collection then radiated out from the hub.

More recently, with the advent of new technologies this hub-and-spoke configuration has been repeated in the context of road infrastructure, in maritime transportation and more recently in air transport. Air transportation in most countries was until recently heavily regulated.

The standard regulatory structure, which also applied to international services, was based on regulating entry and fares on individual links (Button and Stough, 2000). The result was that a carrier would have a pattern of operations of the type seen in Figure 3.5. There would be no focal point and interlining with its own services to provide an integrated network would be very limited. If someone wanted to travel from C to G, for example, the carrier could well offer a service that went C to B to I to G with the plane stopping at each point *en route*. In many

---

[3]   The issue of how equilibrium is attained across congested networks and the use made of individual links is a topic in its own right that is not covered here. Of importance are the generic rules developed by Wardrop (1952) and notably his first principle that at any equilibrium, depending on the degree to which information is perfect and on whether tolls are charged, the sum of either the actual or the expected average user costs, including time, plus the contingent fee should be equal for alternative routes or people would shift from one route to another. This sum should also be equal to the benefits enjoyed by the marginal user.

cases there would be a need to change carrier if, for instance, a passenger wanted to go from A to D and the authorities had given the route license from A to B and from B to C to one carrier, but another was given C to D.

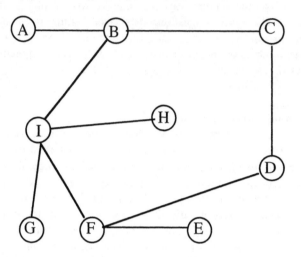

Figure 3.5 Pre-deregulation airline route structure

The relaxation of many of these regulations in many markets has allowed more efficient networks to emerge. The outcome has differed according to the nature of the carriers involved. In particular, there have been important differences between the air cargo operators and predominantly passenger carriers. One reason is that passengers are sensitive to routings while packages, being inanimate, have no such feelings and consignors generally have little preference regarding routes provided time windows are met. Cargo carriers find it easier to focus on mega hubs and to channel considerable volumes of traffic through them at times passengers would see as antisocial. The growth of package services also means that good road access allowing intermodal operations with trucking playing a role in hubbing.

The deregulation of the US domestic air transport market from 1977 showed how market incentives can lead to adoption of hub-and-spoke operations across transportation networks. In Figure 3.6, city H that previously enjoyed only one air link becomes the hub for an entire range of airline services. Why H? In most cases with passenger transportation an airport hub is located in a major city that generates significant local traffic as well as being the point of interchange for transferring flow traffic. The airport must also have the physical capacity (runways, terminals, etc.) to handle the high volume of transit traffic. Its selection is also determined by location – a central position normally allowing for linkages to a larger number of spoke airports. The same types of argument can apply to seaports or rail interchanges.[4]

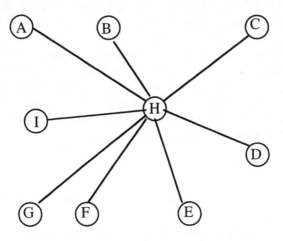

Figure 3.6 Post-US deregulation hub-and-spoke airline route structure

With this form of hubbing structure, flights are funneled in 'banks' into a number of large hubs where substantial numbers of passengers changed aircraft to complete their journeys. These banks involve the coordinated arrival of a large number of flights in a short space of time and then an equally coordinated departure of flights within a narrow time window. Larger hubs may well have up to seven or more such banks a day. Travel time would be longer for many people but fares fell and the range of potential flight combinations available to any particular destination expanded considerably.

3.3.5 Public assessment of network investments
While many networks are provided by the private sector, others are often seen as a public sector responsibility. Private networks are developed on commercial criteria whereas public authorities often used social appraisal techniques and most notably cost–benefit analysis. This involves making network additions that generate a positive increase in consumer surplus. The general principles can be gleaned by considering two roads, one from X to Y and the other X to Z, where Y and Z are

---

[4]   The post office has used this system since its inception in 1840 in the UK and utilizes a variety of modes to feed through their sorting offices each night. FedEx bases its operations on Memphis with banks of trucks and planes feeding packages in each evening to be sorted and dispatched early next morning.

to some degree substitute destinations. Then an improvement in route XY will affect three groups. (It is assumed that all demand curves are linear and that the pre-investment traffic flows on XY and XZ are T_{xy} and $(T_{xz} + R)$ respectively.) The three groups of users to consider are then:

(1)   Existing users who remain on their original routes (T_{xy} and T_{xz}). These will gain consumers' surplus because those on XY will now be using a higher quality facility while those on XZ will benefit from reductions in demand for this route as some former users switch to the improved XY. If this latter traffic diverted from XZ to XY is denoted as R, then the total benefit to those remaining loyal to their initial routes is:

$$T_{xy}(C_1 - C_2) + T_{xz} (D_1 - D_2) \qquad (3.5)$$

where C_1, C_2, D_1, and D_2 are the pre- and post-investment costs by roads XY and XZ respectively.

(2)   Generated traffic consisting of those not previously traveling (G_{xy} and G_{xz}). On average each of these groups of new road users will benefit by half as much as existing, non-switching traffic. The total benefit of the investment to this group is:

$$0.5G_{xy} (C_1 - C_2) + 0.5G_{xz} (D_1 - D_2) \qquad (3.6)$$

(3)   Diverted traffic that switches from route XZ to XY as a consequence of the investment (R). The switch, given the free choice situation, must leave this group better off – it would not have switched otherwise – and the additional welfare it enjoys is equal to half of the difference in benefit between the cost reductions on the two routes,

$$R [(D_1 - D_2) + 0.5\{(C_1 - C_2) - (D_1 - D_2)\}] \qquad (3.7)$$

or

$$0.5 R \{(C_1 - C_2) + ((D_1 - D_2)\}$$

The total benefit (TB) of the investment is the summation of these elements:

$$TB = T_{xy} (C_1 - C_2) T_{xz} (D_1 - D_2) + 0.5G_{xy} ((C_1 - C_2) + 0.5G_{xz} (D_1 - D_2) + $$
$$0.5R \{(C_1 - C_2) + (D_1 - D_2)\} \qquad (3. 8)$$

This equation offers a useful pragmatic basis for assessment. If the *ex ante* and *ex post* traffic flows on XY are denoted as $Q_{xy} = T_{xy}$ and $Q'_{xy} = (T_{xy} + G_{xy} + R)$, and *ex ante* and *ex post* flows on route XZ as $Q_{xz} = (T_{xz} + R)$ and $Q'_{xz} = (T_{xz} + G_{xz})$, then substituting into equation 3.8 gives,

$$TB = 0.5(Q_{xy} + Q'_{xy})(C_1 - C_2) + 0.5(Q_{xz} + Q'_{xz})(D_1 - D_2) \quad (3.9)$$

or more generally the oft-cited 'rule of half',

$$TB = 0.5 \sum_{N} (Q_n + Q_n)(C_n C'_n) \quad (3.10)$$

The rule of half can be applied to transportation schemes that interact with other components of the transport system where demand curves are linear. It must be used with a degree of circumspection when routes are complementary, where demand for the non-improved links may shift to the right, but the broad principle applies. One problem is that there are many possible sequences in which the price changes on routes XY and XZ could follow; each would yield a different level of aggregate social welfare. The general measure set out in equation 3.10 assumes that demand fluctuations are linear in their own prices and with respect to cross-price effects. How realistic this assumption is depends on circumstances but the rule of half has proved a very powerful tool in road appraisal activities.

3.4 FEATURES OF THE MARKET FOR E-COMMERCE

Increased per capita income, changes in the composition of the workforce, intelligent electronic technologies, and the footloose nature of employment, to name a few, have had a major effect on increasing the demand for flexibility in lifestyles and in employment. As discussed earlier, it is often claimed that the late twentieth century marked the beginning of the information age; an age in which knowledge management is a real issue and many organizations' biggest assets are their employees (Hewson, 1999). Partly, this is reflected in the growth of industries in the service sector such as marketing and information technology (IT) that are strongly people dependent, and are essentially concerned with communicating and persuading. These ethereal concepts of human capital and tacit knowledge are purported, in a generic sense, to be driving factors in an organization's success, and essentially they depend on interaction or communication.

It is in this context that communication can be usefully discussed along with its sub-systems, telecommunications and transportation. Many enthusiasts, particularly in the US context, have had high hopes for the favorable impact of communication technology, and specifically the opportunity to telecommute, on traffic congestion (Salomon and Mokhtarian, 1997). These have included predictions about the potential for large-scale vehicle commuting being replaced by virtual offices in the home, at 'village' sites, or on-board vehicles connected by dial-up communication. Linked to this, the growth of e-commerce and the reduced need to physically visit retail outlets is seen as a mechanism for reducing non-work travel, and for simplifying complex journey-to-work patterns.

These expectations, however, often neglect some of the innate features of the Internet. The market for the Internet has complexities on both the supply and demand sides.

On the demand side there is the oft-cited argument that since the Internet is essentially a network activity, it can be associated with network externalities and very strong increasing returns. In the past, Metcalfe's Law, whereby the utility of a network is proportional to the square of the number of people it connects, has been used to support this type of argument. This has dynamic implications.

In general, it is hardly worth joining a small network, but once a certain threshold size has been reached the benefits are explosive. Simple arithmetic supports this. If two cities, each of a hundred people, are joined electronically, this provides 10,000 possible two-way communications. Adding a third city increases this by 20,000 and adding a fourth city by a further 30,000.

The extent of network externalities, however, is likely to be seriously tempered once one introduces variations in the size of markets and in their nature. Cities vary considerably in their population sizes, and the compositions of their populations and industrial bases. Assuming commercial rationality on the part of network suppliers, the law of diminishing returns implies that the most valuable connections will be made first with centers of lesser value being added subsequently.

This pattern was historically appreciated when postal services were regulated or state provided to ensure ubiquitous supply, and why there has been a tendency to encourage cross-subsidization. Without these measures, many links deemed politically or socially necessary would not have been provided.

Looking at the current US situation, in many sectors there is mounting evidence of market concentration, for example 75% of business-to-consumer (B2C) e-commerce is done through five sites (Amazon, eBay, AOL, Yahoo! and Buy.com). The reason is that the market is far from perfect on the supply-side. Indeed perfection may not be desirable if the market is to remain viable. Varian (1999) points to the decreasing cost nature of providing information goods. Information goods have high fixed costs, but then extremely low marginal costs. This poses problems of, what is often termed, an empty core.

A non-core situation can be illustrated by taking the situation of two identical carriers supplying service on a link, with standard U-shaped average cost curves. There is, thus, an assumption of fixed costs. Marginal cost is a discontinuous function of total carrier output and is equal to the minimum average cost of the carriers at two points in Figure 3.7, namely Q_1 and Q_2. The demand for services is represented by the curve D. In this situation if one carrier provides a service then excess profits will be earned.

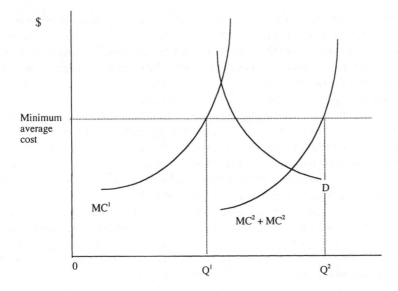

Figure 3.7 Decreasing costs and the empty core problem

Expansion to two carriers, as the second carrier is attracted to the market, will result in both making a loss, since competition will lead them to operate at a price equal to marginal cost. Only if by chance the demand curve intersects the average cost curve at a point coincidental with the average cost curve will a stable outcome emerge. Increasing the number of firms does not affect the outcome until the number becomes very large, at which point the Pareto-optimal number of undertakings is reached.

This type of situation is not uncommon in network industries (Button and Nijkamp, 1998). Regulation of the market and/or direct supply through a monopoly state supplier is one possible policy solution. This was the *de facto* approach in the past of many countries in terms of postal networks, telephone systems, railroads, and air services. The alternative, and less likely to stifle longer-term technological developments, is to allow concentration of supply. This situation is already happening and is largely a function of how network services are provided.

There is no homogeneous product, but rather there is market segmentation. In air transport and shipping this has taken the form of yield management, in the Internet it is rather through 'versioning'. Shapiro and Varian (1998) offer a range of types of versioning that include such practices as 'features and function variations' (the high version has more features and functions); 'image resolution' (low-resolution images sell for a low price, high-resolution images sell for a high-price) and 'user interface' (the professional version has an elaborate user interface; the popular version has a simple interface).

Versioning is important because it involves price discrimination and thereby a mechanism for potentially recovering outlays when there are decreasing costs. Price discrimination, however, is only possible if a supplier has a degree of monopoly power in the market.

Again drawing on the airline parallel, this has been attained through loyalty schemes such as frequent flyer benefits and through mergers of carriers. Loyalty schemes are somewhat different in Internet markets where transactions are potentially more frequent than flights. As with frequent flyer schemes they should also be non-linear involving plateaus above which the bonuses are greater. The discrimination can also be through 'shopbots' whereby the e-commerce company separates out those users who search out lowest cost generic products systematically and those who do not. By holding periodic sales, the careful searcher can get the lowest price, but at the expense of both search costs and forgone loyalty payments. Such segmentation also allows consumer surplus to be translated into producer revenues for the Internet provider.

3.5 CONCLUSIONS

In a way this chapter highlights how little real understanding there is of the economic implications of the Internet and e-commerce. Lack of quantification is a particular handicap for testing alternative theories, but the general neglect of network modeling until comparatively recently is also a limiting factor.

Of course, it could be that the New Information Age is simply a modified replication of the telegraph era, or the telephone age, and that there is really little more economics to be understood. The new technology has features common to many other network activities, albeit with a few idiosyncrasies of its own, and by and large, therefore, its role in society can be explained in traditional microeconomic theories, or at least by rather minor variations to that theory. The Internet simply offers an advanced form of communication that will have implications for the way we work and travel, but fundamentally these will be similar in their implications to early trends in communications technology, *viz*; the railways, telegraph, postal service etc. caused important one-time shifts in the aggregate production function and were then assimilated. The empirical evidence to date does not refute this idea.

The alternative is that the Internet/e-commerce economy requires a new way of thinking and not simply a minor reformulation of traditional theory. The speed of change, the new social values and the complexity of the 'new age' make traditional theories redundant and potentially very misleading. The evidence on this has not really materialized to date. Certainly, there are differences in the way the US economy has been performing in recent years, with low inflation and low unemployment thwarting traditional economic ideas such as the Phillips Curve. In itself, however, this may simply be a reflection of a stepped change in the structure of the economy rather than creating a fundamental change that should reshape economic thinking. Only time will tell which school of thought is correct.

4 TELECOMMUNICATIONS AND TRAVEL BEHAVIOR

4.1 INTRODUCTION

Our concern here is with the way that emerging telecommunications technologies are impacting on personal transportation, and in particular work related travel.[1] In one sense we see it every day as drivers pass engrossed (often illegally) in their mobile phone conversations. But there is more to it than the ability to travel and communicate at the same time. There are complex links between the way we view and use telecommunications and our personal mobility.

Society's affinity with the automobile is not new, nor is it on the wane. This pattern is, as we briefly argued in Chapter 1, partly associated with travel behavior but it goes beyond this because car ownership is seen as reflective of status and independence (Dupuy, 1999). Given this, it is unlikely that future traffic congestion problems, and possibly environmental concerns, will diminish with the continuation of existing traffic policies. Indeed, there are reasons to think that they will worsen. Land restrictions limit the ability to expand existing roads and to develop new roads. In addition, the commute to work is the most common trip made and this commute contributes significantly to road congestion (Mokhtarian, 1997).

More complex commute patterns, more multiple-purpose trips, and increased female labor participation are adding to commuter problems in many cities. From a traffic management perspective, these factors create a conundrum with respect to controlling traffic flows and maintaining traffic safety. They also raise matters of environmental protection and public health.

Some have argued that Intelligent Transportation Systems (ITS) – an infrastructure of networks that includes public transportation, traveler information and vehicle control devices – may be used to increase the productivity of existing transportation infrastructure. However, ITS and road telematic devices – those that merge telecommunications and the microprocessor (Eisenstein, 1999) – remain emergent and are not yet widely available. In addition, the proliferation of these technologies suffers from problems including significant infrastructure costs and associated technology development, implementation, motivational, and

---

[1]   In fact it is even a little narrower than that in that the main focus is on teleworking and little is said about such things as teleconferencing that is becoming an increasingly common business practice. This is left to the next chapter.

management problems, as well as the lack of awareness of the benefits of these technologies by policy makers and consumers.

As a result, many in transportation management are looking to telework as a means of providing an interim, less costly and fairly expeditious way of reducing traffic congestion and traffic related pollution; the 'intelligent transportation approach'.[2] Generally, it is believed that telework has the potential to eliminate or otherwise shorten work commutes during peak travel times since with telework, employees work from home or travel to nearby work centers. Such options provide individuals with increased control over work and family requirements, and provide employers benefits such as lower costs, increased employee morale, and higher productivity.

There has also been interest from the policy perspective in the role that teleworking and the like may play in reducing the environmental costs of transportation, and in particular the pollution associated with the automobile. Cars both create a large amount of environmental damage and produce a diverse range of harmful effects that, it is often argued, require a range of policy options to combat.[3] Whilst not a direct means of internalizing these social costs of transportation by affecting the amount and nature of personal and goods movement it is felt that telecommunications policy may have desirable effects on the problems of traffic and the environment.

Telecommunication advances have created ranges of 'teleprocesses' that afford the development of varied work methods and arrangements for individuals and firms alike (Nilles, 1994). Teleprocesses encompass teleservices (online banking and shopping), but also include telework. Telework is a term that is used quite loosely and has a variety of definitions – the scope of which is either very broad or very narrow. In the literature the term 'telecommuting' is used more frequently. Internationally, however, 'telework' is the more common term. In Europe, telework is a slightly broader concept than telecommuting and refers to work performed from distant locations and does not necessarily substitute for the journey to work.

Nonetheless, telework is generally understood to involve 'using telecommunications to conduct business at a distance and includes videoconferencing, online database searches, facsimile transmission, cellular [and standard] phone calls, voicemail, and electronic mail' (Handy and Mokhtarian. 1995). Technically, telecommuting is a subset of telework; it eliminates or reduces the length of commute trips because work is completed at home or in telecenters; and has direct transportation implications (Mokhtarian, 1991). Here, the terms

---

[2]   For a significant study of the issues involved in the US see US Department of Transportation (1992).

[3]   As pointed out in Chapter 2 within the industrial countries, transportation accounts significant nitrogen oxide emissions (an 'acid rain' gas), carbon monoxide emissions (a toxic gas), particulates (that can be carcinogenic), hydrocarbons (that are the main contributors to 'global warming'), as well as being noisy and visually intrusive.

telework and telecommunications will be used interchangeably. The definition of telework undergirding this book refers to:

> company/government employees in any occupational group working full- or part-time for whom the commute to work is eliminated, shifted out of peak commute times, or shortened through the performance of the work role at home or at an alternative workcenter, and who communicates with the usual place of work using electronic, tele/videoconferencing or other means instead of traveling there.[4]

4.2 COMPLEMENTS OR SUBSTITUTES?

One of the primary reasons behind the push for the increased investigation of telework options is the belief that telecommunication advances will function as a substitute for travel, or affect travel behavior in such a way that peak period congestion is reduced. There is, however, no accepted consensus on the exact nature of the links between telecommunications, and especially teleworking, and transportation use. Two basic hypotheses have been proposed to describe the dominant potential relationship. These are related to notions that information systems may be a substitution or a complement to travel.

4.2.1 Concepts of complementarity and substitutability

Mokhtarian (1997) points out that, 'Historically, transportation and communications have been complements to each other, both increasing concurrently, rather than substitutes for each other. And we have no reason to expect that relationship to change'. But this is not a view all share, and empirical testing is difficult.[5]

Complementarity is, for ease of analysis, commonly discussed in specific terms of enhancement and efficiency, although in practice complementarity is essentially a hybrid of the two.

In the case of enhancement, communication stimulates the need or incentive for travel by precipitating the transfer of additional information, specifically information about available opportunities. A brief e-mail, for example, may spark one to identify relevant information (that may or may not involve transportation) on a completely different project. This type of cross-fertilization, synergy, or

---

[4]   Adapted from the definition used by the US Bureau of Transportation Statistics (1993). The definition excludes field workers who travel in the course of work and self-employed, home-based workers, private consultants and contract workers.

[5]   There have been studies looking at such things as telephone usage and travel that have sought to isolate the substitution and inducing effects of telecommunications on travel. Micro studies of this find a combination of substitution and complementary effects but the ratio seems to be very contextual (Claisse and Rowe, 1993)

enhancement is more likely to occur now, purely as a result of the permeability, magnitude, and timeliness of information flows made possible by technology.

An example commonly used to illustrate enhanced efficiency is in freight transportation, where communications technology makes the supply chain more 'transparent' and, therefore, assists efficiency of scheduling and customer service. In personal transportation, an individual may choose to telework in the morning, avoid the morning peak period of traffic congestion, and drive to work later in the day attending business meetings en route. It is argued that the person's efficiency is improved.

Until recently, substitution has been the more popular of the hypotheses, and one that has been taken on board my many politicians and a painless way of tackling traffic congestion. Salomon (2000) succinctly outlines the theory of substitution with regard to transportation and telework; an increase in the supply and use of telecommunications will result in a diminishing demand for transport services. He asserts, however, that there is little evidence to support substitution. He states, 'Consumers are likely to make their choices on the use of either travel or telecommunications on the basis of which mode better serves their ends.'

Thus, instead of substitution, a more plausible telecommunication-travel relationship is that of travel modification. According to the theory of modification, the availability of telecommunications will modify the demand for travel but not in one unique direction. The realities of the impacts of past communication advances (i.e. the telephone[6] and facsimile), and present research, supports modification of travel patterns with respect to telework.

A complicating factor of the substitution hypothesis is an assumption that the total volume of interactions, whether by travel or communication (e.g., interactions between people or between workplace and employee) is constant.[7] This assumption may not be the case (Albertson, 1977). The Institute pour Frantide shows a gradual increase in passenger transport miles and the number of remote communications in France between the early eighteenth century and late twentieth century. Also in practice, the policies adopted regarding the way the transportation system is used and the way teleworking is treated by companies and government, for example regarding tax incentives, will be influential on the level of teleworking adopted.

Supporting this hypothesis, over time the aggregate amount of all forms of communication has increased. Incomes have risen, car ownership has risen, and socioeconomic life of western economies has evolved to encourage greater levels of interpersonal contact. High growth in the service sector and information industries, for example, has resulted in a greater inherent emphasis on face-to-face

[6]   For an analysis of the effects of standard telephones on travel see Claisse and Rowe (1993)

[7]   Nilles (1994) points out, for example, that as the independent demand for telecommunications grows, opportunities for travel substitution and travel stimulation emerge simultaneously. Given this, a clear trade-off between travel and telecommunication seems unlikely.

communication and the development of interpersonal relationships during work hours.

Drawing on the ideas of Sviden (1983) a more complete picture seems to be, therefore, that the interactions between telecommunications and transportation have potentially three dimensions. In some cases there is complementarity with advanced communications stimulating teleworking, in other cases there is substitution, but in the third case it may stimulate additional interactions involving both some substitution but also some additional travel (Figure 4.1)

The links are thus not always clear and are often more complex than is sometimes assumed. Increasingly, business and pleasure are merging, and networking is a valued skill in contemporary working life. The complexity of social, economic and technological forces can be such that a firm's success frequently depends heavily on continuously adaptive organizational interactions or networks. This can be particularly so in the case of political and social complexity where a meeting face-to-face may be more desirable than a telephone, videoconference or e-mail interaction. Individuals may be more comfortable discussing the complexities and or sensitivities of a project or process in person. The availability of multiple modes of communication, personal and electronic, enhances the range of opportunities for interaction.

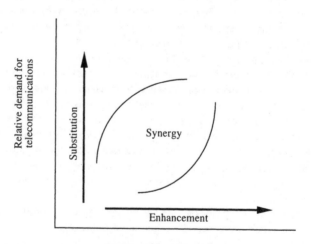

Relative demand for transportation

Figure 4.1 Substitution, enhancement, and synergies

4.2.2 The nature of work

The degree to which telecommunications acts as either a substitute or a complement for transportation will change over time as the nature of work itself changes. The idea of what work entails has historically undergone change as economies have shifted through the centuries from agriculture, heavy industry, manufacturing to an information/knowledge era. We are now moving into a global economic environment. Sullivan (1999) compares the traditional work relationships that generally existed to 'boundaryless' or more individualist career paths that exist today (Table 4.1).

Table 4.1 Comparison of traditional and boundary less careers

	Traditional	Boundaryless
Employment relationship	Job security for loyalty	Employability for performance and flexibility
Boundaries (employers)	1 or 2 firms	Multiple firms
Skills	Firm specific	Transferable
Success measured by	Pay, promotion, status	Psychologically meaningful work
Responsibility for career	Organization	Individual
Training	Formal program	On-the-job
Milestones	Age-related	Learning-related

The locus of control for work and career paths has shifted from the company to the individual. Similarly, telework options increase the levels of autonomy and responsibility for employees. Technological advances and globalization, both of which create the need to use flexible scheduling and work options to meet global service and personal needs, enhance the practicality of telework alternatives for businesses and individuals alike (Lobel et al, 1999). Also, telework is the type of work arrangement that influences individual outcomes like work–family balance, job satisfaction and stress, as well as organizational outcomes like worker morale, productivity, and commitment (Sullivan, 1999). Thus, telework has the potential to further influence the nature of work.

The components of telework's influence on the nature of work are reflected in, amongst other things, increased use of flexible work hours, satellite offices, innovative monitoring systems, and alternative office arrangements like 'hoteling'. Hoteling involves reducing the number of private offices and having employees share or reserve office space only when a workspace in the primary office is needed (Saveri, 1995) while they work at home or are at meetings elsewhere for the rest of their work time. The influence of telework also involves aspects of social connectedness/cohesion as well as several dimensions of trust.[8]

Fukuyama (1996) suggests that the social interaction of workplaces is an important element of fostering a sense of community over individualism. He contends, 'Work and money are much more important as sources of identity, status and dignity ... This kind of recognition cannot be achieved by individuals; it can come about only in a social context.'

---

[8]   Salomon and Salomon (1984) and Shamir and Salomon (1985) offer some insights into the employees' perspectives on teleworking.

Teleworking does interfere with this 'community building' process, if only modestly at this juncture. It can also be said that telework adds a dimension of uncertainty that may not bode well for trust within an organization as 'trust reduces social complexity by going beyond available information and generalizing expectations of behaviors in that it replaces missing information with an internally guaranteed certainty, (Blois, 1999). Diminished levels of face-to-face interaction may reduce trust among managers and staff. Significant increases in the levels and penetration of telework may, however, pose threats to social stability via reduced levels of social capital and shared norms. The reduction in social interaction may create problems for some workers, but not all necessarily.

However, if the costs of videoconferencing equipment and the like diminish, then perhaps teleworking will not have a negative impact on community building or a shared organizational culture. If organizations develop formal strategies to promote the use of videoconferencing and other means of keeping teleworkers 'connected' socially, then a new form of organizational communication may emerge that helps to foster trust instead of diminishing it. The additional communication outlet may help promote increased levels of informal social interaction and cohesion.

Fukuyama (1999) contends that in the case of Silicon Valley informal social networks within the various flat, loosely structured organizations facilitated trust and its economic boom. Therefore, employees themselves may find informal ways to maintain social connections despite being physically separated from the work–place. Also, reconnecting work and home may have positive benefits. Fukuyama states, '...it is if anything more natural and more in keeping with the experience of human beings throughout history that home and work should be co-located'. With respect to identity, telework may help to 'regenerate' some of the family and community norms that have been on the wane.

Giving workers the flexibility to manage their work and family requirements may in the very least reduce stress and improve dispositions and interpersonal interactions. Nonetheless, these types of social and psychological issues are complex and need to be evaluated carefully as there is uncertainty regarding the direction and level of telework's impact at this juncture.

4.2.3 Expanding interactions

Improved and novel transportation technologies, together with additional transportation infrastructure and hardware, have allowed personal interactions to grow considerably over time. These developments, coupled with new demands stemming from changing behavioral patterns have permitted more frequent interactions between the same individuals or groups (a 'deepening effect') and for a larger number of interactions among different individuals (a 'widening effect').

In practice, however, at any point in time there are physical and logistical constraints on the capacity of individuals to meet face-to-face; the transactions costs, to use the jargon of institutional economics, can be very high. This constrained interaction curve is shown graphically in Figure 4.2. Public concerns about the environmental implications of further infrastructure expansion and the high financial costs of such investments, combined with changes in life-styles, suggest that this interaction curve is now beginning to flatten in many countries. It is becoming more difficult and costly to meet face-to-face. Questions can also be raised concerning the marginal social utility of additional transportation infrastructure provision, especially if it leads to additional travel.

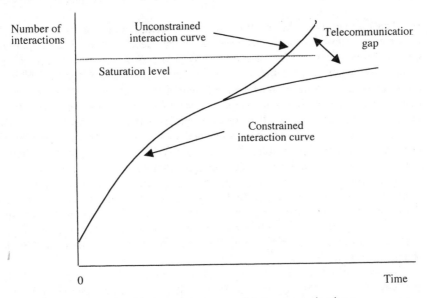

Figure 4.2 The constrained interaction curve and telecommunications

Through telecommunications technology a greater number of interactions are possible because of the empowerment provided through timely (in some cases real-time) information transfer (the unconstrained interaction curve in Figure 4.2). This development means that telecommunications has the scope to not only fill the potential interactions, but also to push up the unconstrained curve. What types of interactions are most efficiently replaced by telecommunications in this process is by no means certain.

4.2.4 Factors affecting interactions
An important factor affecting the nature of human interactions is the complexity and security of the information that has to be transferred. In general, the more complex and sensitive the information, the more important is the need for face-to-face contact. There is also the uncertain issue of the additional amount of interactions that are generated by the very existence of new forms of interaction. What is currently evident is that people are engaged in a wider range of interactions than before and that the net effect is a greater number of interactions in total.

It is useful in looking at the link between telecommunications and transportation to review the sociological context within which personal transportation take place. Much of the early modeling of travel patterns was essentially aggregate in nature and engineering driven. While more recent work has been more closely allied to behavioral types of models, often based in microeconomic theory, it is still in many ways very simplistic. In particular it has traditionally been assumed that people travel to work just to earn an income. Other motivations for making these types of trip are now seen as important and can impact on travel patterns.

The journey-to-work, and the associated traffic congestion, has been at the center of debates on urban transportation policy. Because road space is publicly owned and not provided in a market setting, and consequently road users are not made fully aware of the full costs of their actions on others at the time trips are made, there tends to develop excessive levels of commuter congestion. Excessive congestion is seen as inefficient in a purely transportation sense and, because of the pollution generated, is often an environmental issue. Considerable research and policy-based analysis has been expended seeking a socially acceptable way of limiting the congestion problem.[9] Recent analysis suggests, however, that the issue may be more complex than is traditionally thought.

In much of the transportation and communications discussions, there is the implicit assumption that individuals wish to reduce their travel time, and in particular that involved in the journey-to-work. This has stemmed, in part, from the notion that travel is largely a derived demand existing for the sake of other ends (e.g., to earn an income, shop, transport children or socialize), rather than being an end in itself.

Research in California challenges this assumption, drawing on the findings of a survey of over 1,300 workers that found that only 3% of people desired a zero-to-two minute commute. It showed that almost 50% of respondents preferred a commute of 20 minutes or more. This type of finding would not be inconsistent with the notion of the constant travel budget hypothesis that some traffic engineers have long supported. Such an amount of time spent in traffic congestion may be seen as a reasonable price to pay for a suburban life-style.

Policy makers and researchers focus on the negative impacts of the commute in terms of environmental impacts, congestion, stress and so on, while the positive attributes are not recognized. It can be argued that individuals often value the transition between home and work and the ability to use the time productively. They may also value the opportunity to drive a status-oriented automobile or the chance to experience the sites by traveling. They may value a non-home destination for work because of the social/professional interaction opportunities it affords, the scenic location, or the shopping and other location amenities. There

---

[9]   Ideally many economists would privatize the road network giving explicit property rights to the owners. This would stimulate them to ensure the facilities are used optimally. Failing this, a congestion charge could be levied (the 'Road Price') that would lead to a congestion level acceptable to the public authorities being achieved. In practice, however, efforts to contain congestion have involved a combination of subsidies for public transit, physical traffic management schemes and adding additional road capacity. Continuing high levels of traffic congestion are the result.

are also the opportunity benefits involved in not spending time in a commute such as doing household chores.

Various pressures and constraints appear important for individuals to change their prevailing work routine. In the majority of cases, a threshold level of dissatisfaction with one or more aspects of life was necessary to cause an individual to consider an alternative to conventional work patterns. This dissatisfaction may be manifest in a desire to accomplish certain goals in work, family, leisure or travel.

Constraints could also be manifest in the amount of telecommuting permitted by the nature of the job or by the employer, the availability of suitable remote technology, whether supervisors support telecommuting, and the propensity toward distractions at home. Individual are likely to be more productive if they are easily able to switch off from, and separate, home duties.

As seen in Chapter 2, interest has grown in the travel patterns of the genders, particularly the apparent idiosyncrasies of travel by women. More part-time work, increases in female non-home based travel, partly through a greater proportion of women in the workforce, and flexible employment have contributed to increased demand for off-peak travel. Women remain responsible for the majority of household duties and child care and this leads to more complex travel patterns involving linked trips and greater car dependency. The flexibility, and complementarity, provided by teleworking is likely to be valued by women, particularly those with dependants.

Employers may find benefits in stimulating or facilitating teleworking. The current relatively strong economy in the US, even in the early 2000s, favors employees. Employers, particularly in the information technology sectors experience difficulties retaining high-quality staff, resulting in valuable expertise and tacit knowledge walking out the door. Employers are often creative in terms of the remuneration packages that they offer, but they also need to provide and manage the work environment. More subtly, telecommunications provides the advantage of impersonalizing communication. It may be more advantageous to employers to use telecommunications to emphasize content and minimize social influences, and to reduced socio-emotional communication and increased task orientation that can enhance group work and efficiency. The success of this effort depends on the context and environment in which the telecommunications mediums are used.

According to some psychologists, the interpersonal attraction dimension of social influence is a multidimensional construct, comprising task attraction, physical attraction and social attraction. The more people are attracted to one another, the more they will communicate with one another. But the more they are attracted to another person, the more influence that person has in interpersonal communication. Interpersonal attractiveness can thus enhance communication and detract from it. Strategically employers could use either telecommunications or face-to-face methods depending on the individuals involved and the company's objectives. It provides employees with more options.

From a financial perspective, employers have identified benefits from savings in office space, lighting and utilities by outsourcing to one-person businesses. In some cases, new office buildings are being designed on the premise that workers will 'rent' rather than 'own' space, that is; they will have no dedicated desk, but book one when they need to visit the office (hot desks). Estimations of savings are, however, scant.

In summary, the benefits to employers are largely idiosyncratic, depending on the circumstances and environment of each firm. Transition costs may be large and they are also likely to vary according to the current working practices and fixed investments of firms. Changing working practices is not cost-less and can be disruptive in terms of meeting customer demands.

4.3 TRENDS AND REALITIES FOSTERING INTEREST IN TELEWORK

4.3.1 The potential for teleworking

Teleworking can take a number of different forms. Exact delineation is difficult but there has been a convergence to some standard classification. In the US telework options exist in two basic forms (US Bureau of Transportation Statistics. 1993):

- *Home-based.* Employee works at home 1–2 days/week and spends the rest of the week at the main office or other facility;
- *Regional centers/workcenters* – These centers serve as extensions of the normal workplace, but are located closer to employees' homes, in less congested areas or near public transit locations. Regional centers exist in three primary forms:
  (i) *Satellite workcenters* – These centers are established and equipped by an organization to accommodate its teleworking staff;
  (ii) *Local workcenters* – Teleworkers from different organizations use these facilities and share office space/equipment
  (iii) *Neighborhood workcenters* – These are smaller centers that serve fewer workers, but generally are located within walking distance of employee residences.

Typically, information or knowledge-based jobs are more suitable for telework. That is, jobs where workers' primary activity involves the creation, processing, manipulation, or distribution of information. McCloskey and Igbaria (1998) note that within this context, both jobs with a high division of labor and external control (clerical) and a low division of labor and internal control (professional or managerial) are amenable to telework. According to Nilles (1988), jobs or tasks that are not location dependent and/or do not require significant levels of face-to-face interaction, are likely to be good candidates for telecommuting. Korte and Wynne (1996) suggest the following are possibilities for teleworking:

- Data entry or typing
- Programming or other specialist computing
- Secretarial or administrative work
- Translation
- Financial services, book-keeping or accountancy
- Ordering, information or booking services
- Sales, marketing
- Editing
- Research, consultancy
- Design, architectural work
- Training, education
- Management
- Repair, maintenance.

4.3.2 The up-take of teleworking

As seen in previous chapters, the amount of teleworking still varies considerably from country to country, and also inevitably within countries. But there is, nevertheless a steady growth in its adoption that extends across virtually all countries. Table 4.2, for example, reports the growth in teleworking within the European Union in the 1990s. Although the data are not strictly comparable across years, inverse levels of utilization are clear but so is the overall positive growth path.

Table 4.2 Teleworking in EU countries

Country	Level of teleworking – formal and informal		
	1994	1997	1998/9
Austria	0.35	1.50	2.00
Belgium	0.48	5.3o	6.20
Denmark	0.37	9.70	11.60
Finland	2.50	6.30	10.00
France	0.98	1.10	1.80
Germany	0.41	1.90	5.10
Greece	0.46	0.50	1.30
Ireland	1.40	6.10	7.10
Italy	0.46	0.90	1.70
Netherlands	1.22	9.10	18.20
Portugal	0.56	1.30	2.20
Spain	0.82	0.60	0.90
Sweden	3.77	5.40	9.00
United Kingdom	2.20	7.0	5.50

Source: European Union.

This recent interest in telework is a reflection of the convergence of several important communication, legislative, societal, transportation, and workplace trends. Essentially, advances in communication technology, the growing interest in cost-reduction and retention concerns of employers, and increasing concerns regarding traffic congestion and air pollution have spurred on interest in this burgeoning trend. The following illustrate existing realities and/or trends from various perspectives that influence further investigation into the potentiality of more telework.

Automobile use and environmental concerns
The shape and structure of cities, limits on public transportation availability, and the increasing suburbanization of employment often make car ownership an economic necessity. Americans drive 6.3 billion miles a day, compared to 2.4 billion in 1965 (Consumer Federation of America, 1996). Since 1969 the average number of persons in a household fell from 3.16 to 2.56 in 1990 but the number of cars per household increased from 1.16 to 1.77 over the same period while the popularity of work-linked carpooling declined from 20.4% of all work trips in 1970 to 13.4% in 1990 (Ferguson, 1997). Another study, shows that between 1980 and 1990, the percentage of people driving to work alone rose from 64% to 73% (Russell, 1996).

The result was that congestion grew from seriously affecting 41% of US urban interstate highways in 1975 to 69% in 1993 (Langhoff, 1999). With this came heightened concerns over environmental hazards and costs associated with increased levels of emissions generated by automobiles. In 1996, transportation accounted for 32% of US carbon dioxide emissions. In 1985, about 390 million metric tons of carbon were emitted by transportation sources; by 1996, nearly 450 million metric tons were emitted (US Federal Highway Administration, 1998).

Business concerns
US corporations' sense of space is expanding on a variety of levels: geographic (global markets), physical (virtual offices), and electronic (use of information and telecommunication technology) (Saveri, 1995). In order to develop and retain competitive advantages and/or to increase global competitiveness, the organizational structures of many firms have flattened. Firms have downsized and decentralized their operations in order to reduce costs and overheads, yet at the same time, these actions help to increase market flexibility and responsiveness.

In addition, the nature of work in the information era and the type of workers required for such work, is changing. Work in this era is increasingly less labor intensive and more capital and knowledge intensive. Increased literacy and numeracy skills – not brawn – are required of today's employees. Knowledge based work is facilitated by computerization and automation, and thereby decreases the connection of work to physical spaces. Also, current tight labor markets – particularly within high-technology industries – make it increasingly difficult for employers to find and retain employees with needed skills and talents.

ITS concerns

ITS and telematic technologies undoubtedly have considerable potential to address the nation's increasing traffic congestion and safety concerns – see the more complete discussion in Chapter 7. Some ITS applications like anti-lock braking systems (ABS) have already proven to be effective and are popular features among auto users. Road telematic features, like the OnStar travel information service, are also popular and this type of technology is gaining significantly in its use. However, advanced technologies like voice and speech recognition, forward-looking radar and intelligent cruise control remain costly, emergent technologies that have really yet to take off. Related telematics applications suffer from similar challenges of reliability and upgradeability of features, meeting customer demands for simple, safe, real-time services, and overcoming lingering technical and cost problems (Eisenstein, 1999).

In term of infrastructure, telecommunications, in conjunction with institutional reforms, has played an increasing role in facilitating coordinated responses to incidents and in coordination of traffic management more generally. The challenges here are often far more to do with overcoming institutional constraints than in finding an appropriate technology to adopt. In many cases, public sector infrastructure authorities are lagging private sector on-vehicle systems in application.

Individual family trends

Demographic trends influence the labor market. For example, the 'Baby Bust' cohort (about 45 million persons) in the US is smaller than its predecessor, the 'Baby Boom' cohort (about 77 million persons), therefore fewer young persons are entering the workforce (Gross, 1996). New entrants to the workforce will increasingly comprise more technologically skilled persons who view jobs as temporary (Shulman and Reiser, 1996). Many baby boomers in the current labor market are a part of the sandwich generation – persons that must care for both young children and their aging parents. For example, 47% of US workers are required to provide either child or eldercare; and 66% of parents feel they do not have enough time to spend with their children.

Workers therefore, are seeking more flexible work options to address family obligations. Currently, upwards of 75% of employers now have part-time employment options, about 60% offer flextime options, and 45% offer job-sharing options (Williams, 1996). Thus, telework is viewed as an additional alternative work option that employers can offer employees.

Legislation

Several pieces of important legislation in the US have facilitated the overall interest in telework. They include the Americans with Disabilities Act that requires employers not to discriminate against persons with disabilities and that proper workplace accommodations be made for disabled persons. The 1990 Clean Air Act requires that employer trip reduction and vehicle occupancy programs be implemented for State Implementation programs. The 1991 Intermodal Surface Transportation Efficiency Act provides federal funds to develop telework programs. The 1998 Transportation Equity Act for the 21st Century/TEA Restoration Act, 'builds and authorizes funds for highway improvement, safety, and research programs" (US Department of Transportation. 1998).

Within the federal government, efforts have been made to promote a 'family friendly' work environment. According to the President, family-friendly environments were to be obtained through 'broad use of flexible work arrangements to enable federal employees to better balance their work and family responsibilities ... increase employee effectiveness and job satisfaction while decreasing turnover rates and absenteeism' (Weekly Compilation of Presidential Documents, 1994). Telework options are generally included in such flexible work options. In addition, in 1996, the President's Management Council on Interagency Telecommuting Working Group desired that 'each agency and department make telecommuting part of its overall strategy to improve government services to the American people' (President's Management Council, 1996).

Finally, the National Telecommuting and Air Quality Act of 1999 requires the Secretary of Transportation to make a grant to a nonprofit private entity for the purpose of developing a pilot program for the use of telecommuting as a means of reducing air pollutants. In addition, under Public Law 106-246, the Administrator of the Environmental Protection Agency was required to make a grant for the first year of a 2-year program to implement telecommuting projects in five metropolitan areas. There have been other legislative initiatives; these are intended just to offer a flavor of what has happened.

Technological factors

Technological advances have made it easier and cheaper to communicate across geographic space. The advances have taken place with respect to a broad range of technologies and services including: computer and communications manufacturing, electronic components, peripheral equipment and software, electronic signalization, and communication services (cellular, specialized mobile radio services, personal communication services, cordless, paging, and the like).

In addition the shift from analog to digital infrastructures and decreased dependence on networks, allows for significant increases in capacity (Seth and Sisodia, 1997). Both of these advances provide greater economies of scale, increase the features and services available, and reduce unit costs. The increasing number of technological options and the reduction in costs (as well as the number of persons with Internet access and the widespread availability of fax machines) make telecommuting options more viable – nationally and internationally. For example, in 1930 a 3-minute call from London to New York cost $250 in 1990 dollars; by 2005 the same call may cost $0.10 (Smith, 1996).

4.4 WHAT IS KNOWN ABOUT TELEWORK

The definition of telework adopted has significant implications for determining the actual number of teleworkers, and consequently for assessing the potential impact of teleworking on travel and related behavior. So far we have been very loose in our definitions to allow the conveyance of some general points, but precise definitions are important for quantification and for detecting changing trends over time.

According to the International Telework Association and Council, for example, there were some 19.6 million persons telecommuting in the US at least occasionally in 1999. Another source contended, however, that the number of telecommuters was more in the range of 21 million people – 5% of the workforce (Ruhling, 2000). The estimates of people who telework full-time are even more varied. One estimate asserts that 7.4 million people were full-time telecommuters in the late 1990s (Deeprose, 1999); yet, according to another, there were only 1 million telecommuters (Au, 2000). The only consistent fact seems to be that people prefer to telecommute on a part-time basis – generally one or two days per week (Mokhtarian and Bagley, 2000).

The variation in the figures illustrates that the accuracy of estimates and projections can be contingent upon how telework is defined. Korte and Wynne (1996), for example, explicitly note that, in Europe part of the difficulty in estimating telework figures is that there is a lack of reliable empirical data that makes both local and international comparisons difficult.

Often the definition of telework varies between studies. Distinctions are also often not made between self-employed home workers, contractor home workers, remote workers (i.e., salesmen) and telecommuters. Pratt (2000) contends, 'Because the word telecommuting lacks a generally agreed-upon definition, when it is used in surveys it conveys various images to respondents. Thus, the data collected may be ambiguous and lead to errors of interpretation.' In addition, attempting to rely on employer based data to generate estimates of the number of teleworkers proves problematic because 'Employers themselves are probably not aware of the full extent of telecommuting by their employees, as much of it takes place informally and occasionally' (Handy and Mokhtarian, 1995).

Given such concerns, Handy and Mokhtarian (1996) have argued that to develop sound estimates and produce solid forecasts for teleworking, emphasis must be placed on determining both the penetration and level of telecommuting. Penetration refers to the percentage of workers that telecommute; levels of telecommuting are based on telework occasions (frequency) and refer to the percentage of workers that telework on a given day. Not all surveys attempt to capture these two distinct sets of information. To establish a more consistent definition of telework, Korte and Wynne (1996) outline three required dimensions of telework:

- *Workplace location.* Criteria where work or part of it is to be completed:
  - Partial independence of workplace location from company,
  - Location is temporarily or permanently close to or at the place of residence,
  - Location remote from the company;
- *IT use.* Levels of communication between teleworkers and employers:
  - Low: telephone, stand alone computer equipment, delivery of work/tasks by mail,

- High: telephone, fax machine, e-mail, PC or terminal linked to servers or mainframes, delivery of work/tasks transmitted via telecommunication network;
- *Organizational forms*. Nature/extent of organization for companies and employees vary:
  - Company – relocate functions, outsource, individual or micro-companies are free to locate elsewhere (home, shared office space, etc.);
  - Teleworkers – home-based work, alternate work between home and office, mobile work (work anywhere) and telework centers.

Because of data limitations, and the rather slippery nature of the teleworking concept, information on its up-take and importance in the economy is, therefore, as we have seen, inevitably, poor. Telework is also but one manifestation of increasing technological advances, the degree of up-take of these advances, the use made of them, and the resulting human behavior. Salomon (2000) illustrates the interaction of these components at the individual and institutional levels. Table 4.3 illustrates the increasing complexity society faces with respect to work, service, and social options.

An interrelated component of this complexity is transportation, which is increasingly being influenced by information and telecommunication advances. At this juncture, however, the emphasis is simply on telework and its capacity to make significant impacts on modifying or reducing congestion and pollution. The potential benefits for employers and employees that may be realized from increasing the amounts of telework are summarized in Table 4.4.

Table 4.3 Types of technology advances and their areas of impact

Demand side: Supply side:	Individuals/households	Institutions
Individuals/households	*Social* Telephone, Internet, E-mail	*Labor* Telecommuting
Institutions	*Products/Services* Teleshopping, Teleservices Tele-education, Telemedicine	*Products/Services* E-commerce, Teleconferencing, E-mail, EDI (Electonic Data Interchange)

Generally, traffic and environmental interests in telework have come from its potential effects on accessibility. (Salomon and Mokhtarian, 1998). Telework is conceptualized in many of these works as substituting trips to work while still providing the access (via telecommunication devices) needed to perform work functions. The reduction in the numbers of cars on the road, in turn, facilitates traffic management. Concomitantly, from the environmental standpoint, telework reduces vehicle-miles traveled (VMT) and the accompanying auto emissions. The Clean Air Act Corporation estimates that the average vehicle emits 1 gram of volatile organic compounds; 2 grams of nitrous oxides; and 5 grams of carbon monoxide per mile. Thus, fewer cars on the road generally translates into lower levels of air pollution.

Table 4.4 The nature of the potential costs and benefits of telework

Employer		Employee	
Benefits	Disbenefits	Benefits	Disbenefits
Reduced car parking requirements lowers overheads	Requires employee self-discipline	Greater flexibility in work hours	
Reductions in office space requirements – lighting, space, furniture	Lower productivity (e.g., home based distractions, lack of direct supervision)	Greater flexibility in life-style	Requires self-discipline
Higher staff productivity through fewer interruptions	Less effective communication between personnel due to lack of proximity and/or interaction	Higher productivity through fewer interruptions	Lower productivity due to e.g., home based distractions, lack of supervision
Higher efficiency (e.g., less 'paid' time traveling)	Less opportunity for cross-fertilization resulting from social/professional face-to-face interactions	Lower car use and less fuel consumed therefore money saved	Reduced social/professional contact and lack of stimulation from face-to-face interactions
Less dependent on climate conditions (e.g., snow days)	Provision and maintenance of equipment		
Greater flexibility in work hours	Not all jobs lend themselves to telecommuting causing resentment amongst some staff	Achieve more life goals in a day	Requires dedicated space in the home
Facilitate outsourcing	Increased security problems	Ability to avoid traveling at congested times	Internal household conflicts

A review of various US telecommuting studies reveals that on commute days teleworkers drove about 51.8 miles in the latter part of the twentieth century; on telework days, teleworkers drive only 18.6 miles (National Environmental Policy Institute, 2000). In general, this work concluded regarding telework sessions.

- Average vehicle trips are reduced by 1.1 trips
- Average vehicle miles are reduced by 33–35 miles
- Teleworkers often generate non-commute trips, but total VMT are still lower than on non-telework days
- Teleworkers often generate business-related trips, but total VMT are still lower than on non-telework days.

In terms of the business sector, the implications for the company plays a key role in the penetration of telework (American Management Association, 1999). Businesses normally need commercial or legal incentives, rather than perceptions of environmental concerns, in order to support telework; confronting social concerns seldom has a major positive impact on a firm's bottom line. Compliance with legal mandates, like the 1990 US Federal Clean Air Act, or the Americans with Disabilities Act, is one incentive, as providing telework options helps firms remain in compliance (Piskurich, 1996). There are, however, other reasons that firms establish telework programs including cost reductions (office space, turnover, and relocation); improved productivity and employee morale; and to access new labor markets.

There have also been other studies that have sought to evaluate and allocate the implications of teleworking in economic rather than physical terms. According to the International Telework Association and Council, for example, in the late 1990s, the cost and benefits associated with telecommuting in the US include.[10]

- $2,086 in reduced absenteeism costs per teleworking employee per year (63% savings)
- $685 in productivity gains annually per teleworker (22% increase)
- Retention savings of $7,920 annually for each teleworker retained (avoids replacement cost).

While the uptake of telework is contingent upon organizations offering the option to their workers, the success of telework efforts more critically rests with a voluntary desire of employees to engage in telework, or at least having the opportunity to participate in a new work package of which teleworking is one component. In this context, Mokhtarian and Salomon (1994) sought to identify drivers, constraints and facilitators of telework for individuals. Drivers are factors that provide the incentive, motive, or reason for telecommuting and are seen to include:

---

[10]   An additional rule of thumb is that companies average savings of $2 for every $1 spent on telework programs (American Management Association, 1999).

- *Work-related factors*: aspects of the work environment that are uncomfortable or undesirable for the individual and/or the desire to work independently.
- *Family-related factors*: role responsibilities and/or the desire for more family time.
- *Leisure-related factors:* pursue interests, education, personal improvement,
- *Ideological factors:* promote environmentalism.
- *Transportation factors:* avoid commute; temporarily disabled, etc.

Constraints and facilitators are factors that either encourage or discourage telework and embrace:

- *Awareness of the option*: lack of awareness, misunderstanding;
- *Organizational related*: lack of employer support, managerial disapproval;
- *Job related*: job suitability; availability of technology resources; high costs; and
- *Personality characteristics*: risk averse, social needs, level of discipline; benefit of commute; and conducive household environment.

The individual's decision process to telecommute is complex, however, telecommuters weigh the drivers of, and constraints to, their actions and generally, according to this work, favor telework options 1 to 3 days per week for several reasons including: travel difficulties are avoided; improved concentration and fewer interruptions; increased autonomy; and lower work-related costs (Telework Analytics International, Inc., 1999).

4.5 CONCERNS AROUND TELEWORK

While traffic planners have for many years been exploring the role of teleworking as a means of reducing pressure on congested transport facilities, others, and particularly social scientists, have been more interested in some of the wider problems associated with more teleworking. The concerns are wide-ranging, and some of the key points have been addressed elsewhere which influences their depth here, but they include the following factors.

4.5.1 Confidence and trust
The nature of telework can influence the nature of work leading, for example, to increased use of flexible work hours, satellite offices and alternative office arrangements like hoteling, which involves reducing the number of private offices and having employees share or reserve office space only when a workspace in the primary office is needed (Saveri, 1995). The influence of telework also involves aspects of social connectedness/cohesion and trust.

It has been suggested by Fukuyama (1996) that social interactions at workplaces are an important element of fostering a sense of community over individualism, arguing that, 'Work and money are much more important as sources of identity, status and dignity ... This kind of recognition cannot be achieved by individuals; it can come about only in a social context.' Teleworking can potentially interfere with this community building process. Telework can also create dimensions of uncertainty within an organization and thereby reduce trust among managers and staff.[11]

Much, however, would seem to depend on the technology adopted. If the costs of videoconferencing equipment and such fall then there is more potential for the virtual inclusion of remote workers within a pseudo office environment. By keeping teleworkers socially connected new forms of organizational communication may emerge, helping to foster and retain traditional levels of trust.

4.5.2 Telecommuting choice

The context in which teleworking is used within an organization's overall structure can influence its successful up-take. Mitchell (1996) helpfully outlines several micro and macro parameters that help guide telework discussions and the formulation of telework programs and policies. Micro-level parameters are those that pertain to individuals or a particular firm and include:

- *Person* – skills, attitudes, preferences, etc.
- *Employment context* – single employer, self-employment, virtual firm, etc.
- *Task set* – nature of the work to be completed (concentrative versus. communicative).
- *Nature of external relationships* – customer preference for face-to-face interaction, etc.
- *Locational context* – home-based, telecenters, mobile, etc.
- *Nature of internal work* – level of interaction/interdependency with others, work styles, etc.
- *Technology context* – level of existing technology use, comfort with technology use, costs associated with technology resources/equipment.

More macro-level parameters are strategic factors for firms or regions to assess when considering telework policies. They may include:

- *Geographical context* – regional characteristics.
- *Sectoral context* – impact on different industries; industry bias; strengths of industries, etc.

---

[11]   Trust is important in the workplace according to management scientists because it 'reduces social complexity by going beyond available information and generalizing expectations of behaviors in that it replaces missing information with an internally guaranteed certainty' (Blois, 1999).

- *Product and delivery characteristics* – understanding of attention needed for product/delivery mix; global market issues.
- *Skills context* – consideration of types of skills needed/need to be developed.
- *Regulatory context* – regulations are favorable/unfavorable to telework.
- *Policy context* – the policy focus is to encourage innovation; protect workers, etc.

Taking the time to thoroughly consider these factors reduces the likelihood of a company developing ill-conceived or constructed programs or policies. At the same time, examining these micro and macro factors to potential telework, but also non-teleworking employees, helps those involved better understand the multifaceted nature of telework.

Bernardino and Ben-Akiva's (1996) decision model for the adoption of telework incorporates concerns and perspectives of both the employer and the employee. The motivations and constraints of these parties differ, yet are contingent upon one another. For example, in designing a telework program, firms will consider profitability, teleworking frequency, organizational needs and the like. The types of programs offered to employees will cause workers to evaluate the qualities and characteristics of the offering, their own motivations and concerns, etc., before making a decision to adopt telework as an option. Given that employees are central to the success of telework, it is important to understand and carefully assess factors that influence their decisions to undertake telework.

Mokhtarian and Salomon (1994) contend that the individual decision-making process associated with telecommuting is complex. Social and psychological variables are, however, likely given short shrift by transportation planners when the advantages of telecommuting are considered. Mokhtarian and Salomon note, 'the choice to telecommute is not a classic residential or work-location decision, as the choice is usually to telecommute only part time [1–2 days/week], and again can be motivated by different factors than are included in traditional location models'.

In another study, Mokhtarian and Salomon (1996a) found that about 12% of their sample did not want to commute; a finding that correlates with the 15% of hard core telecommuters and 15% who did not even think about telecommuting found by of Mahmassani et al. (1993) – see Table 4.5. The table also suggests that most employees only favor teleworking under certain conditions. The majority of respondents are only willing to accept telework options provided the employers pay all related costs and only about 35% would be willing to work from home every day provided that they received a pay increase as well as the employer paying all related costs.

In their work, Mokhtarian and Salomon (1996a) also found that telecommuting was an option for only 11% of their sample, and that 68% had at least one constraint on their choice; job unsuitability, manager disapproval, and lack of awareness. They also (Mokhtarian and Salomon, 1996b) found that only two characteristics significantly differ between those teleworking and non-teleworkers: presence of children under age 6 and occupation. Managers are more likely to telecommute, as are those with children under 6 years of age. These findings provide insight into the constraints on the potential size of the labor force amenable to telework and their characteristics.

Table 4.5 Stated preferences for telecommuting program (percentage of responses)

Program scenario	1	2	3	4
Salary same, employer pays all costs	21.6	44.5	22.0	11.8
Salary same, employee pays for new phone number	11.9	25.8	33.4	28.9
Salary same, employee buys PC	9.2	16.0	31.8	43.0
Salary increases 5%, employer pays all costs	34.0	52.1	NA	13.8
Salary increases 5%, employee pays part of costs	16.2	28.2	21.2	58.1
Salary decreases 5%, employer pays all costs	7.9	12.8	21.2	58.1
Salary decreases 10% employer pays all costs	5.2	5.0	12.4	77.4

Key: 1 = Work from home everyday; 2 = Work from home several days/week; 3 = Possibly work from home; and 4 = Do not want to work from home.
Source: Mahmassani *et al.* (1993).

4.5.3 Travel and personal environmental factors

Following the seminal work of Zahavi, and based on global figures, Schafer and Victor (2000) find that on average people spend about 1.1 hours per day traveling. The implication is that in general people have a base level need for mobility. In addition, some people derive a degree of utility from discretionary travel – leisure and miscellaneous travel. Consequently, some people remain undaunted by telework options aimed at reducing their travel, leading Salomon and Mokhtarian (1998) to argue that it is important to ascertain the number of individuals that will travel for unobserved objective and subjective reasons. For example, some people may enjoy the buffer time that commuting affords to transition in and out of home and work roles (Richter, 1990).

A love of cars is also culturally embedded in many societies; inherent in car ownership are status and a sense of freedom and independence (Jensen, 1999).[12] This reality needs to be incorporated into attempts to implement telework

---

[12]   An indication of the attachment to the car is given in Baldassare et al. (1998). In a survey of suburban attitudes on efforts to reduce traffic congestion, only about 20% of solo drivers would be willing to stop driving alone if charged parking fees, smog fees, or congestion fees, and a third said they would not change their current driving patterns if carpools, vanpools or public transit were expanded in their areas. Forty-two percent would not change their existing driving habits if paid a cash bonus by their employer to use carpools and the like.

initiatives, and when making projections about the potential impacts of teleworking.

Jou and Mahmassani (1997) analyzed trip-chaining behavior associated with work trips and found that the phenomenon is more extensive during the evening commute. Numerous non-work activities are performed during the work commute, which diminishes the attractiveness of public transit options; longer commutes afford more trip stops; women make more stops during their morning work commutes; persons over age 45 are less inclined to make stops; persons in lower-wage jobs make fewer trip stops; and workers that like to arrive to work early are more inclined to make trip stops during the work commute. Many of these trip stops are not work-related and would likely involve travel irrespective of the option to telecommute.

In another study, Sun et al. (1998) find that home owners or those buying homes generate 40% more daily trips and 84% more VMT than renters and that living in a single family home versus an apartment or condominium produces 120% more VMT with possession of a car phone generating 52% more VMT and 22.9% more trips. Persons in high-density areas travel 19% fewer VMT than those in low-density areas, and households with low access to their jobs made 17.3 trips and 72.3 VMT, compared with those with high access to employment (15.2 trips and 44.5 VMT). This suggests that a range of location factors influence travel behavior and that telework options may often be dominated by some of these.

There are also issues about retention rates once people have experienced a period of teleworking. Some studies suggest that about half of those teleworking stop after 9 to 18 months (Nilles and Mokhtarian, 1998). The desire to telework seems to be contingent upon life-cycle factors and work/career conditions. Changes in either of these may reduce the desire to telecommute even after initiation. Also, people may tire of working from home given the relative social isolation it can involve.

4.5.4 Business concerns

A range of factors affect the attitudes of employers towards teleworking. Often it depends on where they are in the value chain – some types of business are simply not amenable to large-scale teleworking (see again Figure 2.2) – but there are a variety of other factors that can come into play. The interest here is with companies that have scope for at least part of their activities being conducted away from their premises. Reasons found for not doing so include (Pratt, 1997):

- *Security/privacy costs.* Handheld and loaned computers used at remote work cannot be monitored unlike traditional desktop machines, that increases the threat of viruses, and the potential for unauthorized intrusion, and theft, damage or destruction of information assets and trade secrets.
- *Hidden costs.* Employer liability and property insurance costs exist with formal telework programs; workers' compensation costs can apply to teleworkers; and there may be legal over-time stipulations.

- *Fairness issues.* Generally only certain jobs are suitable for telework; creating positive effects with those that volunteer and are allowed to telework, but resentment by non-teleworkers. Anti-discrimination laws may also play a role.
- *Training costs.* Training is often required for managers and employees to adapt to new procedures and policies, management styles, alternative workplaces, and responsibilities; non-telework employee training and the like are also often associated with formal telework programs.
- *Disruption of team-based efforts.* With telework, higher levels of coordination are required among management and staff that may involve increased equipment and training costs.
- *Limited effectiveness of benchmarking.* Due to corporate culture concerns, it is more difficult for firms to adapt the telework programs of others, leading to unanticipated costs associated with establishing formal programs and use of different telework models.
- *Corporate culture.* In a recent study, 35% of respondents claimed that a resistant corporate culture was the primary barrier in failing to implement telecommuting programs.

4.5.5 Individual concerns

In most countries telecommuting is voluntary and its up-take based upon individual attributes (gender, income, access to equipment, etc.), job characteristics, disposition toward telework, transportation preferences, and the price elasticity of demand associated with telecommuting (Yen, 2000). Because of the range of factors involved, it is often difficult for companies to assess the viability of teleworking or the type of telework structure that would appeal to their employees. The type of repetitive work that may be seen as technically the easiest to monitor from an employees perspective, may also be the type where employees may prefer more human contact about them.

Individuals tend to prefer home-based telework to center-based options, but this may lead to conflicts between personal and business interests in relation to the type of telework adopted. Businesses, for professional reasons, and because of their customer preferences, may prefer center-based options to maximize control of employees (Bagely and Mokhtarian, 1997). Where there is commercial confidentiality involved or security, this may prove a significant handicap to home-working.

4.5.6 Gender/ethnicity considerations

As seen in Chapter 2, gender can in some cases affect travel behavior. McGuckin and Murakami (1999) find in their analysis of trip chaining that women are more inclined than men to make stops at multiple locations during the commute, and also make more trips to and from work. Single men and women with no children have similar commute patterns while in households with children, women have complex trip chains – more so than women without children or men. Single mothers of small children trip chain more than single fathers or dual parent households. Further, investigation by Turner and Niemeier (1997) give support for the household responsibility hypothesis that suggests that the idea that women have greater household burdens and hence choose shorter journey-to-work commutes.

Mauch and Taylor (1997) find that racial and ethnic variations in US travel patterns among men and women are explained by income, status, employment, and auto availability, with gender having a more direct effect on travel. Women make more child-related and household-related trips than men. The gender difference in travel times is 4.5 minutes for whites, and 1.8 minutes for Hispanics. Gender differences for average travel times do not vary much by race or ethnicity; and gender differences in child-related trips during the work trip are 60% for blacks, 152% for whites, and 212% for Hispanics.

This all supports the fact that future telework uptake in the US may have gender and racial biases as well as occupation and location biases. This is turn will affect the types of substitution and complementarity effects that will develop with transportation with more specific implications for traffic patterns.

4.7 TELEWORK POTENTIAL

4.7.1 Overall potential for teleworking

Much effort has gone into looking at exactly how much work travel could be diverted to teleworking. Some of the numbers are clearly spurious, and are often thrown up as part of advocacy campaigns.[13] Nevertheless they do offer some general thoughts on exactly how much work, and with it work travel, could theoretically be affected by teleworking.

The most common breakdown is by function and the separation of those that are more immediately amenable to teleworking. The value chain concept of Porter (1980) offers some general insights into this and, for example, was used by Eldid and Minoli (1995). For example, there is more opportunity for stages involving upper management, human resource management, technology development, procurement, marketing, and sales than there is in inbound and outbound logistics, and operations.

But the immediate up-take of telecommuting by companies will depend not only on potential, but also on the relative savings that can now be attained. This revolves around the particular features of each stage in the value chain. Nilles (1997) offers some general observations on the potential savings that come from teleworking (Figure 4.3). These need to be tied to the type of activities a company or division of a large company is engaged in, and its internal structure.[14] Such

[13]   Ilan Salomon once reported at a seminar in Europe the he had sought to verify the basis of a published forecast that telecommuting would constitute 12% to 13% of trips. He could not find any evidence in the supporting references that provided any basis for this figure.

[14]   This is a topic returned to in a somewhat different context in Chapter 6.

calculations are difficult, especially for outsiders who are not privy to a company's full operational picture.

4.7.2 Potential for teleworking in the US National Capital Region
Labor markets are extremely heterogeneous, not only in terms of the types of industry or production involved but also according to location. There are wide geographical variations in the ways they function and, *ipso facto*, in their potential for widespread adoption of teleworking. Nevertheless, while generalizations are difficult, case study material can prove insightful provided the specifics context of the case study is not forgotten.

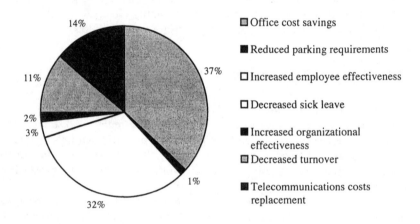

Source: Nilles (1997).

Figure 4.3 Potential savings to employers from teleworking

The National Capital Region[15] is one that suffers from severe traffic congestion and pollution problems. The region ranks among the worst five areas in the US for congestion (Table 4.6). Teleworking has been advocated as a policy option, particularly in Northern Virginia, because of the nature of local employment, particularly executive, administration, managerial; professional specialty; technicians and related; sales; and administrative support. In Virginia some 65% of employment is in these occupations. In addition, Northern Virginia has a large concentration of high technology companies engaged in

---

[15]   The National Capital Region embraces Northern Virginia, Southern Maryland and the District of Columbia. It is characterized by a predominance of service industries and government employment.

telecommunications, Internet industries, and information technology that employ people familiar with the technology of teleworking (Behr, 1998).

In April 2000, the Metropolitan Washington Conference of Governments (MWCOG) (2000) announced a regional telecommuting goal to increase the percentage of telecommuters to 20% of the workforce by 2005. It was argued that if this were achieved there would be 70,000 fewer cars on the road each day. According to the MWCOG, in 1996, 7% of workers were telecommuting in the region; in 1998 this had grown to 12%. It was argued that achieving a 20% telecommuting goal was reasonable given the growth in telework in the region.

Table 4.6 The most congested US urban areas

1. Los Angeles	7. Atlanta
2. Seattle	8. Boston
3. San Francisco-Oakland	9. Detroit
4. Washington	10. San Diego
5. Chicago	11. Las Vegas
6. Miami	

MWCOG sponsored a telework project involving 270 teleworkers from August 1997 to June 1998. It found that 70% were between ages 35–54, with 61% of being female, and with 60% having incomes over $55,000 in 1996. The average one-way commute distance was 25 miles and average commute time was 44 minutes to work and 48 minutes home. Forty percent of participants in the project teleworked one or two days per week and 24% reported that their schedules varied from week to week. Eighty percent worked from home (as opposed to a telecenter) and saved an estimated 97 minutes of commute time on telework days.

Looking at the picture more broadly, however, the MCWOG data show less than 1% of those surveyed participated in telecommuting at least one day per week and that about 50% lived in the Virginia part of the region with lone driving the primary commute mode irrespective of gender or race. Of those who drove alone, the primary alternative commute modes used during the previous year were transit (57.7%) and carpooling (32%). Half of those who changed their commute mode did so because of changes in employment or work hours and to save money.

The region's largest single employer, the US federal government, is a strong promoter of telecommuting options and efforts have been made to promote a 'family friendly' work environment.[16] Telework options are generally included in such flexible work options. In addition, in 1996, the President's Management Council on Interagency Telecommuting Working Group desired that 'each agency

---

[16]   According to the US President, family-friendly environments were to be obtained through 'broad use of flexible work arrangements to enable federal employees to better balance their work and family responsibilities ... increase employee effectiveness and job satisfaction while decreasing turnover rates and absenteeism' (Weekly Compilation of Presidential Documents. July 18, 1994).

and department make telecommuting part of its overall strategy to improve government services to the American people.'

Given the strong federal presence in the region, the Washington metropolitan area benefits from federal resources to support efforts like telework and to conduct small-scale projects. For example, as part of the National Telecommuting and Air Quality Act of 1999, the Washington area will be involved in the Telework Emissions Trading Pilot Program (National Environmental Policy Institute, 2000), whereby test cities received $250,000 to implement an emissions trading program to give incentives for businesses to implement telework programs.

Lowe (1998) examined commuting patterns in the Washington metropolitan area using 1980 data and found that commuting dispersion and complexity increases significantly beyond about 12 miles from the geographic center of agglomeration. These are influenced by the interrelationships between the pattern of residential densities and the various overall patterns of employment concentrations. This suggests that commuting patterns will continue to evolve in this fashion in the metro area as the suburbanization of employment continues. Telework options may contribute to the pattern of intra-county commuting or further disperse commuting patterns as persons move further in to rural areas as the need to commute to work declines.

4.8 CONCLUSIONS

Telework holds promise as a potential mechanism to reduce traffic congestion and air pollution.[17] This alternative, however, is no panacea. There are ample disbenefits and barriers to implementing telework. In addition to promoting the option to businesses, individual employees must possess the motivation to voluntarily telecommute. There are numerous social, psychological, and often, economic factors that must be brought to bear before opting to telework. In addition, the interests of businesses and individuals do not always coincide on matters such as telework sites. Employees largely prefer home-based options. Due to the nascent emergence of telework and/or for management/professional reasons, businesses may prefer employees to telecommute from a workcenter under formal telework programs.

Society's love for cars and leisure driving are cultural factors that come to bear. Research indicates that discretionary driving is a very real phenomenon and is a form of utility that is not easily surrendered (Salomon and Mokhtarian, 1998). There is a core of persons unwilling to accept telework options. Others simply need the commute time to 'unwind' or redirect their focus between other activities, or they simply enjoy driving. Although work trips may be shortened, or

---

[17]   In many ways the enhanced potential that modern communications holds for at least working partly at home is largely in terms of giving wider flexibility to overall life-style. It allows for greater interactions within family units and a much larger choice set in terms of how individuals and households divide up their time.

eliminated, by telecommuting, travel and trip making continues. Trip generation and distance is partially determined by gender, household responsibility, presence of children and income. These are factors that are largely unalterable.

Finally, suburbanization of employment and residences contributes to the shape of the modern urban form. Telework options may promote continued dispersion and complex travel patterns as persons move further into remote areas or it may not. It is too early to predict. In addition to wider options that telecommunications is offering, there are a multitude of other changes that are taking place that are influencing land-use patterns and urban form. Society is multidimensional and so are the forces that shape it.

5 VIDEOCONFERENCING AND WORK TRAVEL

5.1 INTRODUCTION

Trips to and from workplaces in most countries produce the most serious forms of urban traffic congestion; the peaks of the 'rush-hours'. But, as service sector activities form an increasingly large part of the economies of many countries, so personnel movements during the entire work-day become increasingly common. Many service sector activities have traditionally involved considerable person-to-person interactions. Telecommunications has, though, always played its part in both facilitating these interactions and, where appropriate, has formed a substitute; e.g., the telephone replaced many local courier services in the early twentieth century.

The use of modern telecommunications in the workplace as a means of facilitating personal interactions is growing although not always in the ways people had predicted in the early 1980s, and not as fast as some had foreseen. This is not to say that many firms do not conduct regular video and teleconferences, that medical services, and especially diagnostics, are not frequently provided electronically, and that classes are not often conducted electronically and interactively, but rather that the perceived full potential of videoconferencing has not yet been completely realized.

There are numerous ways in which telecommunications may affect the amount and nature of travel whilst working. These include:

- The use of videoconferencing and teleconferencing in place of physical meetings.
- The change of location or timing of a business trip through cell-phone contact while en route.
- The use of lap-top computers and other modern technologies during travel, thus combining work and mobility.
- Financial transfer of assets rather than by physical movements by 'couriers'.
- The use of 'electronic computer classrooms' that reduce the need for students to attend classes.
- Monitoring equipment from a central site.
- Reporting back from locations to a range of inspectors or supervisors simultaneously.

The emphasis here is rather limited and is directed almost entirely at the use of videoconferencing in the workplace.[1]

There are a number of different ways of videoconferencing but they all involve the same broad principles. Technically, videoconferencing entails electronic communication by both images and sound between participating individuals. It differs from rather older, established methods of electronic conferencing, such as teleconferencing, that only links up participants by sound through telephone connections. This means that there it offers major advantages over these older systems terms of the degree of information sent and received.

Each participating group at a videoconference both sees and hears others involved. In physical terms it entails sitting in front of a television like receiver which both provides input from other participants (their images and voices) and, through microphones and cameras, sends information to them. When there are a number of individuals involved at any one location in the conference, specialized studios can be employed involving rather more sophisticated equipment that permits groups of people to participate together. In other cases, where there may just be one individual at each location there are facilities that allow appropriate computers to be used in the office with no special spatial requirements.

The images of participants are often complemented by various other technologies that allow printed material and other physical objects to be seen at the same time, and can also involve concurrent interactions with the World-wide Web and the like.

The gradual universal up-take of tele-education, and videoconferencing involving visual links has, in many respects been rather sluggish compared to early expectations; teleconferencing being taken-up more rapidly. This is despite the fact that numerous studies have, for instance, shown that, in practice, people conducting meetings electronically from their places of work could avoid many work trips. An oft-cited figure is that of the European Conference of Ministers of Transport (1983) that technically 13% to 23% of trips could be substituted by telecommunications and, while many of these may be commuter trips, a proportion involves in-work activities.

Things are, however, gradually changing and the focus here is on the more recent developments in videoconferencing and related technologies in terms of their interrelationship with trips made as part of employment.

5.2 THE DEVELOPMENT OF TELECONFERENCING

The idea of videoconferencing and similar concepts is certainly not new – pioneering systems were demonstrated as early as the 1950s – but as with some other telecommunications media its adoption has been relatively slow. In 1956 AT&T built the first 'Picturephone' test system and introduced it at the 1964

---

[1]   It also focuses on traditional video-conferencing but in addition to this there have been increased sales of videophones. Whether these are taking the place of formal meetings or are a more sophisticated means of informal interaction has yet to be fully explored.

World's Fair in New York, marketing it in 1970 at $160 (current price) per month. In 1971 Ericsson demonstrated the first transatlantic video telephone. By 1986 PictureTel was marketing a conferencing system costing $80,000 (current price) with an hourly line charge of $100. By 1991 the company was marketing a black and white system for $20,000 with a $30 per hour line charge, and a year later AT&T brought out a $1,500 videophone for $1,500.

The next decade saw a rapid movement forward in technology as standards and protocols were established; products such as VocalTec Internet Phone, Microsoft NetMeeting, Virtual Room and Videoconferencing System came onto the market. By 2001 transatlantic surgery was being performed (a gallbladder operation) using a videoconference link, reporters in Afganistan were using $7,950 portable satellite videophones to broadcast live on the war, and commercial videophones were being sold for $570. Now computers and telephones are regularly fitted with video facilities allowing personal meetings to be more interactive.

While videoconferences have been presented as a valuable alternative to certain types of business travel for quite some time, empirical evidence of the rising market share for this medium on business travel behavior has, however, until recently, been hard to find.

Explanations for the relatively slow take-off of the technology normally refer to the fact that for most purposes face-to-face contacts are still more efficient and cheaper in generalized cost terms. But there are other barriers. International use can, for example, be problematic across several times zones, and there may be technical problems and congestion associated with the line. There is also evidence that different nationalities have different preferences when it comes to forms of communication; a study of European academics, for instance, found that, although there emerged a general complementarity between the use of telecommunications and face-to-face meetings, preferences for the various media for communications varied by country (Button et al., 1993).[2]

The world is, however, changing. Costs of videoconference equipment and associated line time have fallen considerably in recent years and are forecast to fall even more dramatically, the quality of image has improved and congestion on transport networks is pushing up the costs of face-to-face meetings.[3] In a comparative study of the possible uptake of new telematic technologies as they

---

[2]   Different priorities in communications can also be seen in the up-take of cellular telephones. In 2000, for example, 25% of the population of Italy had a cell phone, 13% of France's population, 13% of Germany's, 18% of the UK's, 48% of Sweden's, and 13% of Spain's.

[3]   The 'principal-agent' effect has also probably tended to favor personal travel. With the employee not bearing the costs of a business there is a tendency to seek options where there are external benefits (e.g., an extended stay or visit to a new place) and this can lead to a higher personal return for the worker in selecting a mode that allows personal travel. There is some evidence in terms of equipment sales that the down-turn in the global economy following the terrorist attacks on the US in 2001 stimulated increased use of videoconferencing as companies became more cost conscious and as businessmen became concerned about the safety implications of personal travel.

might affect traffic congestion, videoconferencing was singled out to probably be of more short-term significance than most other developments (Button, 1991).

Further, the long-term importance of some forms of telecommunications as possible substitutes for transportation is, as we have seen, a topic of immediate relevance. There is mounting concern over the environmental damage done by transportation and many governments are admitting that fiscal expediency will prevent traditional means of funding infrastructure developments from being used to meet projected unrestrained traffic growth. While, as we have seen much, of this concern relates to peak period, urban commuter movements, it is not absent in the case of work-related travel. The mounting public concern over noise pollution at airports and the fear of the damage done by high-level con-trails is, for example, acting as a significant constraint on the longer-term expansion of air transportation; a major mode used by modern business travelers in a globalizing economy.

On the other hand, technology and continuing economic regulatory reforms, notably market liberalization and privatization, in many countries seem likely to both facilitate the continued improvements in the quality of telecommunications and further bring its real costs down significantly.[4] Societal trends amongst the younger generation, brought up in an 'electronic' world, also mean that personal resistance to the use of videoconferencing and related technologies is far weaker than it was even in the in the recent past.

Although still at a relatively low level, but growing rapidly, world-wide use of videoconferencing would seem to be increasing. A survey of 100 US organizations regularly using videoconferencing in the early 1990s found that videoconferencing had doubled since an earlier 1985 survey (conducted by D.J. Bush Associates and reported in Lehrman, 1991). At a global level it has been estimated that image communication is growing at about 25% to 39% per annum. Some 60% to 70% of it has traditionally been done in the US, with about 25% in Europe and much of the remainder in Japan (Douglas, 1989).

In absolute terms, however, use of the facility is limited. In 1988 the best estimates suggested that fewer than 6,000 units had been installed in the US. Equally, within Europe the up-take has been gradual. In part, high line costs and different standards offered by the national PTTs, coupled with user concern over the quality of service engendered by the crude technology associated with early systems, have hindered the development of the international system.

In this context, we explore some of the recent growth trends in videoconferencing and the future role of videoconferencing as a substitute or complement for face-to-face contacts. More specifically, the impact of videoconferencing on business travel demand is studied by looking at alternatives where the medium enjoys a comparative advantage over alternatives. This economic approach is in contrast to the extensive literature on the technical

---

[4]   This must, though, be put into the context of reductions in the costs of some competing and complementary forms of transport. In the context of medium and long business travel, for example, the advent of low-cost airlines has reduced the costs of using that mode considerably.

aspects of videoconferencing. Further, the literature on the socio-economic aspects of videoconferencing tends to focus in particular on the possibility of fostering its greater use as a means of limiting mounting problems of traffic congestion and traffic related environmental degradation (e.g., Boghani et al, 1991; Button, 1992; Sviden, 1983).

5.3 THE USES OF VIDEOCONFERENCING

Work interactions may take a variety of forms, some more suitable for videoconferencing, but also some easier to examine from an academic perspective. This has resulted in an emphasis on looking at certain types of interactions, but probably the most important being interactions that take place within the employment context. Figure 5.1 offers a simple breakdown of the main typologies of communicative interactions in terms of whether they are essentially person or group driven.[5]

FROM/TO	Individual	Group
Individual	A	B
Group	C	D

Figure 5.1 Various workplace communications interfaces

- *Individual to group communications* (Category **B**) involves such things as research dissemination, education, and the passing down of instructions from higher levels of management. The information being moved normally has limited specific importance and any considerations of matters of confidentiality are minimal. Indeed, often the maximum spread of information is being aimed for. The exceptions to this can be at the higher levels of management where the group involved is clearly defined and information is restricted.
- *Individual to individual communications* (Category **A**) has traditionally been the domain of those interested in language, writing, psychology, education, and personal forms of communication. This has changed recently with economists, for example, being interested in issues of the importance of asymmetry in personal decision-making and in spatial

[5]   This section draws upon Button and Maggi (1995).

analysis where there has been a view that aggregation of group actions provides a basis for macroeconomic analysis.

For the internal working of companies, it is important in terms of decision-making at various levels of management where personal contacts are important and communications down 'ladders' where, again, small numbers of individuals need to be informed. High degrees of confidentiality can be important. Telephone conversations tend to dominate electronic communications for this type of interaction, especially when the parties have enjoyed prior contact.

- *Group to individual communications* (Category **C**) often concerns feedback or planning actions. The aim is that key decision-makers have full, or at least necessary, information from others in the company or from suppliers or customers. Often this can be at a macro-level if higher management wishes to convey information to the larger work force. This fits more with analysis of markets and managerial practices and the flow of information is generally unidirectional, although interactions are not entirely missing.
- *Group to group communications* (Category **D**) are generally at the meso-level involving discussions and the interchange of information at various levels of a company. These often involve regular meetings or 'brain-storming' sessions aimed at tackling specific problems, presenting status reports, or developing futures. Videoconferencing is playing an increasing role in this type of interaction, especially where purpose built facilities offer a high level of sophistication in the techniques available for conveying information.

The role of videoconferencing, and telecommunications in the workplace can also be looked at in another way (Figure 5.2). This is in terms of the time it takes to conduct interactions between people and the nature of the players/actors involved.

Communications with international, or long-distance time dimensions, tend to be more time consuming in many cases if there is to be face-to-face communications, although this issue is finessed a little later in the chapter. Equally, communications with clients is often time consuming because of a lack of full familiarity and the need for bargaining compared to intra-company communications between levels of management. The potential gains for substituting face-to-face communication thus vary according to the function of communications as well as to the scale of the parties involved.

5.4 THE DEMAND FOR VIDEOCONFERENCING

To understanding what is happening with respect to videoconferencing, and also to develop any sensible scenario concerning future developments, it is important to initially gain a better understanding of the market for videoconferencing services.[6] The demand for videoconferencing services is almost always, like transportation services, derived from the end needs of an industrial or commercial company. It is not a final product. There is also a diverse range of costs associated with electing for a videoconference compared to some other form of communication, including face-to-face meetings.

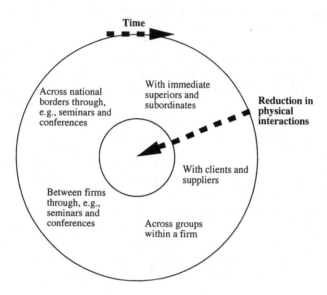

Figure 5.2 Work induced interactions

One way of looking at these factors is set out in Figure 5.3 that provides a schema setting out the types of cost decisions that have to be made when deciding to videoconference.

The immediate financial costs are the most obvious items, and the ones that frequently receive the most attention in studies of the subject. In the past the fact was that these costs were high, both because of equipment and studio costs and because of line costs. The opportunity time costs have received rather less attention although there is evidence that over some distances, the costs of face-to-face meeting can be lower than for videoconferencing; this can, for example, happen when there are significant time-zone effects.[7] Of key importance here are

6   This may be a market external to the user, in the sense that the facility is hired from another company, or public agency, or it may be internal in the sense that the user makes use of his undertakings' equipment. The markets are, assuming companies have reliable internal accounting procedures, essentially the same in practice.
7   Some data on these relative costs in the UK during the 1990s are found in Button (1992b).

the number of participants involved, the number of locations concerned, the distance separating the parties and the length of the meetings.

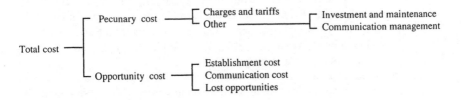

Figure 5.3 The costs of videoconferencing

To help separate the various issues involved in deciding whether to engage in videoconferencing activities it is useful to decompose the costs of videoconferencing versus face-to-face contacts into four main components (see Table 5.1). For simplification, we assume that both communications options are available, that our concern is with a company's long term decisions regarding its communications strategy and that the company is interested in minimizing the longer run average costs of its communications. The relevant costs making up the long run average costs (LACs) then become those in Table 5.1.

Table 5.1 Elements of the long-run average total costs of meetings by videoconference and through travel

	Fixed Cost	Transmission	Time	Distance
Travel	0	0	$(\frac{M}{E_{travel}} VT + \frac{D}{V_{travel}} VT)$	$D \cdot TD_{travel}$
Video	$\frac{I_{video} + CC_{video}}{Y}$	$\frac{M}{E_{video}} TC_{video}$	$(\frac{M}{E_{video}} VT + 0)$	$D \cdot TD_{video}$
Travel	0	0	$(\frac{M}{E_{travel}} VT + \frac{D}{V_{travel}} VT)$	$D \cdot TD_{travel}$

- *The average fixed costs of communication.* In terms of face-to-face contacts these are effectively zero. With videoconferencing there are the initial costs of establishing the communications infrastructure (studios and equipment), I, and of the communications concept (internal restructuring to handle the new media akin to that required with computerization of accounts), CC, and these are spread over the contacts, Y, made.
- *The average monetary cost of transmitting the message.* This embraces the time per contact, M/E, multiplied by the monetary cost of contact per

time unit, TC. Since the monetary contact cost is generally zero for travel when the meeting is held on the premises of one of the participants, this item falls from consideration in the case of travel to meetings.

For videoconferencing, however, there are the fixed and time-dependent tariffs levied by the operator of the line and, possibly, studio rental costs. The actual time per contact depends upon both the function of the message itself, M (for example, how complex it is), and the efficiency of the medium in transmitting it, E.

- *The value of time.* Time has value to individuals and, in general, people prefer to spend the least time possible on any interaction.[8] We denote this value as VT. The full time cost of communication is composed of travel time, D/V (where V is speed) and transmission time, M/E. In the table travel time for videoconferencing is assumed to be zero although in some cases there may be a need to travel to a studio.
- *The monetary costs of distance.* This reflects differing costs of long as opposed to short distance communications and is closely correlated with the distance involved, D, times the distance-dependent tariff, TD.

Thinking of the comparative position of videoconferences in terms of the long-run average cost equations depicted in Table 5.1 raises a number of questions.

What are the implications of the differing cost curves? Much depends on the individual cost parameters, but in Figure 5.4 combinations of LAC curves for face-to-face contact and videoconferencing with respect to the distance apart of the relevant parties are presented that illustrate some of the arguments.[9]

If the slopes of both long-run cost curves are relatively shallow because the information being conveyed is relatively unsophisticated (case A), actual meetings with face-to-face contacts will be the cheaper mode and only if contacts are very frequent per time period will videoconferencing eventually have lower cost. Indeed, casual observation shows that for short distances contacts are frequently made face-to-face even for very banal communication issues.

For more complex communication over long distances (case B) marginal cost is important and, because of the expensive technology required to convey such information electronically, face-to-face contacts will certainly have lower cost than videoconferencing.[10] In this case, however, if communication had a very high utility, it might pay to invest in more sophisticated videoconferencing facilities, with a high fixed cost but lower variable time cost (as indicated by the thick line representing new videoconferencing technologies seen in case D). In case C

---

[8]   In transportation modeling one of the standard approaches to assessing the implications of any change to a transportation network involves estimating the demand elasticity of travel with respect to 'generalized cost', where this latter term reflects the combined money and time (converted into a monetary equivalence) of using the new facility versus the old.

[9]   A rigorous derivation of this modeling framework is contained in Maggi (1993).

[10]   This is especially so if there are time zone factors to be taken into consideration.

marginal contact cost is lower for the telecommunication mode, for example for simple communications over long distances, videoconferencing will prove the lower cost medium except for when there are relatively few contacts.

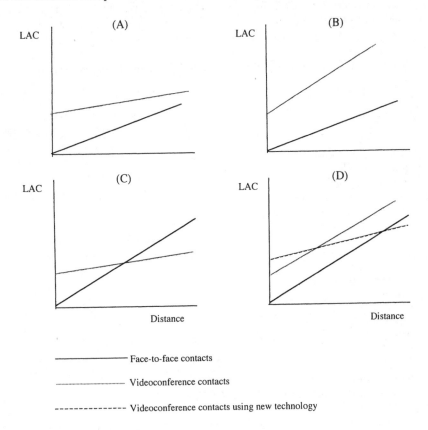

Figure 5.4 Telecommunications–travel cost trade-offs

Second, there is the question of exactly how important in practical terms are the relative items in each of the equations set out in Table 5.1? The evidence we have on this tends to come from stated preference studies (structured questionnaires and surveys) with comparatively little econometric analysis of revealed preferences having been attempted. Although not couched exactly as one would like for exploring the cost models set out in the table, a study of both UK videoconferences users and non-users offers some insights (Table 5.2).

Those already using videoconferencing are inevitably most sensitive to the direct financial costs of use although, equally, the table also indicates a considerable potential sensitivity to the costs of alternatives – the costs of making physical contacts. Image quality – reflecting the efficiency of message and information transmission – is also a significant factor influencing the use of videoconferencing. Recent technology improvements, however, would seem likely to have reduced the importance of this issue. With respect to non-users, the direct cost factor is again important but equally so is access to the facilities and to links, in terms of easier hiring (not a problem perceived by existing users), and the quality of the facilities. There may well still exist a lack of confidence within this group as to the technical and service quality being offered at present.

Table 5.2 Factors likely to influence the future use of videoconferencing

	Not using videoconferencing		
	Not important	Important	Very important
Better quality images	4	4	1
Easier hiring of equipment	3	2	4
Transport costs	6	0	3
Costs of videoconference	3	2	4
Increased travel within company	4	3	2
	Using videoconferencing		
	Not important	Important	Very important
Better quality images	8	8	7
Easier hiring of equipment	16	5	2
Transport costs	7	4	12
Costs of videoconference	5	2	16
Increased travel within company	8	6	9

Note: Uses a sample of 32 undertakings – 9 did not use videoconferencing. Multiple responses were possible.
Source: Taken from Button and Lauder (1992).

Finally, the arguments set out above have been couched in essentially static terms but how inappropriate is this for new technologies? There is an established notion in management science that products go through a life-cycle. The classic form of the model assumes a sigmoid growth curve in sales of the product concerned followed by a decline (see the thin line in Figure 5.5). The product is initially launched but sales are low because of factors such as consumer unfamiliarity, lack of service facilities, high costs of non-mass production, technical unreliability, inadequate complementary infrastructure, and so on.

If it survives this phase then growth in sales occurs as consumer tastes are converted ('bandwagon' effects may also be initiated in some cases, for example when there are considerations of fashion), costs of production fall, sales outlets and service facilities expand in number, and standardization of technical specifications takes place. If the product involves networks of any kind then network economies can emerge that add impetus to the up-take of the product as more people have access to it; this may be a powerful effect in the case of videoconferencing as the benefits of equipment purchase rise as more potential contact possibilities emerge.

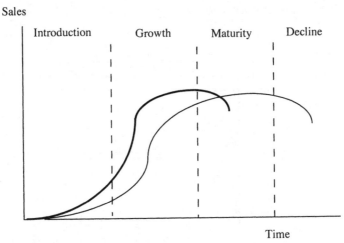

Figure 5.5 The classic product life-cycle

A mature market is reached when long run-marginal costs of production are minimized, product availability is virtually ubiquitous and near saturation of all potential users is achieved; the main market is for replacements. Finally, as new products come onto the market, and the market for the target product reaches replacement levels, so its sales decline.

While this classic framework has an attractive degree of simple and intuitive logic to it, its application to specific 'products' is less satisfactory. Studies have shown that the shapes of life-cycles vary considerably between products and services. While there is some evidence that more technological products, such as videoconferencing, tend to have a fairly long introduction phase, followed by a very rapid take-up and movement to maturity, the pattern is by no means universal. In particular, the move from the introduction phase to the growth phase is extremely difficult to predict.

This is possibly one reason for what, in retrospect, appeared as rather optimistic projections of videoconferencing use in the early 1980s. Essentially, those involved thought that the growth path would be similar to that shown by the thick line in Figure 5.5.

5.4.1 Videoconference use
What do we actually know about the uses to which videoconferencing is put? If one looks back only a few years the evidence was that videoconferencing was finding it difficult to move to the important take-off phase in Figure 5.5. In Switzerland, for instance (Maggi, 1993), the amount of use made of videoconferencing either by the public videoconference studios (Figure 5.6) or by a Swiss multinational chemical firm with its facilities (Figure 5.7) was extremely

limited and evidence of any significant growth was difficult to find. This picture gradually changed with time. The Zurich PTT, for example, and admittedly from a very low base, experienced a 3000% rise in the use of its studios between 1990 and 1991 with parallel growth in self-dialing.

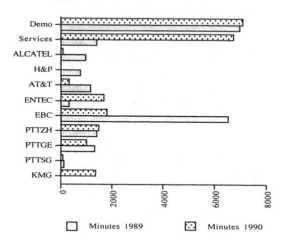

Figure 5.6 Videoconferencing in Switzerland (public studios, 1989/90 in minutes per year).

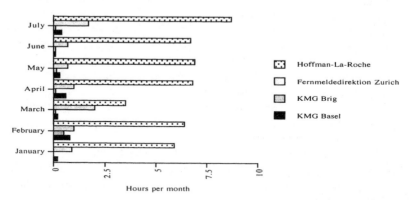

Figure 5.7 Videoconferencing by large Swiss chemical firms (hours per month, 1991)

Sudden, unforeseen, changes in circumstances also seem to be introducing potentially longer-term take-ups of videoconferencing. The Gulf War of 1991, for

---

ll   There was also a major upsurge in the use of teleconferencing during the early years of the twenty-first century as a cheap and flexible means of conducting business without the need for specialized equipment.

instance, led to many companies reducing or stopping employees flying and as a result videoconferencing use rose – for example, in the UK, BT experienced a 50% rise. A key point is that this once-for-all jump in use did not suddenly vanish but became part of the base figure.

The relatively low costs of transportation in the 1990s, partly as a result of deregulation of air transport in many countries, and generally rising incomes, however, tended to stymie significant further growth at that time. The uncertainties engendered by the attacks on the in 2001, the Second Gulf War, and the SARS outbreak provided a further upward jump in videoconferencing. At the local level, mounting traffic congestion in many major cities and at airports adds to the uncertainty of travel.[12]

At the more macro, and technical, level, one can look at the cross-elasticities of demand between transport and telecommunications by applying various econometric models of consumption to national times series data. Work of this kind is scant because of data limitations and problems of model specification. Salvanathan (1991) has attempted such an approach for the UK using the so-called Rotterdam modeling framework and employing times series data for the period 1960 to 1986.

While the work is aggregate, simply separating expenditures on private transport, public transport and communications, and there is no distinction by type of travel or means of communication, it is suggestive that the demand for communications over the period was highly inelastic (–0.12). Further, there is only a low cross-elasticity both between communications costs and private transport (0.08), and between communications costs and public transport (0.03). Similar aggregate work in the Netherlands (Netherlands Organisation for Applied Scientific Research, 1989) also yielded low elasticities and suggests that adoption of telecommunications over the next 35 years will only reduce traffic by 8%.

Of course, it would be inappropriate to directly apply these elasticities to videoconferencing, especially when looking at the significant price falls that many in the industry are still suggesting as possible in the future. The change is not marginal and it is unrealistic to anticipate fixed elasticities over anything but a relatively limited price range. However, in absolute terms, if this elasticity were applied to, say, a fall of 80% in the costs of communications then private transport use would fall by 10%.[13]

Looked at another way, in Great Britain the number of trips made as part of work travel would have fallen in 1985/86 by 0.044 per person per week which aggregates to some 114.4 million work trips per annum – given the nature of the

---

12   There was also a major upsurge in the use of teleconferencing during the early years of the twenty-first century as a cheap and flexible means of conducting business without the need for specialized equipment.

13   This assumes there is no, what traffic engineers call 'latent demand' for road space. Put another was, as trips are transferred to videoconferencing there may well be people why make additional trips as the level of traffic declines thus reducing the time cost of travel. This in turn pushes up the congestion level thus increasing once again the time cost of travel.

substitution effect and the greater incentive to switch communications mode when longer distance interactions are involved, the actual impact on mileage traveled would inevitably have been larger.

5.5 POTENTIAL TRANSPORT EFFECTS

The overall take-up of videoconferencing, as with the larger concept of telecommuting, is seen to have potential implications for the transport system (although not always those of reducing demand) but equally it has possible implications for internal industrial organization, the nature of office architecture, and the location of economic activity. It can also affect the comparative advantages of different locations. These aspects of telecommunications have, though, been less thoroughly explored than the implications of the ability of people to work at home. At the micro level, for example, there is evidence that use of videoconferencing tends to vary between companies. Relatively little work, though, has been conducted, either at the theoretical or empirical level, on this aspect of the subject.

In the past, the slowly increasing use of videoconferencing has often been seen as a way of reducing the costs of work-based travel. Johansen and Bullen (1984) and Salomon (1986) have pointed to the increased awareness by companies of travel costs, including time as well as money costs, and are able to compare these directly with the costs of investing in videoconferencing facilities.[14] In practice, however, the situation is more complex and at the level of the individual company the impact of videoconferencing is seen by several studies to depend on a number of factors.

In the first place, companies vary in the degree to which they systematically cost alternative methods of communication. Some undertakings, however, with in-house videoconferencing systems also operate accountancy procedures to determine when it is cost-effective to replace personal travel by a videoconference. IBM in the US has an on-line system to inform managers throughout the world of the comparative costs. In the UK, GPT, which has an internal videoconferencing system linking its main sites, equally provides details of comparable costs. The costing of the video facility is based on full cost recovery.

Further, some studies suggest that videoconferencing will be used to conduct many types of meeting not previously carried out face-to-face using transport modes (Johansen, 1984). In other words at least part of the demand will be newly generated interactions.

Where there is some potential for transfer, evidence from UK studies is that personal contact is still necessary. For instance, while some 34% of meetings recorded could have been performed by audio only conferencing and a further 10% through the use of video systems some 50% of communications still required face to face contact (Pye, 1976). Bennison's (1986) early work in the field

---

[14] In a way this may be seen as a labor market parallel to the up-take of supply chain logistics in the freight-inventory market.

highlights the potential complexity of underlying relationships involved. His study of a field trial in the UK found that in companies where videoconferencing had become established it had become a complement to face-to-face contact meetings. This confirms findings in Mokhtarian's (1988) US study in Southern California. The indications are that videoconferencing may generate additional trips even if it reduces the average trip length.

To a considerable extent the degree of complementarity or substitution between travel and videoconferencing will depend upon the uses to which videoconferencing can be put within a company, the external environment in which a company operates and the internal managerial structure of the company. Only limited evidence is available on any of these points.

Regarding use, Button and Lauder's (1992) study of UK users found that there was evidence of explicit travel replacement. This was both for domestic and international trips, but no evidence was gained regarding either directly generated additional travel related to the other uses being made of videoconferencing or as a result of time and cost savings brought about by the substitutions which were recorded – see Table 5.3.

Table 5.3 Uses made of videoconferencing in the UK

	Used	Used frequently
In-house training/education	1	2
External education	4	5
In place of international travel	1	3
In place of travel within the UK	2	14
Internal communication	5	9
Communication with other companies	8	9
Setting up video conferences with others	7	1
Other purposes*	4	4

*Use in design and development and for demonstrations were both mentioned twice.
Source: Button and Lauder (1992).

Concerning the external, commercial environment in which companies operate, if we look at the up-take of videoconferencing in Switzerland we see from Table 5.4 that some types of company have adapted more rapidly to its availability than have others. The earliest users, from 1986 to 1989, were mainly multinationals, often with strong US markets or with experience of US equipment. This initial pattern of up-take conforms to what one would anticipate from the product life-cycle model set out earlier in Figure 5.5.

The types of firm initially using videoconferencing in Switzerland tended to have experience of it elsewhere and hence be part of an intra-firm network which removes many of the problems of product familiarity and lack of complementary infrastructure (divisions in other parts of the world already having equipment).

They are also large enough in most cases to justify the use of older, less mobile and flexible videoconferencing technologies.

Table 5.4 Users of videoconferencing in Switzerland

Innovators	Rapid adopters	Major users	Slow uptake	Not using
DMF	Alcatel DEC Du Pont de Nemours Hewlett-Packard Hoffmann-La Roche IBM Sony	ABB Caterpillar ITC Laussanne Nestlé Business Park Swissair Tetrapak UBS	CICR, DFAE Mövenpick ONU Palais Féséral Universités	Alusuisse André & Cie Danzas Kuoni Maus Frères Pirelli SGS Edco,

Source: Adapted from, Perret-Gentil et al (1992).

These multinationals were followed, via a demonstration type effect, by a heterogeneous collection of large Swiss based companies. The official, administrative and educational sectors, which function in an essentially domestic environment, have been rather slower to adopt videoconferencing. They have less experience from outside involvement and this increases the initial impetus to invest in an uncertain product. In other sectors of industry the up-take seems also to have been slowed by the lack of a critical network scale. (For a technical explanation of the benefits of network size, see Katz and Shapiro, 1986.)

Regarding internal company structure, the available evidence is extremely limited, in part because defining business organizational structures is itself a difficult task. Some general points, though, can be made. Figure 5.8 provides some of the standard models of organizational structure of business firms.

As a caveat, it should be remembered that there is an inevitable link between the internal structure of firms and the external environment in which they operate. Multinationals, for instance, which we saw from Table 5.4 were early users of videoconferencing in Switzerland, often have hierarchical or semi-independent unit structures. This makes isolating the independent effects of the external environment from that of company structure difficult.

How videoconferencing influences the face-to-face contacts that take place between the various elements in each form of company structure will, in part, depend on the geographical dispersal of plants, units and so on within a company coupled with its overall size. With larger companies serving large national and multinational markets the structure itself is of greater significance. Essentially face-to-face or videoconferencing contacts within an organization serve a bridging function. The nature of the bridge, however, relates back to the elements in Table 5.1.

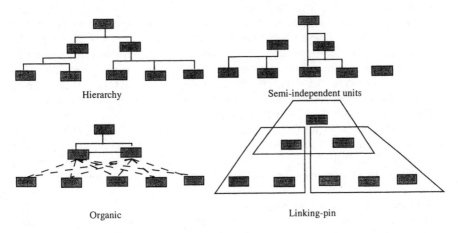

Figure 5.8 Examples of organizational structures

In general, videoconferencing is less good at handling complex messages and where there are significant fixed costs (I) relative to subsequent utilization costs. This suggests that its most likely use is at lower-middle levels of companies where, as we see from Figure 5.8, in virtually all organization structures there are larger numbers of contacts and where the level of information to handle is less complex. There are, though, probable caveats to this. In the semi-independent unit structure these economies of density are markedly lower and it is this type of industrial structure that seems to be growing in some sectors (in part to enhance flexibility and nimbleness of undertakings). It is also less clear how videoconferencing would fit into the link-pin structure where the information flows tend to be rather more focused on subordinate managers than enhanced notions of hierarchical powers.

5.6 FORCES FOR CHANGE

Some of the changes that we have noted in the UK and Switzerland, such as the growth of interest in videoconferencing during the two Gulf Wars, should be seen as exogenous shocks to the system. There are in addition a number of internal developments that are increasingly adding to the up-take of the media.

5.6.1 Changing attitudes of business towards the automobile
Returning to our product life-cycle model, any product gains a market both by attracting new users (business creation) and by taking users from other products (business diversion). In the case of videoconferencing, the diversion effect is likely to be primarily from business trip making and from audio conferencing.

There has, in the recent past been a very rapid increase in business travel, and in particular that undertaken by cars.

The pressure to switch to videoconferencing has been softened in many countries both by the taxation structure regarding company cars and by major road building projects that have limited the build up of congestion on trunk roads. The generalized costs of business travel have, therefore, been kept down although this is now changing and not simply because of rising fuel prices from 2003. For example, a survey of 75 managers of UK companies conducted by the Kristal Corporation in 1991 found that 91% felt that business travel now disrupts work routine and increases stress as well as interfering with family life. The problems of travel caused 21% to lose their temper, 20% to perform badly, 16% to have disturbed sleep, and 13% to take solace in alcohol. While these factors are beginning to exert short-term pressures, in the longer term the types of problems outlined are likely to worsen if traffic growth even approaches the levels forecast.

5.6.2 More user friendly equipment

While many products offer what appear to the manufacturer to be considerable attributes in a purely technical sense it is often user friendliness that is a key consideration for widespread adoption and use. In the case of videoconferencing, this may be viewed in terms of the individual users' reactions to the product and the degree to which the product fits in with the wider activities of the firm. Early equipment involved studios that, while offering many diverse technical features, often proved alien and intimidating to users. It also involved complex arrangements for booking time that reduced its flexibility for managing work patterns.

These limitations are now rapidly being overcome as equipment becomes more mobile and it is much easier to arrange video meetings and get the specific types of service attributes desired. Videophones, for instance, are now becoming available, albeit at relatively high prices, and the providers of videoconference facilities, such as the Swiss PTTs, are recognizing that public studios may not provide the ideal way forward. In particular, systems such the Swiss MEGACOM facility launched in 1992 with its self-dial, wideband features, facilitate easier access to the network. Further, where additional features are being incorporated, they are often facility specific (such as sophisticated electronic encoding devices to limit 'eavesdropping' on confidential conferences) and are essentially purchased as add-ons rather than being charged for irrespective of use.

5.6.3 Links with other technologies

Videoconferencing is only one element of a range of technical possibilities in the telecommunications field. Its widespread adoption and speed of take-up will, to some extent, be influenced by the up-take of other telecommunication systems (for example, telecommuting, teleshopping and distance learning). This synergy effect stems from the degree to which the actual cost of videoconferencing is likely to fall as economies-of-scope can be realized by suppliers of telecommunications facilities as they supply a variety of different but linked products. And also from the reduction in user resistance to videoconferencing as people become more familiar through usage with advanced telecommunication systems in general.

5.6.4 Enhanced reliability

Product take-off requires confidence on the users' part that the service sought will be forthcoming in a reasonably reliable fashion. The early UK system Confravision, for example, suffered from having to use standby television relay circuits. These problems have now largely been overcome and, in any case, the growth in traffic congestion, with its associated impact on reliability of person movements, has changed the point of comparison.

5.6.5 Lower costs

Cost is obviously a primary consideration to business users of telecommunications. In the past complexity kept the price of videoconferencing units high but economies of large-scale production are rapidly bringing these down.

There are two main elements of equipment cost which need to be considered with respect to videoconferencing. First, there are studio costs. Mobility is a relative thing and some current 'mobile units' are in fact far from easy to transport about buildings but they may be used in virtually any type of room. In particular, this means that dedicated studios are no longer required for most forms of conferencing. The new generation of codex is now much smaller than previously and some of the new configurations of equipment take up little more floor space than a desk. The reduced need for studio facilities is also likely to lead to lower labor costs in operating a videoconferencing system within an organization.

Second there are equipment costs *per se*. These have fallen considerably and are forecast to fall very dramatically over the next few years. There are suggestions from those involved in the industry that while portable units in the US in the early 1990s cost in the $30 – 80,000 range (while full dedicated studios can cost $200,000 although this, in real terms, is about 80% lower than in 1981) fell to under $7,500 by the mid-1990s. This is mainly because of economies of scale in production that accompany higher sales as international agreements on standards for interactive video compression are reached and product uniformity increases.

Line costs are the main elements of costs associated with videoconferencing – at present codex costs amount to only about 25% of the lifetime costs of a videoconference network. They are, however, falling dramatically. At the international level, renting time on satellites in the US dropped from about $8,000 per hour in 1981 to less than $300 by 1993. The investment now taking place in fiber optics and the increased capacity of satellite systems is likely to bring these costs down further. Within Europe, costs tend to be much higher than in the USA and in most countries there is central control by the national PTT. Increased competition and the liberalization process, however, are gradually changing these pricing structures.

One option where a company does not have its own videoconferencing units, and probability of the rapid creation of a significant network of likely contactors is remote, is to hire or lease the service and here costs have again fallen considerably in competitive markets such as the US. Conference Express charged in early 1991 between $750 and $900 for a one hour meeting between two US cities, $1900 per hour between New York and Paris, $2500 per hour between New York and London and $3300 per hour between New York and the Far East. On average these charges represented a 60% reduction for domestic videoconferences and a 75% reduction for international videoconferences from the mid-1980s.

5.6.6 Standardization

Very seldom does any product gain rapid market assimilation without either some implicit or explicit sets of standards being arrived at. Without such standards equipment cannot interface efficiently, economies of scale in production cannot be achieved, training poses a problem and service and maintenance costs are high. As has been demonstrated with many products the standardization does not have to reflect the best ultimate technology – one might wait forever for this – and may have serious limitations in the longer term as demand patterns change and technology advances.

Standardization is likely to both bring down the hardware costs of videoconferencing as well as opening up many more opportunities for inter-organizational video meetings. There is always a trade-off when setting standards between an early introduction of a standard, to assist in bringing a focus to development and design, lower production costs and simplify communications, and a later introduction of a better standard, once more of the technical developments have taken place.

The efforts at present, while accepting the potential for improved technology, are tending to focus mainly on the creation of universal standards that it is hoped, will assist in the more rapid up-take of videoconferencing. In the early 1990s the International Telegraph and Telephone Consultative Committee introduced a new standard and manufacturers moved to implementing P*64 hard and software in their videocodecs. There is also discussion of a new standard for multi-way video that seems likely to be accepted in the near future. Such standardization offers both potential for improved quality of picture at any bandwidth as technical developments can be pursued within known parameters and also a wider range of product qualities as equipment at different bandwidths are tailored to meet specific requirements.

Videoconferencing depends upon the availability of adequate and appropriate links between the users' stations. In the past pre-booking systems were required although ideally a public switched service is required to facilitate easy use. At present this does not exist on a European-wide, let alone on a global, basis although the situation is changing as, for instance, we noted in Switzerland.

5.7 CONCLUSIONS

The early optimistic forecasts that videoconferencing would provide, in a very short space of time, a popular and widely used telecommunications instrument for business that would reduce the need for travel to face-to-face meetings were not well founded. In particular, such predictions ignored, on the supply-side, the inherent limitations of the infant technology available, the socioeconomic difficulties of converting to the new media and the high costs of use while, on the demand-side, the capacity of conventional transport modes still provided reasonably reliable and efficient means of facilitating face-to-face contacts.

These forecasts also ignored the possibility of other new technologies that would find a market niche much more rapidly, such as the facsimile, and have tended to divert resources away from videoconferencing. One must also add that the external benefits often derived from business travel (visiting new places, making new acquaintances and being out-of-the-office) may well have been underestimated in these predictions.

The take-off has, therefore, been almost painfully slow. More recently, however, there are signs in the UK and Switzerland, both that many of the underlying parameters are changing and that there is beginning to emerge a more dynamic market for videoconferencing services. Whether this is a genuine take-off and whether it will exert any major influence on business travel is still, though, far from certain.

Given the hindsight of experience in this field, predictions about future trends are perhaps best avoided. What we do find, however, is that there is considerable potential for telecommunications costs to fall in the near future and with them the costs of videoconferencing. The quality and user-friendliness of equipment are also likely to improve. Evidence from users and non-users in the UK suggests that a combination of such changes combined with increasing costs and frustration with the transport network could lead to a greater use of videoconferencing. If so, however, it is extremely unlikely to provide an answer to problems of mounting traffic congestion and pressures for more transport infrastructure capacity but it could help to reduce the intensity of such problems.

6   THE BUSINESS OF E-COMMERCE

6.1 INTRODUCTION

Production methods have changed considerably over recent years, as has the wider logistics supply chain in which they fit. These developments in production have resulted as sea changes have occurred in technology and in management science, but they have also been driven by demands for new products and the emergence of new markets. Significant institutional changes have also been part of the larger process, although cause and effect are seldom easily separated.

These new markets do not only reflect the oft-cited 'new trends in globalization and internationalization' that we have cited in the media, but also represent reformulations of traditional markets as tastes and consumer demands have changed and evolved. But to allow the necessary transactions required to bring together inputs for production, and to take the outputs to markets, so there have also been necessary changes in the ways transportation and telecommunications interact with production.

Logistics at the start of the twenty-first century is as a result a far cry from that of even 25 years ago. To meet the new conditions, producers increasingly demand just-in-time deliveries and collections, trucking is widely used, and inventories are, as a result, far smaller. Part of this trend stems from changes in the transportation system *per se*; the introduction of the container in the 1960s was a crucial development, and the emergence of larger freight aircraft heralded rapid and reliable long-haul services. There have also been major advances in managerial techniques, including finance, and business models, sometimes linked to the shift to service based economies in developed countries, that have integrated transport more fully into the larger production process.

More recently, over the past 30 years or so, there have been significant changes in the way that transportation markets function, both for passengers and freight movements. In particular, formerly very heavily regulated, and in some countries state owned, transportation supplying agencies have been allowed to function in much more liberal market conditions. The UK trucking industry, for example, was deregulated from entry controls (there were no rate setting regulations) under the 1968 Transport Act. Of more importance in terms of the scale of their impacts, and also their wider demonstration effects internationally, were the series of reforms in the US from 1976, when the freight railroad industry began to be deregulated, that culminated in a virtually free market for passenger and freight transportation in the US. Changes followed elsewhere, with the Single European Market initiative freeing up the main western European transportation networks from the early 1990s, and the ending of Soviet domination in eastern Europe seeing that macro-region, albeit slowly, liberalize its transportation markets.

Table 6.1 Major legal changes to US transport regulations 1976–89

1976	Railroad Revitalization and Regulatory Reform Act – removed many regulations over rate setting
1977	Air Cargo Deregulation Act – initiated free competition for air cargoes
1978	Airline Deregulation Act – initiated a phased removal of fare setting and market entry controls
1980	Staggers Rail Act – removed many regulations over line abandonment and gave further freedom in rate setting
1980	Motor Carriers Reform Act – increased entry and rate setting freedom and reduced the role of rate fixing bureaux
1981	Northeast Rail Service Act – enabled Conrail to abandon little-used lines
1982	Bus Regulatory Reform Act – eased conditions of market entry and exit and phased in relaxation of rate controls.

Without these institutional reforms, and complementary ones such as the ending of the monopolies of post offices to carry mail and small packages, the transportation sector would have struggled to more forward as a purveyor of the services that are needed for modern logistics management.

The coordination both within the various elements of the supply chain and between them has inevitably become more complex, as the transportation and telecommunications elements have evolved, and especially as the demands for service quality have risen. The demands placed on rapid, reliable, and, often, flexible telecommunications in this context are considerable. But equally, the developments in the chain would not have been possible without new and innovative telecommunications technology that allows passive monitoring of the system (e.g., through global positioning systems – GPS) and more immediate interventions (e.g., route guidance).

Telecommunications developments have thus both been responsive to the needs of the logistics market but have also been a facilitator and, in some cases, a driver, of change in these markets. The liberalization of many transportation and telecommunications markets around the world has added to the ways in which more efficient two-way interactions can occur.

Although Internet commerce is still relatively limited, it is growing rapidly and it is having a significant economic impact on the supply chain (Borenstein and Saloner, 2001). The most popular purchases over the Internet are items such as books, CDs, electrical components and those goods perceived as having a known quality. The phenomenon is also certainly not purely American. As early as 1994 1.2 million French were buying over the Web compared to 0.8 billion in the US at the same time. Now retails over the web in Europe amount to about $3.6 billion. In the UK by 2002 businesses were selling £23.3 billion of products over the Internet, some 1.2% of total sales – up by 39% over the previous year – and of this £6.4 billion was sold to households.

From a transportation perspective, it is useful to note that 66% of the sales involved goods with the sale of services. Some of this, however, represented a transfer from other forms of telecommunications technology (e.g., computer-based faxes, automated telephone entry and EDI), the use of which fell by about 6%. Overall in the UK, as Internet access has increased – from 10% access in 1998/99 to 40% in 2001/02 – and more people are buying goods and services on-line – surveys have indicated anything between 12.2% and 26% by 2003.

Here, therefore, we turn our attention to examining some of the key interactions regarding the ways in which telecommunications interact with the movement of goods rather than people. Goods movements can be a complex process involving numerous actors, often entail the use of a number of modes of transportation, and can be highly specialized according to the commodities involved and the markets that are served.

6.2 DEFINITIONS OF E-COMMERCE AND GENERAL TRENDS

While the term electronic commerce, or e-commerce, is widely used, its exact definition is rather opaque and measurement is even more imprecise. One reason for this is that it is seen as very much a new phenomenon and that fine-tuning of definitions takes time. Boundaries have to be defined, and interfaces clarified.[1] The result is that a number of alternatives exist.

The Organisation for Economic Cooperation and Development has proffered in a variety of official publications, 'Electronic commerce refers generally to all forms of transactions relating to commercial activities both organizations and individuals, that are based upon the processing and transmission of digitalized data, including text, sound and visual images.' The Commission of the European Union argues that, 'Electronic commerce is about doing business electronically. It is based on the electronic processing and transmission of data, including text, sound and video. It encompasses many diverse activities including electronic trading of goods and services, online delivery of digital content, electronic fund transfers, electronic share trading, electronic bills of lading, commercial auctions, collaborative design and engineering, online sourcing, public procurement, direct consumer marketing, and after-sales service. It involves both products (e.g. consumer goods, specialized medical equipment) and services (e.g. information services, financial and legal services); traditional activities (e.g. healthcare

---

[1]   One of the problems is that much of the activity on the Internet involves browsing or price checking rather than the making of an actual purchase. This has been estimated to amount to over 85% of activities.

education) and new activities (e.g. virtual malls).' And the International Monetary Fund has described it as, '... the business occurring over networks which use non-proprietary protocols that are established through an open standard setting process such as the Internet.' But these are simply a few ideas.

Much depends on the boundaries that are drawn. Figure 6.1 provides a typology in pyramid form with the broadest boundaries being drawn around all transactions involving electronic transfers and credit card transactions and the narrowest limiting itself to electronic business-to-consumer activities where an actual transaction takes place.

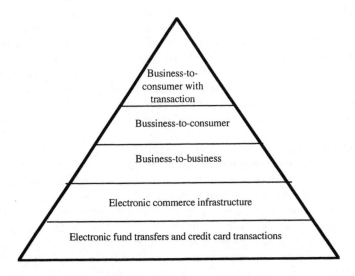

Figure 6.1 Typology of electronic commerce definitions

The definitional problem makes accurate measurement of the extent of e-commerce almost impossible, but there are additional problems in gaining information. Much of the data that are used in debate stem from surveys but these are largely of private, often newly formed companies that have no legal obligation to respond or to give accurate information and involve imprecise definitions of the concept. Indeed, the commercial incentive is to 'talk-up' sales to bolster share prices and market image. The very speed of growth in e-commerce also means that many of the traditional, non-governmental sources of data such as trade associations are still in their infancy and as such struggling to offer a comprehensive range of information services.

The data collected also tend to reflect revenue rather than being measures of value added which is a more conventional measure of economic importance and success. This can lead to problems of double-counting as business-to-business (B-to-B) revenues are added into the final revenues from business-to-consumer (B-to-

C) transactions.[2] The fact that the attraction of many e-commerce sites is their linking of a multiplicity of functions (e.g., search engines, advertisements, travel agencies and directories) compounds these measurement problems if one is seeking details of particular features of e-commerce markets, or emerging trends.

There is also the difficulty that in many cases e-commerce does not reduce the final prices of goods and services and, indeed, in some cases there is a tendency for them to rise. What it can do is to increase the convenience of shopping and purchasing, offer improved product information and increase the choice set from which the purchase may be selected. Traditional accounting techniques of looking at value added had tended to assume product homogeneity but this is the very thing that e-commerce has affected.

The integration of e-commerce into business activities is of longer standing. Traditional merchant practices, both wholesale and retail, have added to them a complexity of separation of businesses into large areas of their activities. They are in some cases required to keep separate accounts for taxation purposes (e.g. in the US e-commerce is state tax exempt) but this is not always the case. Despite these problems, estimates from the US made in 1999 suggest that up to 39% of retailers had plans at that time to sell on-line and this has turned out to be a conservative projection.

Whilst the data may not be very precise, what is clear is that e-commerce is growing and, despite some turbulence in its path, at a fairly rapid rate. This growth is not the result of any one factor but seems to stem from an amalgam of interacting causes. At the forefront is that fact that B-to-B e-commerce increases productivity and reduces business costs. It is relatively cheap to develop an electronic store that is open for global business 24 hours a day and 365 days a year. But linked with this, e-commerce provides near instantaneous feedback on sales and inventories. This allows for the effective creation of supply chains and the adoption of near optimal 'just-in-time' management techniques.

In particular, in the B-to-B context it allows linkages between buyers and sellers that fine tune demand forecasting. The gains from this are particularly noticeable where there is large-scale production with multiple interchangeable components with build-to-order elements such as in the automobile industry. Although precision is distant, estimates suggest that a 20% savings has been attained in the US auto market. As one performance indicator, whereas in the past it took about 10 business days to assemble a car, manufacturers now aim to respond to specific vehicle orders within 3 to 5 days.

As would be expected, the growth has not been even across sectors and industries. Different cost structures, variations in the nature of products, and diverse patterns of demand all play a part in affecting the up-take of B-to-B and

---

[2]   There is evidence that B-to-B e-commerce between very large companies developed more rapidly and is very much larger than B-to-C e-commerce (Organisation for Economic Cooperation and Development, 1997).

B-to-C e-commerce. Table 6.2 offers a very broad indication of how various sectors have reacted to the new telecommunications opportunities.[3]

Table 6.2 Shifts in the business model from physical to electronic markets

Sector	Degree of business substitution
Music	Radical
Publishing	Radical
Transport	Partial
Information services	Mixed evidence
Retail banking	Radical
Marketing and advertising	None

There is nothing surprising. At one level, written material can easily be delivered electronically as can music both between companies and to the final consumer – indeed in the latter context, the i-Pod and like may be seen as a logical extension of radio and television that have been delivering music to the home for many years. In addition, where physical products are sought, books or compact discs are easily transportable and purchases are generally made on the bases of reviews, recommendations, or previous experience of material by an author/artist, actual contact with the product is not required for decisions on purchase.

Equally, banking requires no physical movement of assets and there has long been a tradition of moving 'money' electronically by telegraph, for example, by Western Union. Again, modern telecommunications has added to the quality and the number of options available to banks rather than producing a sea change in the fundamental ways in which they work. As such they have transportation effects, but more in terms of continuing an ongoing trend. In other areas, such as marketing and advertising, personal contacts still seem very important in many cases, and in others the masses of advertising material that companies and individuals receive through the mail, in newspapers, and as fliers seems to continue unabated.

6.3 DEVELOPMENT IN TELECOMMUNICATIONS, E-COMMERCE AND PHYSICAL DISTRIBUTION

The development of telecommunications has already impacted significantly on the freight transport sector. It is now an integral part of modern supply-chain

---

[3] These types of sector differences are also borne in evidence from the consumer side of B-to-C business. In the UK in 2002 the four most popular services on the Internet involved books, hotels and travel, tickets for events, and music.

management, of which transport is a central component, and is especially relevant for just-in-time activities.

As each producer and manufacturer strives to gain market power, the elasticity of the supply chain is critical in ensuring quality (e.g., the cold chain requires goods to be maintained at or below a certain temperature and delays can affect quality and the production life-cycle), convenience, and time compression. Customers are increasingly able to shop around at a minimal cost for a product and service that satisfies their individual needs. From a producer perspective, this equates to the threat of competition and the opportunity for greater market share.

6.3.1 Aspects of B-to-B e-commerce and B-to-C e-commerce

The growth in the e-commerce market in its various forms is already having implications for the demand for transportation and on land use. These effects are essentially of two kinds. There is a traffic generation effect because e-commerce leads to greater efficiency in the overall production process and is a trade-facilitator and in this role stimulates economic growth and with this greater demands for transportation services.[4] This is further driven by the reverse logistics part of the process that has to do with the return of mis-delivered goods or those not wanted by unsatisfied customers. There are diversion effects as various types of activities make different uses of advanced telecommunications services and with this develop in different ways with individual demands on transportation services[5].

While it is possible to deliver some goods online – e.g., airline tickets and music – most goods ultimately have to be produced, shipped, and consumed. The growth in B-to-B commercial interactions is stimulating greater sophistication in supply-chain management and furthering the development of just-in-time production. Traditional inter-business activities involve a buyer looking for inputs or a supplier seeking purchases for its goods and services. Any transactions involve the two parties finding each other – e.g., through advertising and intermediaries – then negotiating a deal – e.g., over quantity, price and specifications – and finally dealing with billing, delivery payment, and transportation. E-commerce is designed to automate processes and, in so doing, ease facilitation at all stages of the process, but affects the types of transaction – e.g., at the most aggregate level B-to-B or B-to-C e-commerce – and industries in different ways. The gains may be considerable and diverse.[6]

---

[4]   The relationship between land-use and transportation is still not fully understood. The normal economic approach is to treat transportation as a derived demand; derived from the demand for final products. There is an argument though, that it may well act as a stimulus for economic growth in some cases.

[5]   One example of this is the automobile-manufacturing sector where the early twentieth century idea of vertical integration and organizational governance has given way as the result of electronic markets to outsourcing and reliance on markets to obtain components on the best terms.

[6]   Lucking-Reiley and Spulber (2001) provide an economic assessment of the types and magnitudes that B-to-B e-commerce can generate.

The development of such features as auto-exchange web sites like Ford Motor Corporation's ConsumerConnect (Kerwin and Stepanek, 2000), for example, are aimed at reducing inventory holdings, lowering transactions costs, permitting tailored or customized vehicles, and fostering faster delivery. The savings in doing business in this way can be substantial, with estimated savings up to 39% for electronic components, 20% for computing, 25% for forestry products and 22% for machining. These savings have implications for delivery patterns involving smaller consignments and more frequent deliveries. Added to this, e-commerce helps improve the efficiency of the freight transportation industry by as much as 15% to 20% (Cohn and Brady, 2000).

The largest advantages, but also the greatest challenges, from B-to-C e-commerce come from slightly different sources, The B-to-C e-commerce market is likely to become more oligopolized as the benefits of economies of scale, scope, and density in hub-and-spoke systems develop, along with the economies that come from large scale warehousing and automated handling systems. Mergers as well as growth within individual undertakings would seem inevitable.

Delivery patterns depend very much on how the major suppliers develop their logistics. Much of the traffic in the US, for example, is handled by UPS (55% of the 1998 Christmas e-commerce delivery market), the US Post Office (32%) and FedEx (10%). Some short-term changes in market share are inevitable as, for example, FedEx restructures its operations to meet the emerging market conditions, and some new players have entered the market, but there are longer-term, structural issues as well.

The freight transportation sector, an industry that in the recent past had been notoriously slow in adopting new technology and cultures, has shifted its focus to developing strategic alliances with shippers. In the case of maritime transportation the first alliance emerged in 1994 when APL, OOCL, MOL and Nedlloyd formed the Grand Alliance and by the end of 1999 only MSC and Evergreen remained as major carriers outside alliances. Relations involving alliances are more than ever concerned with interpersonal communications and trust. In some cases carriers have physically located personnel in shippers' offices to facilitate this process, linking individuals technologically and personally to effectively communicate with customers and clients in a timely manner (Taylor, 1999).

6.3.2 B-to-C e-commerce users

The extent to which B-to-C e-commerce affects transportation and land-use also depends on the types of markets it penetrates. Market research into e-shopping has generally found that the physical shopping experience is attractive to some people, particularly women.

For example, in apparel retailing, displays are manipulated to attract female shoppers; they are interested in finding something that looks and feels right. Studies distinguish the female shopper from the male, arguing that female shoppers browse, are interested in what is new, and touch garments. Men, on the other hand generally go shopping to satisfy a need ('target shoppers' and not 'impulse buyers'; they have a purpose and are often reluctant to try new trends. In addition, with the increasingly popular outlet malls and discount centers that can be found in many places around the world, offering designer labels at discount prices, leisure shopping becomes a quasi-sport.

On-line shopping largely eliminates the experiential aspect of shopping, but what it can do is widen the possible choice set. Statistics of the type cited earlier regarding car purchasing show a great deal more on-line window shoppers than purchasers. Consumers frequently use the Internet to gather information about products, and depending on the perceived reliability of product quality and suitability, many are still purchasing off-line. However, there is some evidence of the reverse with consumers viewing goods at a mall and then buying on-line at lower prices. Again, this shopping pattern depends on the type of product and the attitudinal predisposition of the consumer.

There is a fairly strong correlation between Internet use, type of employment, and income, and this inevitably affects the types of people who are most likely to buy on-line. In the UK, for example, 67% of classes A and B (essentially 'professional' people) were Internet users in 2002, as were 75% with incomes over £30,000 per annum who used it, as did 54% of those earning between £17,500 and £30,000. The age of users is also important, especially for forecasting purposes, and 56% of those aged between 15 and 24 years were Internet users, 63% in the age band 25 to 34, 58% in the band 35 to 44, and 50% in the band 45 to 50 years old (Office for National Statistics, 2002).

These patterns of Internet use have implications for likely levels of future engagement in e-commerce and the subsequent effects of this for the transportation system, and, in the very long term, land-use. As an example, it is the middle class and income range that tend to dominate suburbia where deliveries and collections impose the highest economic and social costs. To date, however, this aspect of the subject has not been thoroughly explored.

Internet transactions involving more local deliveries, such as groceries, have grown slowly with the leader in comprehensive service, Peapod, the on-line grocery company, only covering about 8% of the US population (Peet, 1999). While some companies such as Streamline in Boston have provided free refrigerators to allow them a flexible delivery schedule, a major problem is providing a guaranteed delivery time. In the short term, it seems unlikely that e-commerce will make a significant impact in this area and hence it is unlikely to reduce traffic at supermarkets.

6.3.3 B-to-B developments

The largest up-take of electronic commerce in monetary terms is in B-to-B transactions that now amount to well over $114 billion annually in the US or about 80% of total Internet transactions. For example, Ford, DaimlerChrysler, and General Motors are transferring all their purchases to the web over the next few years via a single e-hub exchange for auto parts and General Electric has been rapidly moving in that direction. Internationally, Sears, Roebuck and Carrefour have moved to an Internet retail exchange to handle the $80 billion they spend annually with suppliers.

One explanation for these developments is that B-to-B transactions are purely commercial in their orientation, there is no utility involved in the act of shopping *per se*, and because of their frequency of purchase, they generally involve a known quality. They effectively cut transactions and search costs. In contrast, consumers often enjoy the act of shopping and require non-quantitative information about products. That is largely why, although as many as 40% of car buyers consulted the Internet at some point, only 2.7% of new car sales in the US in 1999 took place on-line.

The growth in the e-commerce market in its various forms is already having implications for the demand for transportation and on land-use. While it is possible to deliver some goods online (e.g., airline tickets and music), most goods and services ultimately have to in some way be produced, shipped, and consumed. The rise in B-to-B interactions has been stimulating greater sophistication in supply-chain management and furthering the development of just-in-time production but the effect is not even across countries or sectors.

The B-to-C e-commerce market is likely to become even more oligopolized as economies of scale and scope are realized. Delivery patterns will then depend very much on how the major suppliers develop their logistics. Much of the Christmas traffic, as we noted earlier, is handled by UPS with the US Post Office and FedEx having somewhat smaller roles. Some short-term changes in market share are inevitable as FedEx continues restructuring its operations to meet the emerging market conditions, but there are longer-term, structural issues. It is within this context that there have been noticeable changes in the way freight transportation services are supplied and used. Although different regions may have different propensities toward readily adopting new communication technologies, the capability of the Internet as a medium for consumer shopping is real and is requiring changes to the logistics process.

6.4 REACTIONS OF THE TRANSPORTATION SECTOR

The implications of more extensive use of information systems in commercial activities have impacted, and continue to impact, on transportation, both in terms of personal travel and in the ways in which the transport component of the logistics supply chain functions.

6.4.1 Transportation logistics chains

Handling the changing location needs of modern, information based transportation logistics chain has been proving in recent years to be one of the greatest challenges confronting both industry and public sector policymakers. Industry has to make long-term capital investments in physically fixed capital such as warehouses, depots, and transshipment facilities, whilst land-use planners have to accommodate the new needs of the transportation sector within much larger planning requirements. Continual change and technical progress introduces additional commercial and political risk into these decisions.

The implications of the demands of telecommunications driven modern logistics on the spatial distribution of transport terminals, warehousing and storage would *a priori* suggest a greater concentration of activities nearer the urban core. This can be understood by consideration of the simple notion of a transport chain described by Vermunt (1993) and set out in Figure 6.2.

It is at the beginning and end of any freight movement that handling is undertaken and this is normally in urban or suburban situations; although there are some greenfield facilities emerging. It is at these points (sometimes referred to as the 'last-mile problem') that the more intricate decisions in the transportation chain must be made. The emergence of hub-and-spoke distribution structures provides a dynamic impetus to this effect. As freight traffic grows within urban areas and as a consequence of more inter-urban movements originating and terminating in cities so this handling component has been growing disproportionately.

The urban component of a trip is also the point at which freight transport interacts most seriously with passenger transport and the point at which most immediate environmental impacts become apparent. It is, therefore, that part of any movement that attracts the most policy attention but it is also for that part that it is most challenging to develop publicly acceptable policy solutions.

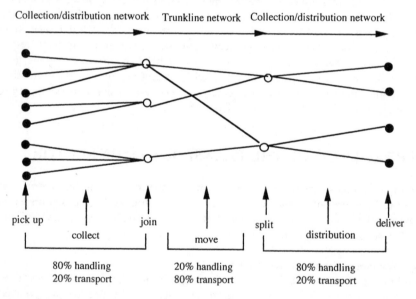

Figure 6.2 Structure of the transportation chain

6.4.2 Trends in the local delivery market

The Worldwide Web has allows individuals to shop and purchase a wide range of items from the convenience of their homes or offices. Such shopping can be done 24 hours a day, on a global scale, and without the time losses associated with physical searches and purchasing. This has led to new structures of distribution emerging with, in many cases, goods being taken directly from manufacturer or distribution center to the home or the office. The major change is in the transportation element of these activities; the distributions center, although often computerized to some extent, has generally evolved more slowly (Anderson et al,. 2003).

The nature of the change that has occurred can be illustrated in Figure 6.3. In the upper diagram the traditional pattern is seen – producers send their goods to distribution centers from which they are taken to stores and shops to be selected and collected by the final consumers. The overall pattern of transportation, including that of shoppers is fairly complex and the overall amount of transportation is considerable with, in the final delivery link, few economies of scope or density being possible.

The lower segment of Figure 6.3 shows the pattern of goods distribution that is now emerging as people use the Internet more intensively to e-shop. In this case the manufacturers send their wares to distribution centers that then, after electronic purchases, distribute them to the final customers. In some cases there are refinements to this picture with the distribution center being bypassed as direct deliveries take place. Additionally, the final deliveries are expresses or other public carriers that combine trips affording transportation economies.

Potentially, significant volumes of goods could be delivered directly from the manufacturer or a major distributor to the customer, who could be located anywhere on the globe. This affects both long-haul and local transportation systems. While the trend in recent years has been to increase the productivity of long-haul carriers through the more efficient use of larger vehicles as more advanced information systems have been introduced and third-party logistics have been developed, distribution resulting from Internet shopping is also increasing the population of delivery vans.

In the 1980s, coincident with a trend toward reducing inventories and a greater focus on customer service, a trend toward smaller quantities of product and more frequent deliveries was observed (ter Brugge, 1991). In Japan, the average weight of goods carried on each trip dropped by 36%, from 3.8 tons in 1980 to 2.4 tons in 1990 (Harutoshi, 1994). For a constant aggregate amount of production, more vehicle movements are required to transport these smaller quantities. This change often entails larger vehicles operating trunk hauls through transshipment and consolidation facilities with collections and deliveries by smaller trucks.

The high growth in Internet commerce is leading to an increase in demand for delivery vehicles, especially those suited to local delivery work. Growth of 15.3% and 25% for small/medium and larger vans respectively, has been reported. Fedex also stated in 1999 that it saw delivery of business generated by Internet transactions as a key to its future growth. If a proliferation of commercial deliveries to residential areas results, there will likely be concerns about the environmental and aesthetic impact of delivery trucks.

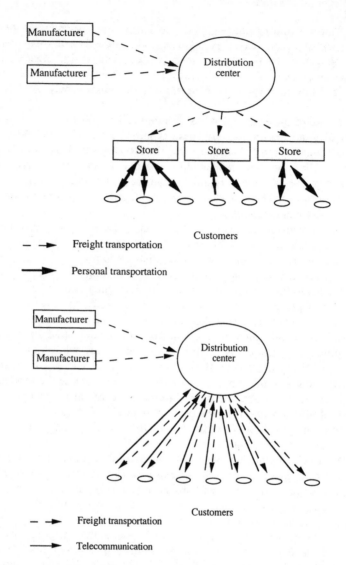

Figure 6.3 Traditional (top) and emergent (bottom) distribution systems

The distribution of Web-based purchases has in the past sometimes proved to be problematic. The online toys market offers a case study. In the US there were many disruptions to deliveries over the Christmas period in 1999 – e.g., Toys'R' Us was fined $350,000 by the Federal Trade Commission because of a breakdown in its order and delivery system – and the problem extended to many other countries. In Australia, for example, major on-line retailers such as d-store and

ToySpot admitted their fulfillment systems were inadequate over that period (Gardiner, 2000).[7] These types of problem now seem much less frequent and in 2003 the on-line sales of toys and video games was up by 33% over the previous year.

The legacy businesses that expanded from traditional retailing into Internet activities have generally found their warehouse and distribution centers ill suited to e-commerce. Companies in the US such as Land's End and J. Crew with a tradition in mail order business had less difficulty, but the transition is still far from smooth. The new suppliers of e-commerce services have generally been inexperienced in inventory control, general logistics and have found problems in containing costs. Many e-commerce companies are now constructing large automated warehouses to handle the picking-and-packing of their sales to ensure an acceptable level of customer service. These developments take time and this has meant that distribution costs have often been higher than they need be.

From a more general traffic management perspective, this growth in B-to-C commerce does not always result in improved traffic flows. People still like to shop and, with increased leisure time, the evidence is that it remains a major recreational activity. Even those who do shop from home now free up time[8] that can be used for other activities that may themselves, involve travel. What it appears electronic retailing does is enhance social welfare by widening individual choice and providing more efficient ways of gaining information. For those in the supply-chain there are economic gains, or else they would not be used, that in competitive markets are ultimately passed on to final consumers in terms of lower prices.

6.4.3 Outsourcing

The new technology based logistics systems are often expensive, can involve specialized labor, and may require considerable capital outlays. This leads to potential economies of scale and scope that make their deployment by smaller undertakings inefficient. As seen by some of the problems in the late 1990s, modern logistics is also a complex business where specialist skills and experience are often needed. This has resulted in a considerable amount of outsourcing of logistics services.[9]

---

[7]   These teething problems are perhaps not surprising given the complexity of global supply chains. Remaining with the toy industry, global shipment involves, on average, 27 parties.

[8]   Looked at from another perspective, shipping costs are seen as one of the main deterrents to shopping for physical goods online. Consumers often did not appreciate their own time costs of collection at stores but now delivery charges make these transactions costs transparent. They can make more informed choices about the costs of using their time for leisure rather than personally collecting merchandize from stores.

[9]   Aoyama et al. (2005) call it disintegration in the sense that traditional in-house supply chains are being broken up and contrast the effects of outsourcing with the integrating effects of mergers and acquisitions.

Outsourcing has thus grown in importance with, for example, companies such as UPS, DHL, ODW Logistics, Penske Logistics, and C.H. Robinson Worldwide playing a prominent role for long-distance distribution in the US. Figure 6.4 indicates the scale and growth in logistics outsourcing in the US. This change implies the potential for considerable consolidation with limited additional vehicle movements if distribution remains oligopolized. The Internet has helped foster confidence in outsourcing solutions. Logistics management is evolving to what can metaphorically be referred to as the 'glass pipe'; it is emphasizing the need for transparency to the client. Delays are visible which places greater emphasis on the connectivity of the supply chain, *viz*; integrated transportation networks, seamless information exchange, good communication and coordination.

Communications technology allows businesses to reduce the quantity of paper transactions, which in freight movement, especially regarding import/export activities, can be extremely high, and to provide customers with information on where their goods are in the chain. Having paid for the goods, customers are understandably anxious to keep track of the physical movement of their investments – that is, where are the delays, where is the commodity in the chain, what is the estimated arrival time?

In many cases some of these challenges are being met by the formation of vertical alliances between individual actors in the logistics chain. As we have seen these alliances are more than ever concerned with interpersonal communications and trust and can entail carriers physically locating staff in shippers' offices, creating linkages of technologies and personal to that allow more efficient communicate with customers and clients.

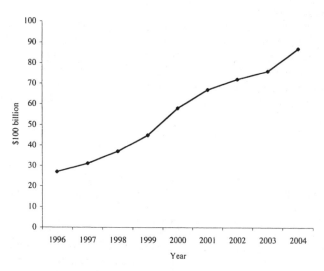

Figure 6.4 Outsourced logistics in the US by revenue

Outsourcing, along with internal efficiency considerations within the transportation system, has also been a force behind the growth in third-party logistics. This involves the growth of consolidators and integrators that provide custom designed delivery systems for industry. The aim is that the three 'logistics flows' – of goods, of information and of financing – complement each other. The entire US logistics market is over a $1 trillion a year, the third-party logistics market is worth about $50 billion but, in contrast to the overall growth rate of about 4% per annum, third-party logistics is growing at over 15%. Perhaps the best, and largest, examples of this type of activity are found in the electronics components, consumer electronics, pharmaceuticals, cars, and fashion industries. In the case of automobiles, the global nature of the supply chain and the nature of the product means that a typical vehicle is made up of over 10,000 components that are produced around the world and companies such as TPG organize owner-operated vehicles to ensure just-in-time delivery to assembly plants.

The setting up of transportation exchanges has stimulated the outsourcing trend in some contexts. These exchanges are portals that connect available loads to available trucking space on a dynamic basis. In practice, these exchanges have enjoyed variable success but many are unprofitable and success seems more common when a single player dominates an exchange. Nevertheless, studies in the UK suggest that in recent years exchanges have reduced empty running in the UK by some 20%.

6.4.4 Depot and transshipment locations

As we have seen, many of the challenges involving goods movements now center primarily on urban activities and the last mile problem. Urban transportation logistics pose management and investment challenges not only for those supplying and using the services but also for those that are responsible for the associated physical transportation infrastructure. It is as much a public policy issue as one for commercial management.

The potential problems of urban and, increasingly, suburban traffic congestion and local environmental degradation in areas in close proximity to loading/unloading, transshipment and consolidation points are a political concern to public authorities. Information on the degree to which logistic suppliers geographically concentrate their activities and the types of logistics operations that are more prone to spatial clustering is important if efficient transportation strategies are to emerge. The information sources on this, however, remain relatively limited.

The increased use of e-commerce, combined with intelligent transportation systems (ITS)[10], impacts on the way logistics suppliers locate their facilities, although this should be put in the context of more traditional considerations. There are also some fundamental issues for logistic service suppliers about whether there are advantages of location economies of

---

[10]   Many of the relevant issues are considered in more detail in Chapter 7. For more on ITS see Stough et al. (2003).

grouping certain types of activity in specific parts of urban areas. This may be in terms of access and land costs but also may involve issues of availability of complementary services such as vehicle maintenance, labor pools, etc.; in other words traditional agglomeration considerations.

No attempt is made here to offer any abstract model of why urban logistics suppliers may or may not decide to cluster but rather we look at the clustering phenomena itself and offer some thoughts on how developments in telecommunications may be influencing this. The empirical analysis presented makes use of geographical information systems (GIS) to examine the spatial clustering of urban logistics activities.

There has been considerable discussion within the ITS community of how GIS data can be used to enhance the performance of freight carriers within cities and more generally. In particular, it has been seen to offer the potential for improved computerized vehicle routing and scheduling. It also has been advocated for planning the routing of hazardous materials and for real-time fleet management, and applications are now emerging in these areas.

Button et al.'s (2001) study concerned itself with the extent to which market trends in the provision of urban logistics services, including those associated with changes in telecommunications technology and use, are leading to geographical clustering of warehouse, storage, and other urban transport facilities. Disaggregate data for 1999 from two large US urban areas (Detroit and Washington–Baltimore) show the extent to which clustering of logistics centers has occurred.

The areas studied differ in their economic geography in that one is characterized by a high involvement in government work and because it has a very significant high technology (both telecommunications and biotechnology) industrial base, while the other has a long history of heavy industry, most notably the automobile industry, and has recently been trying to modernize its core economic activities.

Figure 6.5 looks, on the left, at the spatial distribution of warehousing alone in the consolidated Washington–Baltimore MSA. Warehousing locations are seen as empty squares. The expected concentration around Washington and Baltimore is clear. The more comprehensive picture on the right shows trucking and courier locations (not involving air freight terminals) as filled squares. The spatial pattern that emerges is similar in many ways although there are far more trucking/courier locations outside of the main centers of population. This would confirm that much of the handling, that is largely a warehousing function, takes place in or near the ends of movements.

While such maps can only be indicative of the situation in the region they do provide some visual impressions of what is happening regarding the local geography of logistics terminals. A cursory look at the data point spread provides an impression that logistics centers are not randomly spread. The focus of much of the activity on the main road arteries is clear.

A more concentrated pattern of location is observed for Baltimore than for the Washington/Northern Virginia area. This would seem to reflect the differing population densities but may also be influenced by the rapid recent growth in economic activity along major transport corridors in Northern Virginia as high-technology industry has spread westwards from Washington along a corridor to Dulles Washington International Airport. The more traditional port activity in Baltimore accounts for the more compact pattern that is observed around the port or waterfront areas.

Figure 6.5 Warehousing (left) and warehouse and trucking/courier (right) in the Washington–Baltimore consolidated MSA

Figure 6.6 provides a more detailed spatial picture of distribution of trucking/courier and warehousing and storage locations in the Baltimore MSA. This indicates that there is a much greater spread of warehousing and trucking facilities at the micro level than at the broader regional level of analysis. But it also shows again that one cannot treat these types of activities as being the same. The clustering of warehousing appears much more focused on the urban core area than is the case in the Washington/Northern Virginia area.

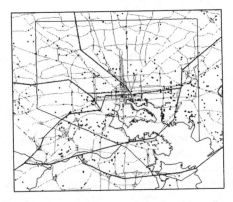

Figure 6.6 Warehouse and trucking/courier locations in the Baltimore MSA

Turning to the area around Detroit; as with the Washington-Baltimore area case, the left element of Figure 6.7 shows the distribution of warehousing and storage and the right element warehousing and trucking combined for the Detroit MSA. In Figure 6.8 there is more detail of the pattern found in the urban core of the area.

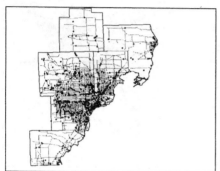 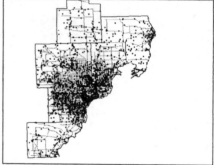

Figure 6.7 Warehouse locations (left), and warehouse and trucking/courier locations (right) in the Detroit MSA

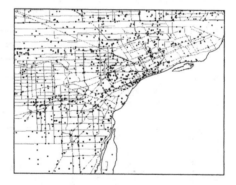

Figure 6.8 Warehouse and trucking/courier locations in core area of Detroit

The spatial pattern would not seem to be that different to that found in the Washington–Baltimore region. In particular, the trucking/courier element is much more spread across both the larger MSA and the core city area than is warehousing and storage. Whether there is actual clustering or not and, if so, to what types of logistics activity it applies is not clear, however, from the visual presentation. It would appear that warehousing does have a more dispersed pattern, with more facilities on the main arteries but whether this is statistically significant cannot be discerned.

Visual presentations are, therefore, useful for highlighting general patterns but lack statistical rigor. Near-neighbor analysis can offer a more structured way of assessing spatial patterns.[11] The findings for the Washington–Baltimore MSA using this technique are that neither the geographical spread of warehousing nor that of trucking are random; indeed, only two types of warehousing and storage (farm products and refrigerated warehousing, both of which are perhaps to be expected) emerge as having a random distribution.

Spatial disaggregation also shows a proclivity towards clustering with only two counties deviating. A simple comparison between trucking and courier services and warehousing implies rather more clustering within trucking in the region, while at a lower level of industrial aggregation, activities such as local trucking with storage, courier services, and general warehousing and storage seem to be more clustered than other forms of local logistic support facilities.

Detroit throws up similar patterns to the Washington–Baltimore area with little support for the notion that trucking/courier and warehousing/storage facilities are either randomly or regularly distributed, although clustering seems to be a somewhat weaker phenomenon.

Technology advances that initially led to the adoption by transport companies of such procedures as electronic data interchange (EDI) and subsequently to Web based systems have produced innovative management leading to developments such as advanced supply-chain management. With these changes have come new ideas on how urban logistics should or could be structured.

To maximize the potential efficiency gains of these new technologies and management practices, it is important that local planning agencies supply transportation infrastructure and management of the existing networks and have good information on where change is occurring and how it is likely to progress in the future. Enhanced modeling is part of this but its practical use is limited in the absence of good data. Understanding the pattern and clustering of trucking/courier bases and warehousing is important in modeling where future traffic flows will concentrate.

That clustering does occur seems to be a reality although the degree of clustering does differ between the cities and between the sub-categories of trucking/courier and warehousing that have been isolated. Why this is the case requires a different type of analysis to that applied here, one that tests causal linkages. This study has limited itself to the more basic question of describing the nature of the clusters and has made no attempt to analyze why they occur as they do.

---

[11]   Near-neighbor analysis is used to identify situations where a distribution of points, or locations is clustered, random or scattered. A random pattern of locations consists of points that are situated in locations with equal probability. Each location occurs by chance and is independent of all other points. A non-random pattern may either be a cluster or it may be dispersed. In the former case, spatial dependence between two or more points implies an attraction for common locations, associated, for example, with economies of agglomeration of some form.

6.4.5 Security

The events of September 11th 2001 in the US and subsequent major terrorist attacks in Spain and the UK have brought security to the fore of transportation policy. While most of the attacks to-date have involved passenger transport modes, there are clear concerns about the role that containers may play as a means of carrying weapons to sensitive sites. The actions to contain the threat that this poses to the logistics system involve extensive use of various types of information technologies and telecommunications.

The topic of security to the supply chain is a complex one. Security, which traditionally involved pilfering and damage, has involved into something altogether more sinister. Unlike safety, security involves 'game playing' with those intent on causing physical and psychological damage, and actual events are relatively small in number. It is therefore technically more a matter of uncertainty rather than actuarial risk. These are inevitable arbitrary actions, given the lack of any Gaussian probabilities regarding potential attacks, that involve a high level of judgment and embrace concerns about public confidence as well as the potential physical threats and damage.

To retain public confidence in the logistics network, there is a need to ensure that the dangers of terrorist attacks are kept within acceptable social limits. There are clear issues about the best ways of achieving this in a purely technical sense, e.g., what should be the role of technology, what should be the extent of private sector involvement and what degree of resources should be placed on prevention as opposed to managing an attack or subsequent recovery?

The underlying nature of the broad challenges confronting authorities, both public and private, when seeking to develop strategies aimed at optimizing security is illustrated in Figure 6.9.

If the issue were one purely of risk then it is conceptually possible, using standard economic cost-benefit analysis principles, to determine the optimal safety level. With upward sloping cost (C) and benefit (B) curves for additional security the optimal safety level would be S. This picture is, however, excessively simplistic and a number of refinements are needed to gain added reality.

First, the fact that benefits of security can be both in terms of limiting material damage and affording psychological 'comfort' to the population means the benefit curve can be decomposed separating out the material damage component (B*) from the full effects[12].

Second, regarding costs, it assumes that C is a minimum cost of security curve that will determine the resources needed to provide any given level of security and that the authorities will pursue actions that ensure the costs of security follow this path. Given the multidimensional nature of the threat to maritime security, the scale and form of the industry, and its international character, it is a complex matter to define this curve. The potential for significant

---

[12]   There is no clear relationship between material and psychological benefits and the divergence seen in the figure is purely illustrative; indeed calculating such a relationship is difficult.

X-inefficiency emerging is considerable in situations like this where objectives tend to be opaque and many costs are only indirectly borne by those responsible for the security provided.

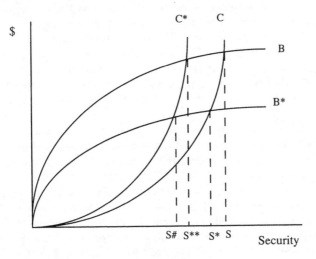

Figure 6.9 Optimal security expenditure

The problem may be compounded if there is asymmetrical information involved concerning the potential effectiveness of security measures. This can allow capture by purveyors of security equipment and systems and with it sales of over costly items. The effect is that in practice, the cost curve may be higher than the minimum possible at C*.

Given these complexities a number of sub-optimal possibilities emerge. Ignoring the psychological benefits that go with greater security could lead to levels of security {S – S*} below the social optimum, but even allowing for these psychological effects, if costs of providing security are not minimized then security will be deficient by {S – S**}. If both full benefits are underestimated and costs are not kept to a minimum then a level of security $S^{\#}$ would be supplied that is well below the optimum.

Defining these curves is far from simple, and there are interactions. Knowledge of the psychological benefits from enhanced security is scant involving such things as political perception, opinion polls and occasional elections. Concerns about security threats are or can be heightened by media coverage, and by its nature people have poor information about how effective various security initiatives are; and those with the lesser amounts of information tend to be sub-optimally cautious. Enhanced intelligence, combined with public confidence in this intelligence, essentially increases the information base. This type of action effectively pulls the B down towards B* but full convergence remains unlikely.

More generally, while useful, this type of risk analysis has limitations when dealing with terrorism. Essentially, the difficulty is the one highlighted earlier, namely that the benefit curve of additional security cannot be estimated in actuarial terms; it is about uncertainty and it is seldom about marginalism. A common approach to dealing with this type of uncertainty problem is to seek out situations of vulnerability and to develop strategies that can reduce this vulnerability or that may provide flexibility if there are attacks on vulnerable points. Comparisons with similar but not identical situations where risk can be assessed can sometimes add insight. A significant degree of subjectivity and 'expert opinion' is, however, inevitably involved, and it is almost impossible to judge success.

Telecommunications is important in this type of uncertain world. It has an obvious role in terms of intelligence gathering although this is perhaps outside of our domain. Within the more traditional confines of the logistics supply-chain, telecommunications enhances tracking of consignments (especially through the use of GPS), can provide advanced information on the nature of cargoes that are being shipped, and offers external surveillance at depots and en route. It is also important in the parallel financial chain that mirrors the movement of goods and provides information on the nature of funding involved. These features both help to reduce the number of 'incidences' but also instill a degree of public confidence in the logistics system. They do, however, come at a price and given the intangible nature of security – success is difficult to measure – there is the potential of adopting excessively sophisticated and costly 'solutions'.

6.5 CONCLUSIONS

Logistics have changed considerably over the past 20 to 30 years. There are many interacting factors that have contributed to this, but the advances in telecommunications have certainly been a major contributing influence. The impact has been on both the demand side and the cost side. This chapter has looked only at a few of the key trends and patterns that have emerged. What is clear, however, is that, unlike the past, many companies now take their logistics seriously rather than treating it almost as a residual fixed cost in their production function. Larger companies now have board members with skills in the area and most employ trained personnel to carry out logistics functions. Specialist logistics providers have grown in number and importance.

Telecommunications, together with the advent of the container and other technological and managerial developments, now allows greater flexibility in the movement of goods combined with enhanced capacities through GPS technologies and the like to track consignments. This has helped reduce inventory costs in the production chain, as well as offering a superior quality of service to final customers. There has been something of a lag in the system as the physical distribution, with the need to adjust assets and minimize stranded costs, has sought to keep pace with the information systems changes that are taking place. This is inevitable given the differing capital intensity and nature of capital deployed by these elements in the chain but there is evidence of major restructuring of physical distribution now taking place.

7 TELECOMMUNICATIONS AND INTELLIGENT TRANSPORTATION SYSTEMS

7.1 INTRODUCTION

There have been significant changes in the way in which transportation policy is now viewed and, while this is particularly so in the context of urban transportation, the reassessment covers all forms of movement. Moving people and goods around cities has always posed challenges. Much of the movement has been during limited periods of the day, the 'rush-hours' and of the week. It has largely been unidirectional during those periods with inward flows during the morning and outward movements in the evening. It has always, even before the advent of the automobile, imposed considerable environmental costs on those living in urban areas. Whilst the problems of noise and atmospheric pollution differed when the horse-drawn vehicle dominated, they were perceived as being as serious as the particulates, aromatics, nitrogen oxide and other gases are today.

Added to this, many inter-urban modes are now posing serious challenges to policy-makers. Many freeways are regularly congested in the US and in several European countries, as are many large airports and seaports. The efforts to reduce some of the worst effects of urban pollution have brought some successes but more substantial volumes of intercity movements have inflicted increased noise nuisance on those around airports, freeways, and high-speed train lines and the growth in long-distance transportation has contributed to the rise in global warming gas emissions.

One way to confront these challenges is to transfer physical movements into telecommunications contacts. In previous chapters we have considered the ways in which substitution of telecommunications activities may provide a viable alternative to many of the physical movements that now take place on transportation systems. The picture that emerged was somewhat opaque. Teleworking, videoconferencing, e-commerce and the like may reduce certain types of movement, at certain times of the day, and over some parts of the network but the overall effect need not necessarily be a social gain.

We are not concerned with the issue of complementarity and substitutability here. We shift to a somewhat different topic, that of intelligent transportation systems (ITS). ITS has many facets and not all are relevant to our discussions. What ITS seeks is to make more efficient use, in the broadest sense, of transportation networks. It aims to enhance the ability of physical transportation infrastructure through the better management of flows and direction of traffic. Examples include new and sophisticated traffic signals, electronic toll collection, use of global positioning systems to keep track of fleets of trucks and buses, and use of acoustic and infrared sensors and video cameras to monitor traffic conditions.[1]

7.2 ELEMENTS OF ITS

New technologies, collectively known as ITS or the variants 'intelligent transportation systems', 'advanced transport telematics', or, in Europe, 'information and communications technologies', are in some cases radically altering the ways in which transport systems perform. They will also fundamentally change the ways in which we provide transport infrastructure and services and the ways in which people use that infrastructure and those services.[2]

There is no unique definition of ITS. They all have similar threads concerning the use of new technologies for the improvement of transport systems and the realization of economic and social benefits.[3] Some of the definitions stress these impacts, whilst others are more concerned with identifying the relevant technologies. For example, ITS America defines it as; 'ITS is a broad range of diverse technologies that holds the answer to many of our transportation problems. ITS is comprised of a number of technologies, including information processing, telecommunications, control, and electronics. Joining these technologies to our transportation system will save lives, save time and save money.' Similarly, ITS Canada, Inc. defines it as, 'ITS, an emerging global phenomenon, is a broad range of diverse technologies applied to transportation to save lives, money and time. The range of technologies involved includes micro-electronics, communications and computer informatics, and cuts across disciplines such as transportation engineering, telecommunications, computer science, financing, electronic

---

[1]   For an overview of ITS see Taylor (2001) and for some case studies see Stough (2001).

[2]   Telecommunications may also be used in a number of indirect ways to manage transportation systems that are not covered here, as pointed out by Jovanis (1983) in the context of work scheduling and transit use.

[3]   There is a tendency to consider ITS with regard to surface transportation, and in particular to road and rail transport; this is in part because of the capture of the jargon by those most focused on these modes. In fact, ITS is better treated more widely. Airline services embody a mass of ITS telecommunications technology, both on the ground, in air navigation services, and embodied in the aircraft, to allow aircraft to take off, avoid collisions, cruise, be tracked, and land safely. Similarly, the maritime sector has sophisticated self-navigation devices, automatic pirate alert-warning equipment, weather and course-adjustment technologies, and anti-collision technology in abundance. In addition, there are 'intelligent vehicles' that embody such automatic features as impact airbags, inertia-real seat belts, and hybrid engines that switch fuel source for economical driving, but since telecommunications are not involved they are not considered here.

commerce and automobile manufacturing. The annual world market for ITS is estimated to be $24 billion by 2001 and $90 billion by 2011, and access to this market is vital to the transportation and related technology sectors.'

Whilst in Europe we find ERTICO adopting, 'ITS are the marriage of information and communication technologies with the vehicles and networks that move people and goods. "Intelligent" because they bring extra knowledge to travelers and operators. In cars, ITS systems help drivers navigate, avoid traffic holdups and avoid collisions. On trains and buses, they let managers optimize fleet operation and offer passengers automatic ticketing and real-time running information. On the road network, ITS systems coordinate traffic signals, detect and manage incidents and display information, guidance and instructions to drivers.'

There is a complex array of technologies capable of application to transport systems. A common feature of many of the emerging technologies is the growing reliance on communications and information. Focusing on roads, the biggest impending change is in the amount of communication and the flow of information between the 'components' of the road transportation system; essentially the actors involved in the system. At present these components largely work in isolation but there is likely greater efficiency when there is coordination and one aim of ITS is to make sure that the increasing interaction between them will involve minimum conflict.[4]

Three broad components of any transportation system may be identified:

- *Roads and tracks*. These embrace not only the fixed infrastructure but also structures and organizations supporting the road network. This includes the road pavement, rail tracks, guideways, bridges, underpasses, road furniture, signs and vehicle detectors, and the authorities that build and manage a transport network, and any commercial enterprises that sell transport-related services.
- *Vehicles*. These are the mobile units of capital that make use of the infrastructure. They include all the locomotives, carriages, vessels, craft, cars, motorcycles, trucks, buses and bicycles driven on the roads.
- *Users*. These are essentially the final consumers of transport services and are often key decision-makers. They are all those who use the systems, as drivers, operators, passengers, customers and service recipients.

One of the main challenges is to reconcile a number of key interfaces and resulting interactions that exist within this structure. The role of

[4] While there has been considerable effort put into developing ITS technologies, rather fewer resources have been devoted to evaluating advanced transport telematics projects and where evaluations have been conducted they have focused mainly on technical evaluation, safety, and impacts (Bristow et al., 1997). Equally, and related to the evaluation matter, there have been only limited attempts to fully model the impacts of transport telematics (Chatterjee et al., 1999).

telecommunications within the ITS framework is to facilitate flows of information across these interfaces so that the resultant interactions are efficient. The main interactions can be summarized as:

- *Trackway vehicle interactions.* These interactions require the flow of information between the infrastructure and the vehicle with no direct intervention by the users. At present, this flow does not exist for the vast majority of users. This is a basic element of many emergent telecommunications applications, however, including vehicle tracking – often using global positioning systems (GPS) and identification systems, electronic toll collection, advanced traffic control and automated highways.

- *Trackway user interactions.* Technologies that involve communication between the road infrastructure and the user are increasing in their importance and sophistication. Historically, information was static and directed equally to all road users. Advisory speed signs on curves in roads are an example. The move is now toward providing information that is increasingly dynamic (real time) and personalized. For instance, different vehicles (such as large trucks, passenger cars and motorcycles) may be given different advice about the speed at which to negotiate a curve. Information about the current status of roadways and traffic, public transport or environmental conditions is being collected in many cases and synthesized by relevant authorities and passed on to system users.

- *Vehicle user interactions.* The level of information provided to the user by the vehicle is changing rapidly. Conventionally the only information we receive from the vehicle largely relates to its own performance (speed, engine revolutions, engine temperature, fuel level, tire pressures, etc.). Sensors and computer systems are gradually being built into the vehicle to provide route guidance information to drivers and provide safety and environmental warnings.

- *Trackway vehicle user interactions.* Technologies that involve communication from the roadway to the vehicle then to the user provide another layer in the road operating system. The technologies include such things as vehicle navigation systems that provide real-time information, vehicle dispatch systems and driver and public transport information systems installed in vehicles, at bus and tram stops or computer kiosks, or made available through computer networks.

- *Other interactions.* The new technologies also enable each of the system components to collect and process more and richer information. By using a wider range of sensors and exploiting high-speed communications and computing, road authorities can access more information about current traffic conditions. This information can then be used to forecast through networks to provide lead indicators to emerging bottlenecks, react to incidents more quickly and adjust traffic lights to ease congestion and reduce pollution. Vehicles are quite simply becoming 'smarter'. Sensors and onboard computers are available that can monitor the condition of the vehicle, the roadway and the driver to optimize vehicle performance and help to protect the driver.

ITS technologies of one or another kind are used throughout the world, and in countries such as Japan and Europe governments have adopted formal ITS policies akin to those that have been pursued in the US. But adoption often lags behind technical know how. Japan, for example, with its strong central government, densely concentrated population and complex travel patterns has pursued largely planned transportation, strategies and its consumer electronics industry, has paid particular attention to national ITS policy, and has relatively well-developed ITS traffic control and vehicle navigation systems (Giannopoulos and McDonald, 1997). Nevertheless, as in many other places, however, there have been institutional limitations to their full deployment by the public authorities.

Europe, like Japan, has generally denser populations than the US, and also like Japan, many of its nation states have more of a tradition of strong central government than the US. For these reasons some European nations have been particularly aggressive in promoting ITS; Germany, for example, in the development of government industry partnerships to deploy traffic control systems; France in deploying the Minitel computer system permitting household access to transportation information; and more generally in Europe in the posting of information on electronic variable message signs.[5]

Yet, as, a whole, national differences have frustrated efforts at European-wide ITS planning, and in many cases more integrated local governments with coordinating powers have often been leaders in applications (e.g., posting of real-time information on parking availability at various urban locations at edges of cities, projected travel times to certain exit points on circular roads, common electronic 'tags' for toll collection and paying parking fees, electronically controlled traffic signals.

The US's ITS program began in earnest with the 1991 Intelligent Vehicle-Highway Systems (IVHS) Act, which led to spending $250 million annually on ITS research, testing of pilot projects, and development of national standards. The program was extended by the 1998 ITS Act, which called for the same spending levels but a reorientation from research to deployment of ITS. Today governments at all levels in the US spend an estimated $500 million annually on ITS, and private industry spends a like amount.

---

[5]   Chatterjee and McDonald (2004), in a study of variable message signs across a number of European cities, found that, despite some poor positioning and use of systems by authorities, motorists gave favorable responses regarding their usefulness and that generally they improved travel times and generated environmental benefits.

7.3 APPLICATIONS AND BENEFITS OF ITS

Since ITS represents a generic concept, with definitions varying with agency and situation, it is difficult to provide a full list of applications and their transportation impacts. Additionally, ITS in some cases is taking over functions that were previously served by more traditional technologies – e.g., the electronic collection of road tolls rather than the manual collection – thus having a variety of implications on public finances and the like as well as on transportation. A few examples, however, offer insights into realized and potential benefits.[6]

7.3.1 Areas of ITS application

Traveler information systems
Transportation users need information to make decisions and transportation systems managers use information to enhance the performance of their networks, often by manipulating it to influence user behavior.[7] Traditional signage was static and generally incapable of giving real-time information about such things as incidents on routes, travel time to key junctions in the network, availability of parking, the arrival time of the next bus, tram, or train, or weather conditions.

The evidence is that travelers do respond to information flows although not always in a complete or consistent way. One reason for this is that different people 'read' information in different ways. Another reason is that transportation users realize both that not all information offered electronically is completely accurate and that it may not be in their individual interest to follow the advice given. For example, there is a tendency to trust what is visible to a driver rather than that displayed on a sign or relayed through an on-board device. Additionally, regular users of a network tend to respond differently to information than do infrequent users. One issue is that regular users of a system may find excessive displays of information regarding such things as regularly occurring congestion simply distracting (Benson, 1996).

Safety
Transportation accidents account for many lives each year – e.g., about 40,000 road deaths in the US – and far more major injuries. While transport in purely

---

[6]   ITS is often seen as sitting on two 'pillars' – Advanced Transportation Management Systems (ATMS) and Advanced Traveler Information Systems (ATIS) – because from a policy perspective the former affects the behavior of the entire driver population in the road cases whereas the latter affects individual driver behavior. But these pillars are seldom strictly separable (indeed used correctly there may be strong positive synergies) and, thus, the temptation to strictly do this here is avoided.
[7]   Transportation planners and traffic managers now use a variety of modeling techniques not just to examine how transportation users respond to passive information systems but also to see how they may influence travel behavior more broadly – see Bonsall (2000).

actuarial terms is becoming safer and the chance of being killed in a transportation accident is falling, the social and economic costs of traffic accidents are still high. The reduction in the risk of being involved in a fatal accident is partly due to safer equipment – e.g., crumple zones on cars, safety belts, and safety glass in windscreens – and better infrastructure design – e.g., safety barriers, better road surfaces and drainage, and clearer sight lines. There are also human elements involving driver training and testing, and actions to reduce alcohol consumption. ITS, however, has also placed a role.

In terms of road transportation, information systems forewarning drivers of hazards allow appropriate preemptive changes in driving strategy. ITS monitoring systems provide information to traffic authorities in many large cities as to where incidents take place and allow for both a rapid response by the emergency services and scope for warning and redirecting traffic.[8] In terms of other modes, the degree of safety input can be even higher. Modern air traffic management systems provide information and traffic control that have made flying the safest mode of transportation with virtually no major incidents due to aircraft colliding, and with adverse weather no longer creating a major safety issue.

Road pricing
Charging correctly for road use would add enormously to the economic efficiency of economies. Leading economists such as William Vickrey and Alan Walters have long argued that with appropriate technologies that keep the costs of collection to the authorities and the road user to a minimum, then the optimal way to deal with road traffic congestion is to charge the users of roads for the impedances that they impose on other users; 'road pricing'.

Simple schemes, such as area licensing introduced in Singapore during the 1970s, showed just how powerful the pricing tool can be in influencing potential car users to change mode, share their vehicles, retime their trips, re-route their trips, and in other ways make better use of scarce urban road space.[9] Manual technologies, such as displaying a pre-purchased permit when in a designated area, are unsuitable in more complex situations where there are numerous charging points, or where greater sensitivity is being sought in terms of achieving target traffic flows.

ITS has offered a number of technical ways to meet these challenges and some are now widely used. A variety of automatic toll collection systems based upon transponders are now in widespread use across the world and these provide a more efficient mechanism for pure revenue collection than traditional toll-booths with their associated local congestion and high labor costs. In 2003 charges were

[8]   The relatively simple ITS device of providing a common number for cellular phone users to report incidents in Massachusetts, for example, not only improved response time but also reduced incident waiting time by 40%.
[9]   An electronic charging regime subsequently replaced the manual system.

introduced for vehicles entering the central area of London with payment possible electronically and management and enforcement through electronic license plate identification.[10]

The Norwegians introduced from the late 1980s a series of cordon-pricing regimes, 'toll rings', around a number of their cities (Trondheim, Bergen and Oslo). These essentially involve payment for entry to the city and are designed to raise revenue for transportation projects. The geography of Norway, with its mountainous terrain and small cities with limited access points, makes this a relatively straightforward way of charging road users. The monies are collected through both electronic and manual systems.

Over time, as practical experience has been gained and as technology has developed, so the systems have become more technically sophisticated. In all cases, the initial technology was not state-of-the-art but well tested to ensure that minimal operational problems would arise. In the US, The FASTRACK HOT lanes on an eight-mile section of I-15 north of San Diego are priced on a real-time basis and run parallel to free lanes. Stretches of private road in Orange County California are priced in accordance with a pre-established timetable.

Security
The events of September 11th 2001 in the US heightened concern in that country about the security of transportation systems; concerns already felt in a number of other countries where terrorists had targeted virtually all modes of transportation.

In the past security had mainly focused on the preventing of theft and pilfering but the use of aircraft as weapons, and the appreciation that other forms of transport could be used in a similar role or as transporters of weapons, has resulted in new priorities. ITS has traditionally played a role in security in terms of providing information and location systems to allow rapid response to incidents and in helping in the recovery of stolen vehicles. The recent trend has been to enhance these roles with more sophisticated and integrated ITS systems being installed by security and responding agencies and with the adopting of large scale identification and location systems for road vehicles, aircraft, ships, and containers. Chapter 6 offered a more theoretical basis for the role of telecommunications in the context of freight transport.

Some of this is market driven, with companies fearing the impact of an incident on their business, but much is being mandated by national and international agencies. The impact of these types of actions, as with all security

---

[10]   Within the charging zone, traffic has fallen by 16% (some 50,000 fewer cars being driven in the charging zone daily), congestion, as measured by the difference between night and day-time speeds, has fallen by 30%, and traffic emissions of nitrogen oxide and particulates both by about 12%. Bus service irregularities have fallen by 30% and disruptions due to traffic delays by 60% while overall bus speeds in the charging zone have risen by 6%. There has been little impact on traffic in zones adjacent to where the charge is levied.

activities, is difficult to access, but in terms of transportation efficiency there are clear burdens that would be even more onerous without modern ITS technologies.

7.3.2 Benefits of ITS

So far we have focused on issues that are being addressed by ITS, the capabilities of the emerging, mainly telecommunications based technologies, their applications, and the way that the relationships between transport system components will change. The larger question, however, concerns the nature and magnitude of the benefits that the technologies will deliver. These are often difficult to quantify and value with any precision, but there are some indicators.

The benefits will likely be delivered by combinations of technologies working together towards the overall aim of making transportation systems better serve the community, in both urban and rural areas. Improved traffic control, better information about traffic conditions and transport options, better vehicles and improved public transport will work together to make it easier and more efficient to use the various transport networks. ITS will also improve the utilization of existing infrastructure and can certainly reduce the need to provide more roads and road transport services. In addition, reduced environmental impact can result from more efficient usage of the road network by more environmentally friendly vehicles.

Quantification of the individual benefits that new technologies will deliver is still in its infancy, although there are a number of studies now emerging. In many instances the overall benefits are likely to be case-specific, not generic, and will depend on the characteristics of each city or region and the combination of technologies that are in use. In addition, many of the technologies are complementary and their full benefits will only be delivered when they are all in place.[11]

Garrett (1998) cites European research suggesting the following likely improvements in transport systems performance achievable by 2017, from the systematic implementation of ITS technologies:

- a 15% increase in survival rates from road crashes;
- a 50% reduction in road fatalities;
- a 25% reduction in travel times;
- savings of 40 hours per traveler per annum through the use of automatic traffic control;
- a 50% reduction in delays through improvements in public transport priority;
- a 25% reduction in freight costs through improved efficiency of freight movements and fleet operations, and

---

[11]   Taylor (2001) summarizes the likely benefits from the various technology categories.

- a 50% decrease in pollution in city centers through the use of advanced traffic management systems.

There remains a need for ongoing independent examination of the magnitude and extent of potential benefits. For example, a relatively recent German study by Baum et al., (1999) indicates that there may be optimal levels of ITS implementation below that of full implementation across a vehicle fleet. They considered the introduction of a system of tandem vehicles for long-distance freight traffic on freeways, in which a vehicle driven by a human operator is shadowed by one under automatic control (i.e., the driver is actually controlling two vehicles at once). An economic analysis indicated that, for the travel data used, the best result was for only 20% of vehicles to be equipped with this system.

Booz Allen and Hamilton (1998) provide an attempt at identifying and quantifying the system-wide benefits of ITS. They focused on four key inputs to the assessment of benefits:

- specification of current and future costs of performance measures such as road crashes, congestion levels, pollutant emissions, and economic costs of transport;
- identification of ITS applications where sufficient information existed to permit quantification of safety, congestion, travel time, emissions and fleet efficiency benefits;
- consideration of the potential levels of application of ITS within the national context, and
- assessment of the current level of and projected increases in ITS implementations over a given time period (1997–2012).

The Booz Allen and Hamilton review of international experience suggested a wide range of benefit–cost ratios associated with ITS applications, ranging from 1.4 (for a freeway management system (INM) in Kansas City, US) to 62 for a Texas state-wide traffic signal coordination program (ATC). Typical results were for ratios of between 1.5 to 3.5. On this basis they calculated that the net present value of likely net benefits of ITS deployments in Australia in the period 1997–2012 was estimated to be between $1.61 billion and $6.19 billion.

7.4 DEVELOPMENTS IN ITS

The EU, US and Japan have large-scale R&D programs aimed at researching, developing and trialing ITS applications. The current total budget for these is about $0.6 billion per annum. In large measure this is a response to chronic traffic congestion coupled with environmental problems and resistance to building more and more roads. The international R&D programs cover the full gamut of applications.

The application of ITS technologies is seen to have the potential to deliver significant benefits to road users, road system administrators, and, when there are environmental gains, to the wider population. The technology and its benefits, however, cannot be considered in isolation from a wider community context. Inherent in any major technological change, there are a range of economic, social, legal, regulatory and institutional issues that can affect the adoption of ITS and the form that it takes. In terms of the impacts of ITS, these include: privacy; information ownership; legal liability; equity; uniform standards and legislation and regulation.

These are large issues that are not fully explored or resolved here but there is an opportunity to introduce the circumstances in which they arise, to look at how they will affect individuals and the community as a whole, and to raise some important questions that should be addressed by the community. Many of the community issues, especially those affecting individuals, will arise because ITS allow components of the road system to interact in new ways and information to flow between the components to an extent and in ways that have been impossible in the past. Added to this, societal changes have made many more sensitive to privacy issues that almost inevitably conflict with any change that facilitates freer flows of information.

Current transport technology is largely impersonal and operates on the basis of averages and totals. Each vehicle, each driver and each transit passenger is treated equally and the way that the system is presented and responds is the same for every user. In future this is likely to change as more efficiency is sought from the transportation system and as technology responds. ITS will allow roads and vehicles to recognize individuals and to communicate and respond on a personalized basis. In some circumstances this interaction will occur automatically. There is also the capability to collect, integrate and disseminate information collected over a wider region to provide an overview for strategic decision-making. The impact of new and emerging technologies as noticed by individual members of the community is changing their perception of the system as:

{Impersonal, Manual, Local} $\Rightarrow$ {Personalised, Automatic, Wide Area}

Most current road system technologies are impersonal, and manual to the extent that interaction between the user and the road system is largely under the user's conscious control. Current technologies also appear to operate on a small local area (single vehicle or intersection), even if this perception may be incorrect. For example, a red light is perceived to apply to that particular intersection, whether or not it is part of a coordinated traffic control spanning a large area. Emerging technologies are allowing road, vehicle and user interactions that relate to specific individuals and occur automatically, possibly without direct input by the user.

7.5 ISSUES IN THE INTRUCTION OF ITS[12]

The upsurge of interest in ITS in the 1980s and 1990s came about not only because of the availability of new telecommunications and related technologies but also because it had become demonstrably clear that many of the traditional ideas of solving transportation problems were either incompletely thought through or impractical. This was particularly true regarding urban traffic congestion but also applied to some elements of environmental damage.

The traditional approach to handling increased urban traffic volumes was to build more roads. Where traffic was non-terminating this meant the construction of by-passes and ring routes. For traffic, mainly commuter traffic, actually destined for or originating from the city center then major radial arteries were constructed. In many cases these were elevated and added nothing positive to the urban architecture. At the same time for movement within the city public transit was subsidized and in many cases capital-intensive rapid transit facilities were built. The two elements, road construction and public transit investment, represented a largely engineering approach to the problem.

Inter-urban transportation policy followed similar lines in most countries usually driven, however, with a somewhat different underlying rationale. Rather than the additional physical capacity being seen as a mechanism for reducing traffic congestion, road capacity was seen as an integral part of regional policy and as a mechanism in larger countries for fostering political and social integration.

Making better use of both existing facilities and new capacity became an important part of the policy debate. Introducing ITS on a large scale, however, has proved difficult in most countries. There is no single reason for this but rather a number of, often interacting, factors have been at work.

7.5.1 Privacy and information issues
In the early days of ITS there was widespread concern that surveillance technologies and motorist databases envisioned for some applications would generate a privacy backlash.

The first group of community issues arises because ITS can personalize the road system to such an extent that it possible to automatically identify and capture information about the activities of particular road users. For instance, automatic vehicle identification allows individual vehicles to be identified and tracked. If the technology is used on public vehicles (such as buses, ambulances, police) or commercial vehicles then monitoring can be justified on the basis of control and operational efficiency. Community support is probably guaranteed for such applications. In addition, automatic vehicle identification on a voluntary basis, such as in the freeway travel time monitoring systems in some US cities (Levine and McCasland, 1994), is also likely to achieve widespread acceptance. When

---

[12]   Benson (2005) offers an overview of some of the institutional challenges involved in adopting ITS.

private vehicles are identified and their movements traced, however, then there are immediately issues of privacy and ownership of information. The major concerns in western societies at present may rest more with the possible revelation of one individual's movements to other individuals associated with that person, rather than by a concern about state or government spying on its citizens, but even these concerns should not be trivialized.

In the event it has been found that usually there are simple solutions to protection of individual privacy. For example, data on a driver's speed used to calculate traffic flow is destroyed as soon as its immediate usefulness is over, typically after 15 minutes. One ITS surveillance technology, use of cameras to enforce red-light running laws, is controversial, but the safety benefits are seen in many jurisdictions as outweighing the threat to privacy.

7.5.2 Legal issues

In the early days of ITS there was considerable concern that a complex of legal problems could present formidable barriers to the development of ITS. In the event, a sensible and conservative approach to deployment of ITS all but eliminated liability and privacy problems, and procurement and intellectual property rights, although matters of concern, have proven tractable.

Privacy issues aside, there are other legal and legislative matters that need serious consideration in the implementation of new technologies, because they imply or require a large-scale change in the allocation of responsibility for transport behavior, especially for road networks. The ability to identify individuals can also be used as a mechanism for enforcement of regulations; for instance, the strong interest in Europe at present concerning intelligent adaptive speed limits whereby a vehicle itself will be informed about the prevailing speed limit by a roadside device. Various alternative methods might then be applied to limit the speed at which the vehicle can travel or to inform the driver of the speed limit. Already there is discussion about the use and implications of such systems for speed limit enforcement (Malenstein, 2000).

Further, these fundamental changes in the ability to identify individuals and to remove some elements of vehicle control from individual drivers immediately lead to questions of legal liability. Identifying the vehicle and identifying the driver are two entirely different processes. Most technology is linked to the vehicle but vehicles can have many different drivers. Under current legal regimes the vehicle owner is usually responsible for the vehicle and liable for any offences committed by the vehicle. The onus is on the owner to identify the driver. This issue of the vehicle versus the driver will become more important as automatic vehicle identification technologies become more widespread.

Similar issues of responsibility and legal liability also arise where there is information flowing from the roadway to the driver or between the roadway and vehicle. Driver information systems and automatic vehicle control are examples. Who will be liable for an accident on an automated highway or for problems that arise if a driver follows directions provided by a driver information system? The current principle is generally that the driver is in control of the vehicle and cannot transfer any liability but this would need re-examination.

Some ITS deployers may only design their systems to avoid anticipated risks, such as the identification of congested routes without the nomination of alternatives, to avoid possible liability issues. Nevertheless this strategy may of itself weaken the value of the information that is supplied, and thus lessen its impact on and credibility to travelers.

In summary, while in the early days of ITS there was widespread concern that use of new information technologies might spawn a host of devastating lawsuits, for example, should alternate route recommendations lead motorists into unfamiliar territory resulting in accidents, or should hands-off-the-wheel automated highways result in massive chain collisions, in fact ITS applications have not involved risky procedures like recommending specific alternate routes, and also backed away from futuristic research that might have produced risky technologies.

7.5.3 Equity and opportunity

Concerns have also been raised that the effects of ITS will be felt differently across the community. Not all members of the community have equal access to the technology or to the information and related services that it can provide. Will the greatest benefits accrue to those in the community with the greatest ability to pay? Similarly, not all members of the community are equally comfortable using information based technologies. As with all new technologies, the rate of acceptance and ability to utilize the technology will vary within the population. This means that ITS technologies should be introduced in ways that are easy to use and accessible for the majority, with responsibility for wholesale changes to be accepted by government, as in the case of the introduction of electronic road pricing in Singapore, where the government paid for the retrofitting of the necessary hardware ('in-vehicle units') to all vehicles registered in the island republic (Menon and Keong, 1998). In other situations parallel systems may be required, such as the provision of roadside variable message signage alongside the in-vehicle ROG and DIS systems available to some, so that all drivers are informed to some degree about downstream traffic conditions.

ITS may also produce changes in accessibility, travel behavior and the pattern of traffic flows. For instance, driver information systems or electronic tolling may encourage drivers to change their routes, timing, and patterns of trips. This has implications for the distribution of economic activity in the city. It will benefit some areas but equally will disadvantage others.

There are already many examples of the use of ITS around the world and the pace of adoption of technological solutions to road system problems is sure to quicken. Most applications of advanced transport technology, however, are aimed at areas where road system usage is high, in terms of traffic congestion, heavily used public transport and many trucks. This means that the technologies are probably being felt first and most extensively in the largest cities where road system problems are most acute. Yet perhaps there are advantages, at least in social and political terms in initial implementations of ITS systems such as electronic road pricing in smaller cities where the impacts may be felt less severely. The 'toll rings' of the Norwegian cities may be good examples in this regard.

7.5.4 Standards and institutions

Standards and institutional change relate to the creation of an environment in which the technologies can deliver maximum benefits with minimal negative impact on the community. The need for standards has already been established since without them there is a danger of having a random mix of incompatible technologies. This has immediate implications for the community in terms of ease of use and cost. It is inconvenient and costly to swap between different systems and to have more than one piece of equipment to do the same job. Likewise it is important that laws, regulations and institutional structures keep pace with changes in technology.

Standardization does not require the adoption of a single technology at the expense of all other alternatives, but may be accomplished by the use of 'open architectures' that allow alternative systems to work together. There is, in other words, the need for interoperability that allows access to an entire system irrespective of specifics of, say, the on-vehicle technology.

There are also important issues relating to public acceptance and implementation. Many of the proposed technologies involve significant changes to the way that road users interact with the road environment. The success of these and other technologies largely depends on the level of public acceptance and willingness to utilize them. There is a danger that potentially beneficial technologies may not be adopted because they become associated with negative issues such as enforcement and invasion of privacy.

There are also problems associated with managing the implementation of technological solutions. For many proposed systems, the full benefits will not be realized until a large percentage of the vehicle fleet is fitted with the required instrumentation or a large proportion of the road network is equipped with advanced instrumentation and signage. As a result, initial benefits may be small and there will be significant challenges associated with managing the transition period until full benefits are realized.

The US has sought to address these issues in several ways through federal policies. The 1998 ITS Act, for example, states: 'The Secretary [of Transportation] shall develop, implement, and maintain a national architecture and supporting standards and protocols to promote the widespread use and evaluation of intelligent transportation system technology as a component of the surface transportation systems of the US'.

The overall ITS standards-setting strategy adopted by the federal government has been to rely primarily on collegially developed standards, using existing standards development organizations, while holding in reserve two federal coercive powers – the authority to hold rule-makings to impose standards, and to withhold federal funds from jurisdictions failing to develop a systems architecture incorporating federally established standards. Superficially, the record of standards-setting looks impressive and as of June 2004, the US Department of Transportation reported that 73 ITS standards had been published and 9 were awaiting publication.

Adoption in the marketplace has, for a number of reasons, been less spectacular. Many standards were promulgated without adequate technical testing, or if there had been technical testing, they were not tested in a working environment (Transportation Research Board, 2004). A second problem is that the level of detail in ITS standards has been inconsistent, leaving opportunities for confusion. For example, it is not unusual for manufacturers whose basic device conforms to the National Transportation Communications for ITS Protocol, add on a feature offering competitive advantage whose adherence to the Protocol is at best unclear.

Even when standards can realistically be set in a dynamic environment, it is as likely that they will emerge from the struggle for market dominance – as with important software standards for the personal computer set through the market dominance of Microsoft – from a national standards-setting organization. In particular, setting national standards administratively may by its nature be unsuited to a technologically dynamic environment.

Another fundamental problem is that many ITS technologies are better suited to standardization at the local or regional level than the national level especially when they do not require interactions among system components; there is no reason why a traffic information and management center in Chicago, for example, should be able to communicate directly with its counterpart in Los Angeles. Successful implementation is sometimes hindered, however, where there are multiple local jurisdictions with a diversity of interests and powers.

7.5.5 Government leadership versus the market

The overarching public issue confronting ITS in many countries is the appropriate role of government, in particular the degree to which the government should guide the evolution of the ITS industry. In the period since the 1991 federal IVHS Act began the US national ITS program, an important policy question, for example, has been the degree to which ITS technologies can now stand on their own and compete directly with alternative transportation practices, and the degree to which ITS still merits protective nurturing by government. National legislation provides that the federal government should direct preparation of a ten-year program plan, and should also develop a national systems architecture with supporting standards and protocols.

The self-sufficiency approach, 'mainstreaming', commits ITS to the direct support of the full range of traffic operations – management of traffic signals, commuter traffic, incident response, highway work zones, special events traffic, and regulation of commercial vehicle movement. ITS can play a major role in all of these services, with advanced traffic control devices like advanced programming of traffic signals (including 'adaptive' traffic signals whose cycle breaks adjust continually to accommodate changing traffic flow patterns), ramp metering, electronic toll collection, and advanced traffic information systems.

The argument for mainstreaming is that improved traffic operations are vitally important – for example, at least half of all metropolitan area congestion in the nation is due to operational rather than infrastructure problems – and by supporting traffic operations ITS can find its best utilization.

The alternative perspective is that ITS still includes a large number of technologies that are not yet fully proven and accepted throughout the transportation profession, but nonetheless hold great promise. This is particularly the case with highly advanced concepts, such as 'hands-off-the-wheel' automated highways in which vehicles are guided by roadside or 'in-road' control systems. From this perspective, ITS services are still an essentially infant industry meriting special treatment and that, absent central leadership, uncoordinated stovepipe applications of information technology to transportation will proliferate.

7.6 CONCLUSIONS

Precise definitions are often difficult, and in achanging world can be limiting. Intelligent transportation systems represent a wide range of technologies, approaches and policies that are aimed at meeting a diverse, and sometimes opaque, set of objectives. Perhaps the common element is that they make use of telecommunications to influence the use of more conventional transportation infrastructure – roads, rail track, seaports and airports.

The ability to better manage transportation networks is of mounting importance in many countries where there are sever problems of traffic congestion that is extending beyond the traditional challenges posed by the urban 'rush-hour' both in terms of the geographical spread of its effect and its duration throughout the day. From the engineering perspective, the prospect of further expansion of traditional hardware is limited and where a variety of new environmental and security challenges are emerging innovative approaches are clearly needed. From the economic perspective, ITS can offer more cost effective ways of making use of scarce resources and help to meet wider social objectives, but only if efficiently deployed; it does seem to be a panacea for solving all transportation related problems.

The up-take of ITS has been patchy across modes, circumstances, and spatial jurisdictions. Certainly, much of the potential for ITS felt to exist in Europe and the US 20 years ago has not been realized. This would often seem to be as much the result of institutional issues as technical problems, although not all ITS 'solutions' have produced all that was promised even when implemented. What seems to be occurring is that there is now more interest in the piece-meal adoption of some ITS where it has clear local advantages, with more sophisticated, system wide approaches being viewed with a degree of circumspection and taken up where network economies can be clearly demonstrated.

8 TELECOMMUNICATIONS AND THE 'NEW GEOGRAPHY'

8.1 INTRODUCTION

Most of the discussion of the interaction between transportation and telecommunications has focused on essentially short- and medium-term considerations; the effects of teleworking on commuter traffic, the role of informatics in making better use of roads, and the importance of modern communications systems in shaping just-in-time production management. From a political perspective this is understandable; there are a variety of pressing social and economic issues that need addressing at this time.

There are, however, indications that over the medium- and long-term the changing roles of transportation and telecommunications may have fundamental effects on the way land is used (Abler, 1975). This is not always a matter of governance changes, in the sense that it is discussed Chapter 3, but rather that for technical reasons it takes time for land-use patterns to change; there are often 'stranded' costs associated with leaving on old location, and search costs for new sites can be time consuming.[1]

Technology has shaped the physical landscape over the centuries, and been a consistent determinant of human land-use patterns. The ability to control fire changed methods of hunting, and then allowed for agriculture to develop. Stone Age technology led to the extermination of many animal species that had trickle down effects on the plants that grew. Moving rapidly forward, as components of this technology pressure, communications and transportation technologies have been key elements in the way that human geography has evolved and in the way in which we live. Whether the technology changes have been the consequence of necessity, or have themselves been drivers is a topic of endless enquiry.

The nature of the links is certainly extremely complex and still not entirely understood; not least because the forces at work have not been constant over time. The result is that there are very many issues involving, in particular, directions of causality that still stimulate considerable debate. The links can also involve a number of intervening and interacting steps via things as diverse as public health and mechanisms of political control that make specification of analytical models

---

[1]   This is not to say that there have not been changes in governance. For example, with the increased physical mobility in US society that, most would agree, has been in part due to the shift to a more service oriented economy, there have been changes in the ways housing may be financed.

challenging. Added to this, land-use has been a subject of public intervention and markets are inevitably far from perfect. This makes empirical investigations and appraisals problematic even today in the age of global information systems (GIS) that provide an abundance of spatially coded information.

Intellectually there have also been significant changes in the way many economic-geographers now view the forces that influence the economic development of various regions, and with this the spatial distribution of activities; we have moved into the era of what is often called the 'New Geography'.[2] This shift reflects two wider trends in economics.

The first is the increased technical rigor that has found its way into the discipline and allows greater clarification in the tracing out of cause and effects. The second is the move away in many pieces of analysis from the assumptions of neo-classical thinking with its focus on perfect markets, to embrace more realistic such as indivisibilities, various forms of scale economies, asymmetric information, and game playing by individuals, public institutions, and firms.

These changes have been paralleled, and from the perspective of empirical testing, supported by new quantitative analytical tools that allow for the explicit statistical problems associated with cross-sectional analysis of data across physical space; 'Spatial Econometrics'. Added to this, there has been something of a resurgence in interest in the role of institutions shaping production and consumption patterns, including their spatial distribution. Traditionally, with the exception of a small group generally seen as at the periphery of main stream economics, institutional structures (including informal institutions as well as legal contracts) were not considered important by economists. Those taking the opposite position, it should be said, did not until recently help their case by being largely antagonistic towards their main-stream brethren rather than putting forward a coherent and rigorous theory of the role of institutions.

But first some background on the way links between communications, transportation and land-use have evolved over time. Land-use patterns change slowly, and legacy effects are seen everywhere, but recent times have witnessed more dramatic changes than ever before and it is helpful for a fuller understanding of the forces at work, and the constraints in play, to take a longer perspective.

8.2 EARLY DEVELOPMENTS IN LAND-USE PATTERNS

8.2.1 Some history
The hunter gathering societies of 5,000 years or more ago lacked the technology to store food or ensure a constant flow of substance at any particular location. Concentrations of populations were simply not efficient for more than a few

---

[2]   These developments mirror larger changes in economic thinking that have involved such creations as 'New Growth Theory' and the 'New Institutional Economics'.

families. The control of fire helped hunters and offered enhanced abilities to pursue their food gathering but at the same time destroyed local woodlands and pastures necessitating continual migrations. It may have enhanced the tendency for families to group more but not for permanency of communities.

There are debates about its origins but agriculture and animal husbandry changed this way of life and introduced more permanency in people's life-styles. The plough allowed large-scale arable farming and the creation of production surpluses that stimulated urbanization. This in turn was reinforced as larger social groups formed and conflicts emerged; towns and cities became safe havens. The size of city-states remained small, however, limited by the productivity of the surrounding hinterland and the ability to transport food from it. Additionally, communications between these unitary entities was poor, and trade limited and difficult.

As nation states emerged, and empires grew, change took place. Communications became more important as an element of political control and as a necessity for military mobilization. Smaller towns grew as essentially communications service stations providing staging points for riders and runners, and at sea as victualling points for ships. Improvements in roads and wagons, and in the logistics of the moving written communications (e.g., early state postal services) allowed gradual refinements to this structure, but in essence it remained unchanged until the Industrial Revolution. Transport and communications were slow and unreliable until well into the Industrial Revolution..

The canals, more efficient sailing, and then steam vessels and the railways initiated an age of faster transportation, and perhaps of greater importance, reliable major infrastructure initiatives, such as the Suez and Panama Canals, that provided the basis for modern global commerce.

Industrialization also brought about modern cities and subsequently metropolises. Cities had largely grown up as safe havens surrounded by walls or located in easily defended terrain. The inability to store fresh food or gain access to potable water, together with a poor understanding of hygiene and public health, generally made them unattractive places to live. There were clear trade-offs, therefore, for individuals to make. There average age of people, and their physical structure (including height), seems from archeological evidence to have fallen as urbanization occurred; a pattern that persisted to the early part of the twentieth century.

Changes came to urban life in the mid-nineteenth century as improved sanitation reduced the incidence of many diseases and more generally made cities more habitable. Housing design and construction improved and, into the twentieth century, the arrival of electricity reduced pollution and transformed living in apartments and small urban houses.

More recent times have also seen the on-going developments in telecommunications, and their interactions with transportation, having a somewhat different impact on the contemporary human geography landscape (Kotkin, 2000). Improved local transport – trams, metro systems, buses, and the automobile –

increased the length of commuter trips, and with this brought about changes in urban geography. In a different context, developments in military transportation and military communications have altered the ways wars are fought and the protection offered by large cities has vanished as a result.

8.2.2 Underlying patterns

While there are some specific features in this history some generic and fairly robust things also emerge. Patterns of location are shaped by technology, for example, in at least two important ways. First, the technology itself makes use of land and affects the way economic production is undertaken. In the transportation context, the move to large sea-going ships produced ports and fostered trade. The advent of the railways, by enabling rapid, reliable, and relatively cheap movement between distant locations, fostered the concentration of economic activities at nodal points in the system – they rapidly developed hub-and-spoke systems. These nodes, both ports and railway centers, were limited in their impacts on local urban form until the development of the tram, the bus, and local truck distributor systems.

But there is also a second way that location is influenced by technology. All forms of technology require inputs of various raw materials. The building of early mercantile fleets denuded much of the Mediterranean shores of timber and the quest for food at sea led to the extinction of the dodo. The railways required coal and steel, and, in the US case, the local bison were nearly exterminated to feed the construction teams. This led to a second location force, that of productive concentration around these sources of raw materials – the mining and steel towns in the rail example.

The information age has not changed these fundamentals but what it has done is to introduce new variables and parameters into the equation and modified some of the traditional ones. The importance of place and location is increasingly being seen not only in terms of physical factors, either raw materials or man-made infrastructure, but more in terms of concentrations of human skills in densely populated areas.

The traditional neo-classical economic theories of location focused on raw materials, technological advantage, and physical access. The latter, however, was a twin-edged sword. Setting aside the particular issues of natural resource based spatial concentrations, access enhanced the potential of a location but at the same time encouraged migration into an area. Internal mobility within the region would decline as congestion costs increased and land values at the best locations increased. This in turn would reflect back on higher transportation costs. Because of this decline in comparative advantage, investment would leave the area to seek other locations where congestion was lower. The outcome would be a gradual evening out of production across space, although this may take generations rather than just years.[3]

Some of the more recent ideas concerning information-based activities suggest there is much more of a proclivity for what has in the past often been called 'cummulative-and-circular causation' in the macroeconomics literature. Essentially the idea, often associated with Gunnar Myrdal, is that, because of scale economies, wealthier areas simply get wealthier and poorer areas even poorer

The modern variant of this theory is less driven by industrial scale effects of the traditional kind, and more by the ability of technology-rich areas to continually up-grade their information base. Basically, the argument is that modern 'high-technology' industry is footloose in that it does not rely excessively on traditional spatially immobile inputs. In particular, the choice of location for a firm is thus much more elastic. Since firms and individuals are not homogeneous this provides more scope for electing to locate in places that offer the best portfolio of desirable features. In terms of the service sector, for example, the geographical concentration of share trading at Wall Street is no longer necessary.

This does not necessarily mean that there will be an even spread of activity across space but rather that location choice will alter, and is indeed is already altering. There is near agreement amongst geographers that there will still be concentrations of economic activity but they will be in different places and of different forms.

Much of what is happening in terms of the spatial pattern of economic activities, both production and consumption, is being influenced by interactions between telecommunications and physical transport movements. Urban forms, for example, are no longer as simple as once thought and in part that is due to changes in telecommunications and transport.

8.3 TRADITIONAL MODELS OF TRANSPORT AND URBAN LAND-USE PATTERNS

8.3.1 Traditional urban forms

Economists have, as we have seen earlier, paid relatively little attention to the interactions of transportation, location, and information flows until comparatively recently; Wise (1971) being an exception. Production and consumption in many analytical economic modes are treated as taking place on uniform, boundaryless plains. Land is seen as a factor of production but largely treated in terms of its output potential when combined with labor and capital with scant regard for its location.

---

[3]   There are some exceptions to this view. Kaldor (1970), for example, suggested that, because of economies of scale and of agglomeration in manufacturing that outweighed congestion cost effects, there would be a tendency for growth to expand in areas that already had a strong industrial base.

Much of the early interest in land-use patterns, at least those that had a transport element in them, had to do with agriculture – von Thünen's work on the influence of distance on production in the mid-nineteenth century being the best known. These theories focused on the weight of produce and their transport costs; everything else being equal you grow the heavier crops nearer the town or village where they are to be consumed.

More germane to the core of this book are the translations of the underpinning of this work into theories seeking to aid in the understanding of urban form, and the domains of cities.[4] It must be said, however, that this understanding is still far from complete and without a coherent framework discussion of the interactive role telecommunications and transportation play in shaping city form and size is inevitably rather piecemeal.

Translating the basic von Thünen framework into a theory of urban form gives us the concentric pattern of urban land-use abstracted in Figure 8.1. Local transportation is ubiquitous (and with this communications flows are ubiquitous), in the sense that there is a constant cost per mile of traveling, and expensive. This combined with agglomeration economies from companies situating in proximity with one another, results in production and jobs being focused in a central business district.

The central business districts themselves tended to grow considerably in nineteenth century and expand as commercial centers. But in doing so their forms changed. The advent of improved communications was one factor that fostered this, as first reliable postal services grew and then, perhaps more important, the telegraph emerged.[5] This allowed information on fashion and news to flow more freely and rapidly, stimulating retail activities, in particular, to expand and concentrate at urban centers. Only larger stores, however, were in a position to fully exploit this, adding industrial concentration, with moves to the 'super stores' of the time, to that of spatial concentration; by 1900, for example, there were over 1,000 department stores in the US. The location of these stores, themselves, influenced the shape of the central business district as well as the land-use surrounding it.

In these concentric cities, those with lower incomes tend to live around the central area to economize on transportation outlays. Many large cities in the

---

[4]   Much of the current analysis of urban form, size, and size distribution stems from the emergence of the 'New Urban Economics'. Until the late 1960s and early 1970s urban economics tended to be largely descriptive and institutional in its nature, and was mainly concerned with specific problems involving such things as urban transport, housing, and public finance. The New Urban Economics represented the introduction of more rigorous and consistent tools of microeconomics that provides holistic framework within which urban issues may be analyzed and public policies can be developed. Hirsch (1973) provides a somewhat dated, but good account of these developments.

[5]   Standage (1998) talks of the telegraph in terms of it being the 'Victorian Internet'.

nineteeth century were, and some remain, major recipients of immigrants, both domestic and from other countries, and this led to special concentrations of various ethnics groups within these income rings. The resultant rise in land-prices from this spatially focused demand leads to high populations densities in the inner zones as poorer people also economize on the amount of residential land they rent or buy (apartments being common). Middle-income groups can afford to spend more on transport and on land and, in consequence, tend to live on larger plots further out. The wealthiest groups live on the edge of cities to avoid the congestion in the center and commute to work; the costs of travel being a relative small part of their income and greater flexibility in work hours often allowing them to avoid rush hour traffic.

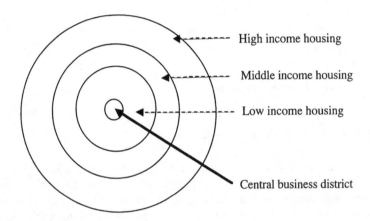

High income housing

Middle income housing

Low income housing

Central business district

Figure 8.1 The 'concentric' pattern of urban land use

The advent of mechanized transportation, initially the trams and suburban rail systems and then the automobile, affected the relative costs of access within cities. The concentric city was focused because of the centralized orientation of long-distance transportation. But then local transportation improvements, for both passenger and freight movement, emerged. Close proximity to trams lines or suburban rail termini, and then major arterial roads with bus services offered significant savings in generalized transportation costs. The result was a distortion to the concentric pattern of urban land-use with residential areas expanding out along the new transportation arteries; the early appearance of suburbs. The axial pattern of land-use emerged (Figure 8.2). The star-shaped pattern still retains the various zones of income groups but each is extended out along the transport arteries.

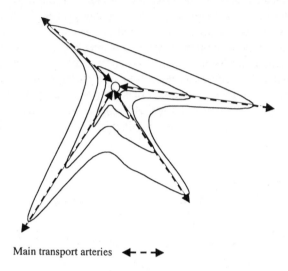

Main transport arteries ◀ – ▶

Figure 8.2 The 'axial' pattern of urban land use

The more contemporary trends, initially in transportation and more recently in communications, have led to somewhat different patterns of urban land-use that have in many instances been reinforced both by prevailing land-use planning policies and by changes in the industrial bases of many cities. Automobiles have afforded greater mobility for locations away from the main arteries. Production technology has moved towards more emphasis on the horizontal layout of plants and away from physically vertical processes; 'greenfield' sites have become attractive. They also offer space for parking provision and for 'work-related' social facilities; golf courses and the like (Button, 1988; Johansson and Westin, 1987).

The result of this has been the emergence of multi-nuclei cities where the land-use pattern is less focused on a central business district and more on a number of specialized sub-centers – e.g. business parks, educational complexes, leisure and recreational areas. Housing estates, while often socially separated, tend not to be in zones around a core but rather in blocks or groups, often with supporting social infrastructure. This is not a new pattern entirely, but this type of spatial concentration tended to be more of a micro-feature of land use within central business areas (e.g., many central areas have long had their business district, their market district, the theatre district, and so on) where various forms of agglomeration were important. New forms of production and goods, combined with changing tastes and income, have expanded scale effects and added new ones.

Advances in telecommunication should perhaps be seen more as a facilitator of this trend than a strict driver; the main forces for this pattern of land-use being more in terms of widespread automobile ownership and changes in the types of goods produced and the production management adopted (Harkness, 1974). Improved telecommunications has allowed it to evolve more efficiently. On the demand side, rising middle class incomes and pollution in many cities led to an outward exodus away from locations around the core.

But it has also been a function of conscious land-use planning policies in many cities where authorities have sought to internalize many of the external economies of production. They have also often been driven by social motivations involving improving the housing stock for the poorer groups in society and making available more communal services. This has not always worked, however, as seen in the move away in the 1990s in many cities from the large residential estates that were constructed in the 1960s. Added to this, have been privately 'master-planned' cities – almost self-contained communities in terms of leisure activities and shops, such as Irvine in southern California and parts of Houston – that cater more for the higher income groups seeking security in numbers as well as high-technology employment opportunities.

8.3.2 Edge cities
More recently Garreau (1991) has highlighted further changes in the form of the emergence of 'edge cities'. Whereas multi-nuclei constructs involve a number of highly specialized centers, edge cities, in contrast, are self-contained social and economic entities that have emerged adjacent to or within the boundaries of older cities; Tysons' Corner in Northern Virginia may be seen as an edge city of Washington DC. They have ties to the longer established entities but are largely independent of them.

Figure 8.3 offers a very simple idea of what the mapping of an established major metropolitan location with an associated edge city may look like. It assumes concentric patterns of land use for simplicity, although many edge cities actually grown on major transportation arteries leading from the legacy area and are in effect located on arms of what may be seen as an underlying axial city land-use configuration. The figure also simplifies the interface between the various land-uses where the old and new cities merge; for example, because of alternative employment opportunities in the traditional core or the core of the edge city there may be 'corridors' of residential areas that feed through the rings of income categories.

These edge cities contain their own employment base, retail and a diverse range of housing. Often there are complete ranges of social services – hospitals, schools, and colleges as the local tax base is strong enough to support them. Because they are more recent constructs, or have taken land that formed part of the traditional city catchment area that had a lower economic value, there is an inevitable tendency for the edge city to have more service related and technology jobs, than the older city.

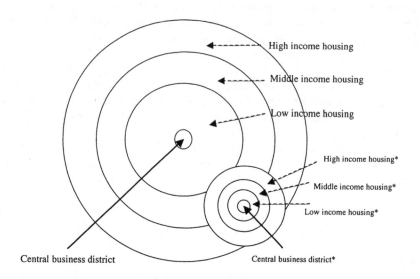

High income housing

Middle income housing

Low income housing

High income housing*

Middle income housing*

Low income housing*

Central business district

Central business district*

Figure 8.3 Simple representation of the edge city concept

The negative impacts of traffic congestion, high crime rates, and the poor quality of the environment, that are often found in the older core have inevitably contributed to their formation, but so has the positive growth of the service sector (Higano and Shibusawa, 1999). Services, as we have seen, now dominate employment in most developed economies and many service-based industries are heavily dependent on telecommunications. It is this type of industry that generally forms the economic base of an edge city, and even if there are other forms of employment these are often tied to information-based activities.

There may also be other reasons to anticipate the continued growth in edge city type activities and that is to do with the structure of the emergent logistics of many forms of activity. In the case of the majority of e-retailing the major players focus their operations around massive 'fulfillment centers'; in the US Land's End has such a center at Dodgeville, Wisconsin that is the size of 16 American football fields. Since these centers need have no physical link to Web servers, but require good access to freight transportation arteries with minimal local congestion, they often locate in proximity to but outside of large cities. Given their employment potential, they may form another nucleus for the emergence of an edge city.

8.3.3 Systems of cities

What this sort of analysis does is provide some basis for explaining the internal spatial structure of cities; what it does not do is explain either why individual cities are located where they are or the relative size of different cities. In the past, technical limitations of transportation and the inability to store agricultural surpluses provided a simple explanation of why cities emerged where they did. This type of rationale is much less strong in modern industrial economies, although an inevitable legacy effect remains.

At one level, while there have been numerous empirical investigations that have shown cities are not simply random occurrences in space but seem to have some pattern to them, there are debates that can be traced back to the 1950s focusing on what produces ordered relationships between urban areas. Not all, however, even agree on the nature of this distribution. Some when ranking cities by population have found that the resultant spread conforms statistically to a Pareto distribution, but others have found a rank size distribution. This type of analysis is essentially descriptive, however, and more concerned with clarifying data than explaining it.

One school of thought aimed at offering an explanation for urban hierarchies, has traditionally looked outside the cities in the sense of being concerned with markets for the goods and services that cities produce, and seeing them as exporting entities growing in line with these external demands. Another school places emphasis on the internal supply-side and, especially, on agglomeration effects.

Distance, and with it transportation and communications, are given somewhat different treatments in these models. In the demand driven framework, issues of market access are important, whereas in the supply driven approach congestion and impedances within cities that affect efficient production come far more to the fore.

There are variants on these models but none offers a conclusive explanation of why some cities grow faster and larger than others. Perhaps we should not be too surprised at this. Economists are poor at explaining economic growth more generally at the national level where the systems are less open. But there are also institutional factors involved. Cities do not operate in perfect markets, and neither does transportation and telecommunications systems, which means that a large element in the distribution of city sizes is inevitably due to government policies.

8.3.4 Rural areas matters

While there has been an increase in urbanization in virtually all countries, this still leaves a significant number of people who live and work in rural areas. The modern economics of agriculture, despite almost universal subsidies in the wealthy nations, has led to considerable increases in labor productivity and with this a shedding of workers, indeed in France only about 3.5% of the workforce are in agriculture. The growth of service industries that are relatively footloose, coupled with the extensive networks of retail, entertainment, medical, and other essential services that can be accessed by telecommunications has, in part, softened this blow to the labor force (Clark, 1981; Clark and Unwin, 1981).

This decline in the traditional rural population, however, does not mean that the rural life-style, in a somewhat modified form, has entirely lost its attraction. There are many who are now choosing to move to the countryside to live. Many of these are retired people who seek the pure peace and quite of a less hectic life, but who can still retain contact with many of the attributes of urban life through telecommunication. Suburbs, of course, can provide a sort of 'Neverland' combining the features of rural and urban lifestyles.

Others live, and pursue their careers, in rural areas; albeit not in the traditional types of job found in such places. They make use of telecommunications to tie in with information systems and with their employers. Many of those living this way are from the creative classes, engaged in a variety of professions that require less immediate interaction with other parts of companies, or they work on a freelance basis.

There are some who argue that the ubiquitous nature of telecommunications will ultimately dominate the economies of agglomeration that have been the backbone of recent urbanization processes. There will be no particular advantage of living close to others. This will eventually lead to the demise of urban life-styles; there will be a *Death of Distance*, to cite the name of a well-known book (Caircross, 1997). The link between work and leisure, whereby 'going to work' entails pleasurable social interactions as well as economically productive activities, will break down and work will be done independently of any particular location. Globally, firms will locate at the lowest cost centers, be dispersed, and will be able to avoid the high cost/high taxation areas.

Such trends are, however, are likely to be very long-term if they are a genuine change in human behavior, rather than a transient phase, and far from simple to extrapolate (Kolko, 1999). There are many stranded costs to be considered if cities really were to be abandoned. If this were to take place then the pattern of human settlement would effectively revert back to that of older rural society with the difference that there would be no real link to land quality in the traditional way. Indeed, many areas that are not the best for farming (e.g., mountains, coasts, and arid areas) may be the most attractive. But this is a more a matter for futurists and sociologists than for speculation here.

8.4 THE SPACE–TIME PRISM

While it is quite easy to trace out the changing pattern of land-use, at least in its general form, more comprehensive theories offering explanations linking travel time, telecommunications, and land-use are less readily available. The notion of the 'space–time prism' and activity patterns developed by Hagerstrand (1970) provides one useful basis for looking at urban development. Black (2001), in particular, has used the methodology in this regard. The basic idea is essentially a development of the longstanding economic model that increased choice enhances utility. In this case, as one gains flexibility due to more flexible working practices so the area of a person's space time prism expands.

Figure 8.4(a) provides a diagrammatic representation of a fairly standard space–time prism for a conventional working day. A commuter has some flexibility in the journey to work (which starts here at 7.15 am to ensure arrival by about 8.15 am), some time is also free during the lunch break to leave the office to do minor tasks, and on the way home after work that finishes at 4.30 pm. Coffee breaks may also add some flexible small space time increments but it is unclear how useful these are. The space–time prisms are dislocated somewhat to reflect the movements in space and the fact that there is a particular beginning and location at the start and the end of the day.

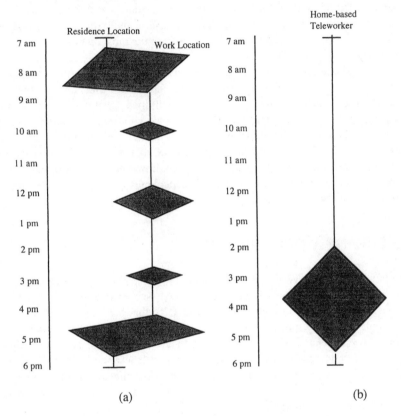

Figure 8.4 The space–time prism concept

Black looks at what may happen if rather than commuting to an office, the worker teleworked from home. This would give the person more control over the time used in commuting, coffee breaks, and a lunch break. He assumes, however, that the constraints of beginning (at 7.15 am) and ending the working day (at 6.00 pm) at home still apply.

Figure 8.4(b) shows a possible resultant pattern. The worker could construct his day in a number of ways, but at the extreme there is nothing to stop the worker collecting various blocks of time 'saved' and then using them all at once. For example, the worker could start work at 7.00 am and work straight through until 2.00 pm, and then spend the remaining four hours driving around. Whether this will happen is conjecture, but it is one possibility and has implications for urban form as it does for the more immediate case of traffic management.

Certainly, there would seem to be a strong case that telework could well lead to more travel if there are economies of scale and scope to be enjoyed from having larger blocks of discretionary time available. Indeed, one finds this even with the introduction of 'flexi-time', itself often facilitated by the advent of new communications within the conventional workplace, that has fostered more complex commuter trips as individuals make use of the freedom to add activities (shopping and collecting children from school are the most common in the US) to a formerly linear commute.

For land-use patterns the ability and willingness of individuals to act more flexibly within their new space–time prisms influences the need for the micro-location of activities, and also the way these activities are supplied. Economies of scale in supplying educational services for small children, for example, may be affected by the greater flexibility parents have in their dropping-off and collection times. Similarly, retail outlets can disperse more as the conventional radial routes no longer dominate commuter trips. This does, however, pose problems for those planning transportation infrastructure. The demands on transportation networks with inevitably be both temporally and spatial different.

8.5 THE 'NEW GEOGRAPHY'

The latter part of the twentieth century and the early part of the twenty-first have seen a renewed interest in things spatial. This has been tied to the availability of new data sources, with the development of GIS, that have resulted in an almost inevitable output of more informed empirical analysis. Globalization has led to interests be stimulated with regard to more macro issues as policy debates about its significance and consequences have taken place. These, and other developments have had their effects across a range of academic disciplines as people have sought to understand change. The result have produced diverse views as one might expect in a still evolving situation.

The 'New Information Age Society' is largely immersed in the dynamic world of communication. One could argue at one level that the increasing proportion of complex goods produced and services provided in the modern economy has led to a greater proclivity toward human and company interaction. Advanced telecommunication systems are rapidly evolving to fill niche markets, enhancing efficiency of business and personal life through flexibility and timely information flow, as well as offering a range of generic services. Penetration of Internet connections into workplaces and households, as observed in western economies, has allowed consumers to browse and search for services and products, communicate between 'desktops', and, on average, access apposite information in a more timely manner than ever before. This may be thought of as a mechanism favoring neo-classical mechanisms for spatial convergence of economic performance.

Counter to this have been the 'New Growth Theory' arguments advanced by the likes of Robert Lucas (1990), Romer (1990) and others that the 'New Information Age' leads to the cumulative-and-circular divergence of economies. The regions or cities that have an initial advantage in information systems will enjoy a variety of internal and external benefits that will allow them to develop their advantages further. Their position has been supported by a body of empirical evidence, largely stemming from the new approaches to economic convergence measurement of Barro and Sala-i-Martin (1992), showing that regions are not converging significantly in their economic performance and certainly not in a way consistent with neo-classical analysis.

The economic argument for the decline in spatial variation, and indeed the potential end of cities, ties in closely with the degree to which electronic communications are substitutes for face-to-face contact (Gaspar and Glaeser, 1996). As we have seen the evidence on this is far from clear. Empirical analysis is constrained by data limitations and the difficulties of testing for causality over a short time period. There has been a tendency historically for urbanization to be unevenly spread, but often to broadly follow a consistent hierarchical pattern (Krugman, 1996).

Whether this pattern is sustainable in the context of the widespread use of the Internet is uncertain and even quite rigorous quantitative analysis has failed to produce a conclusive result.

The empirical work presented by Moss and Townsend (1998), for example, is very much in line with the larger ideas of Romer and Lucas and the more localized analysis of Krugman. There is a high correlation in the US between those urban areas that have a high concentration of information intensive functions, or of technology industries, and the concentration of deployment of Internet technologies. They find a limited network of highly interconnected metropolitan areas that dominate the national network with economically distressed areas often being left behind.

Zook (2005), by exploring the geographical origins of domain names, also provides support for spatial concentration. Attempts to explore this situation using more sophisticated econometric analysis by Pelletiere and Rodrigo (1999), however, produced much less conclusive evidence.

This lack of any confirmation that the spread of Internet supply is in accord with the neoclassical convergence theory is also tending to be replicated in terms of physical distribution. The developments in information systems and e-commerce more generally have led, as outlined above, to a tendency to concentrate interchange and consolidation at a limited number of nodes. The focus of FedEx, the major carrier of e-commerce generated goods movements, in Memphis has been complemented by the city becoming a major trucking center and an important node in all the main railroad networks in the US. Geography has played a part in this but the information revolution has consolidated the hub-and-spoke nature of freight transportation.

These findings that largely refute neo-classical economics may not be that surprising, however, in light of the standard Vernon (1966) theory of product cycles. When new products emerge they tend to be located in regions with high quality labor and access to specialized information. Time erodes these needs as the product becomes more standardized. The Internet is too new to be able to ascertain whether it will follow this pattern or not. The situation at present is that economic and related theories abound linking the Internet and e-commerce to land-use developments, but the empirical support for any of them is still extremely tenuous.

8.6 CONCLUSIONS

It takes many years for the impacts of major technology shifts to be felt. The impact on urban form that the advent of railways brought about took time, many decades, to be felt and the concentric cities that followed were only partially formed when new forms of local public transport and then the motorcar emerged. Suburbia was a major result of the latter but this is still taking place some 80 years or so after the innovations of Henry Ford.

The 'Computer Age' was first talked about in the 1960s, but many of the impacts of the information technology that were foresee are only really beginning to be felt in the first decade of the twenty-first century, and often in quite different forms. New technology and its use has to meet social needs as much as offering a more efficient way of doing existing activities. As Williamson indicated, there are some things that are embedded and not easily changed.

Many factors influence land-use patterns, some natural but others related to human involvement, deliberate or otherwise. Communications act both directly in influencing location patterns, and indirectly by influencing the use and form of the transportation systems. They can also act as a more general facilitator. But the effects can take considerable time to emerge as society physically repositions itself to exploit these technological changes and as the authorities reform the institutional structures that set the parameters in land markets.

At the global level, it is clear that many of the traditional economic notions of comparative advantage need at least to be modified as more mobile factors of production become important. Information is certainly not ubiquitous and access to such things as broadband is far from space neutral – physically there are many places without it and elsewhere its costs vary quite significantly by location. Nevertheless, these factors can be acquired and consequently their acquisition will affect location patterns.

As a result, while globalization seems likely to continue, it will affect different parts of the world differently. Similarly, at the micro level some locations will remain more attractive for production and for living, but which they are, however, may well differ as a result of the telecommunications revolution. Perhaps the one lesson from the past is that predicting the implications of technology shifts on such slow moving things as land-use patterns is not to be taken lightly.

REFERENCES

Abler, R. (1975) Effects of space-adjusting technologies on the human geography of the future, in R. Abler, D. Janelle and A. Philbrick (eds) *Human Geography in a Shrinking World*, Scitiate, Duxbury Press.

Albertson, L.A. (1977) Telecommunications as a travel substitute: some psychological, organizational and social aspects, *Journal of Communication*, 27, 32–43.

American Management Association (1999) The basics of a successful telework network. *HR Focus*, 76(6), 9.

Anderson, W.P. Chatterjee, L. and Lakshmanan, T.R. (2003) E-commerce, transportation and economic geography, *Growth and Change*, 34, 415–432.

Aoyama, Y., Ratick, S.J. and Schwarz, G. (2005) Modeling the impact of business-to-business electronic commerce on the organization of the logistics industry, *Geographical Analysis*, 37: 46-68

Au, W.J. (2000) The lonely long-distance worker, *PC Computing*, February, 42.

Autor, D.H. (2001) Wiring the labour market, *Journal of Economic Perspectives*, 15, 25–40.

Bagely, M.N. and Mokhtarian, P.L. (1997) Analyzing the preference for non-exclusive forms of telecommuting: modeling and policy implications, *Transportation*, 24, 203–226.

Baldassare, M., Ryan, S. and Katz. C. (1998) Suburban attitudes towards policies aimed at reducing solo driving, *Transportation*, 25: 99-117.

Banister, D. and Stead, D. (2004) Impact of information and communications technology on transport, *Transport Reviews*, 24, 611–632.

Barro, R.J. and Sala-i-Martin, X. (1992) Convergence, *Journal of Political Economy*, 100, 223–51.

Baum, H., Schulz, W.H., Geissler, T. and Shulze, M. (1999) Methodological and empirical approach for the cost–benefit analysis of the CHAFFEUR system, in *Proceedings of the 6th World Conference on Intelligent Transportation Systems*, Toronto, WCTR.

Behr, P. (1998) Technology industry rivals the federal workforce. *Washington Post*, September 14, FO5.

Bennison, D.J. (1986) The use of videoconferencing by companies participating in the British Telecom Visual Services Trial, *Teleconferencing and Electronic Communication*, 5, 386–398.

Benson, B.G. (1996) Motorists attitudes about content of variable-message signs, *Transportation Research Record*, 1550, 48–57.

Benson, B.G. (2005) Implementing intelligent transportation systems, in K.J. Button and D.A. Hensher (eds) *Handbook of Transport Strategy, Policy and Institutions*, Amsterdam, Elsevier.

Bernardino, A. and Ben-Akiva, M. (1996) Modeling the process of adoption of telecommuting: comprehensive framework, *Transportation Research Record*, 1552, 161–170.

Black, W.R. (2001) An unpopular essay on transportation, *Journal of Transport Geography*, 9, 1–11.

Blois, K.J. (1999) Trust in business-to-business relationships: an evaluation of its status, *Journal of Management Studies*, 36, 197–215.

Boghani, A.B., Kimble, E.W. and Spencer, E.E. (1991) *Can Telecommunications Help Solve America's Transportation Problems?*, Cambridge, Mass., Arthur D. Little.

Bonsall, P. (2000) Information systems and other intelligent transport system innovations, in K.J. Button and D.A. Hensher (eds) *Handbook of Transport Modelling*, Oxford, Elsevier.

Booz Allen and Hamilton (1998) *Intelligent Transport Solutions for Australia: Technical Report*, Canberra, ITS Australia Inc.

Borenstein, S. and Saloner, G. (2001) Economics and Electronic Commerce, *Journal of Economic Perspectives*, 15, 3–12.

Bristow, A.L., Pearman, A.D. and Shires, J.D. (1997) An assessment of advanced transport telematics evaluation procedures, *Transport Reviews*, 17, 177–205.

Brög, W. (1984) Man and his transport behaviour. Part 1. telecommunications and transport – scientific no-man's land, *Transport Reviews*, 4, 99–102.

Button, K.J. (1988) High-technology companies: an examination of their transport needs, *Progress in Planning*, 29, 77–146.

Button, K.J. (1991) Transport and communications, in Rickard, John H. and Larkinson, John (eds) *Long Term Issues in Transport*, Aldershot, Avebury.

Button, K.J. (1992a) Transport, videoconferencing and the environment, paper to the Regional Science Association International Conference, Majorca.

Button, K.J. (1992b) Videoconferencing and work travel, in *Canadian Transportation: Competing in a Global Context*, Banff, CTRF.

Button, K.J. (1993) *Transport, the Environment and Economic Policy*, Cheltenham, Edward Elgar.

Button, K.J. and Lauder, D. (1992) *Videoconferencing*, London, UK Department of Trade and Industry.

Button, K.J. and Maggi, R. (1995) Videoconferencing and its implications for transport: an Anglo-Swiss perspective, *Transport Reviews*, 15, 59–75.

Button, K.J. and Nijkamp, P. (1998) Economic stability in network industries, *Transportation Research E*, 34, 13–24.

Button, K.J. and Stough, R. (2000) *Air Transport Networks: Theory and Policy Implications*, Cheltenham, Edward Elgar.

Button, K.J. and Taylor, S.Y. (2001) Towards an economics of the internet and electronic commerce, in S.D. Brunn and T.R. Leinbach (eds) *The Wired Worlds of Electronic Commerce*, London, Wiley.

Button, K.J., Brown, P., Fischer, M., Maggi, R., Ouwersloot, H., Rammer, C., Rietveld P., and Salomon, I. (1993) *Academic Links and Communications*, (with) European Science Foundation, Aldershot, Avebury.

Button, K.J., Kulkarni, R. and Stough, R. (2001) *Clustering of Transport Logistics Centres in Urban Areas,* in E. Taniguchi and R.G. Thompson (eds) *City Logistics II*, Kyoto, Institute of Systems Science Research.

Caircross, F. (1997) *Death of Distance*, Cambridge, Mass., Harvard Business School Press.

Chatterjee, K. and McDonald, M. (2004) Effectiveness of using variable message signs to disseminate dynamic traffic information: evidence from field trials in European cities, *Transport Reviews*, 24, 559–585.

Chatterjee, K., McDonald, M., Paulley, N. and Taylor, N.B. (1999) Modelling the impacts of transport telematics: current limitations and future developments, *Transport Reviews*, 19, 57–80.

Claisse, G. and Rowe, F. (1993) Domestic telephone habits and daily mobility, *Transportation Researh A*, 27, 277–290.

Clark, D. (1981) Telecommunications and rural accessibility: perspectives on the 1980s, in D.J. Banister and P.G. Hall (eds) *Transport and Public Policy Planning*, London, Mansell.

Clark, D. and Unwin, K. (1981) Telecommunications and travel: potential impact for rural areas, *Regional Studies*, 15, 47–56.

Cohn, L. and Brady, D. (2000) B2B: the hottest net bet yet? *Business Week*, January 17, 36–37.

Commission of the European Communities (1992) *Green Paper on the Impact of Transport on the Environment: A Community Strategy for Sustainable Development*, Brussels, COM(92)46/FIN.

Consumer Association of America (1996) *Clean Cars, Clean Air: A Consumers Guide to Auto Emission Inspection and Maintenance*, Washington, DC, Consumer Association of America

Deeprose, D. (1999) When implementing telecommuting leave nothing to chance, *HR Focus*, October, 13.

Douglas, S.M. (1989) Sharper focus is trained today on image communications, *Communications News*, February, 25–26.

Dupuy, G. (1999) From the 'magic circle' to 'automobile dependence': measurements and political implications, *Transport Policy*, 6, 1–17.

Economides, N. (1996) The economics of networks, *International Journal of Industrial Organisation*, 14, 673–699.

Eisenstein, P.A. (1999) Telematics maps the road to the future, *Automotive Industries*, 179(11), A3.

Eldid, S. and Minoli, D. (1995) *Telecommuting*, Boston, Artech House.

Elton, M. (1979) Substitution for transportation, *Telecommunications Policy*, 3, 257–259.

European Conference of Ministers of Transport (1983) *Transport and Telecommunications*, Paris, ECMT

Ferguson, E. (1997) The rise and fall of the American carpool: 1970–1990. *Transportation*, 24, 349–376.

Fukuyama, F. (1996) *Trust: The Social Virtues and The Creation of Prosperity.* New York, Free Press Paperbacks.

Fukuyama, F. (1999) *The Great Disruption: Human Nature and the Reconstitution of Social Order*,New York, The Free Press.

Gardiner, G. (2000) Dot com logistics, *Logistics and Materials Handling*, 9, 11–16.

Garreau, J. (1991) *Edge City: Life at the New Frontier*, New York, Doubleday.

Garrett, A. (1998) Intelligent transport systems – potential benefits and immediate issues, *Road and Transport Research*, 7, 61–69.

Garrison, W.L. and Deakin, E. (1988) Travel, work, and telecommunications: a view of the electronics revolution and its potential impact, *Transportation Research A*, 22, 239–246.

Gaspar, J. and Glaesar, E.L. (1996) *Information Technology and the Future of Cities*, Cambridge, Mass., National Bureau of Economic Research, Working Paper 5562.

Giannopoulos, G.A. and McDonald, M. (1997) Developments in transport telematics applications in Japan: traffic management, freight and public transport, *Transport Reviews*, 17, 37–59.

Gross, H. (1996) What really explains weak consumer spending? *Perspectives*, 11 (April), 3.

Hagerstrand, T. (1970) What about people in regional science? *Papers, Regional Science Association*, 24, 7–21.

Handy, S.L. and Mokhtarian, P.L. (1995) Planning for telecommuting: measurement and policy issues, *Journal of the American Planning Association*, 61, 99–112.

Handy, S.L. and Mokhtarian, P.L. (1996) Forecasting telecommuting. *Transportation*, 23, 163–190.

Harkness, R. (1974) Communications, innovations, urban form and travel demand: some hypotheses and a bibliography, *Transportation*, 2, 153–193.

Harutoshi, Y. (1994). Demand forecast and financial feasibility of new freight transport systems, *OECD Seminar TT3 on Advanced Road Transport Technologies,* Paris, OECD.

Hensher, D.A. and Button, K.J. (eds) (2000) *Handbook of Transport Modelling*, Oxford, Pergamon.

Hewson, D. (1999) Start talking and get to work, *Business Life*, November, 72–76, London, British Airways.

Higano, Y. and Shibusawa, H. (1999) Agglomeration diseconomies of traffic congestion and agglomeration economies of interaction in the information-orientated city, *Journal of Regional Science*, 39, 21–49.

Hirsch, F. (1977) *Social Limits to Growth*, London, Routledge and Kegan Paul.

Hirsch, W.Z. (1973) *Urban Economic Analysis*, New York, McGraw-Hill.

Illegems, V. and Verbeke, A. (2004) *Moving Towards the Virtual Workplace: Managerial and Societal Perspectives on Telework*, Aldershot, Edward Elgar.

Jensen, M. (1999) Passion and heart in transport – a sociological analysis on transport behavior, *Transport Policy*, 6, 19–33.

Johansen, R. (1984) *Teleconferencing and Beyond: Communications in the Office of the Future*, New York, McGraw-Hill.

Johansen, R. and Bullen, C. (1984) Thinking ahead: what to expect from teleconferencing, *Harvard Business Review*, March–April, 164–174.

Johansson, B. and Westin, L. (1987) Technical change, location and trade, *Papers of the Regional Science Association*, 62, 13–25.

Jou, R.-C. and Mahmassani, H.S. (1997) Comparative analysis of day-to-day trip-chaining behavior of urban commuters in two cities, *Transportation Research Record*, 1607, 163–170.

Jovanis, P. (1983) Telecommunications and alternative work schedules: options for managing transit demand, *Urban Affairs Quarterly*, 19, 167–190.

Kaldor, N. (1970) The case for regional policies, *Scottish Journal of Political Economy*, 17: 337-348.

Katz, M.L. and Shapiro, C. (1986) Technology adoption in the presence of network externalities, *Journal of Political Economy*, 95, 822–841.

Kerwin, K. and Stepanek, M. (2000) At Ford e-commerce is job1, *Business Week*, February 28, 74–78.

Kolko, J. (1999) The death of cities? The death of distance? Evidence from the geography of commercial internbet usage, presented at the *Cities in the Global Information Society Conference*, Newcastle-upon-Tyne.

Konezny, G.P. and Beskow, M.J. (1999) *Third-party Logistics: Improving Global Supply Chain Performance, Minneapolis*, Piper Jaffray Equity Research.

Korte, W.B. and Wynne. R. (1996) *Telework: Penetration, Potential, and Practice in Europe*. Amsterdam, IOS Press.

Kotkin, J. (2000) *The New Geography*, New York, Random House.

Krugman, P. (1996) *The Self-organizing Economy*, Oxford, Blackwell.

Langhoff, J. (1999) A telemanager's index: the definitive roundup of telecommuting statistics, *Home Office Computing*, 17(April), T6

Lehrman, C.K. (1991) Videoconferencing comes down to Earth, *Public Relations Journal*, 45, 23–7.

Levine, S.Z. and McCasland, W.R. (1994) Monitoring freeway traffic conditions with automatic vehicle identification systems, *ITE Journal*, 64, 23–28.

Lowe, J.C. (1998) Patterns of spatial dispersion in metropolitan commuting, *Urban Geography*, 19, 232–253.

Lucas, R.E. (1990) Why doesn't capital flow from the rich to poor countries?, *American Economic Review*, 80, 92–96.

Lucking-Reiley, D. and Spulber, D.F. (2001) Business-to-business electronic commerce, *Journal of Economic Perspectives*, 15, 55–68.

Maggi, R. (1993) Videoconferencing: economic arguments on an overrated communication mode, in J. Casti, D. Batten and R. Thord *Communication Networks*, Berlin, Springer.

Mahmassani, H.S., Yen, J.-R., Herman, R. and Sullivan, M.A. (1993) Employee attitudes and stated preferences toward telecommuting: an exploratory analysis, *Transportation Research Record*, 1413, 31–41.

Malenstein, J. (2000) Know your limits – a rejoinder, *Traffic Technology International*, April/May, 15.

Mauch, M. and Taylor, B.D. (1997) Gender, race, and travel behavior: an analysis of household-serving travel and commuting in the San Francisco Bay Area. *Transportation Research Record*, 1607, 147–153.

McCloskey, D.W. and Igbaria, M. (1998). A review of the empirical research on telecommuting and directions for future research in D.W. McCloskey and M. Igbaria (eds) *The Virtual Workplace*, Hershey, Idea Group.

McFadden, D. (2001) Economic choices, *American Economic Review*, 91, 351–378.

McGuckin, N. and Murakami, E. (1999) Examining trip-chaining behavior: comparison of travel by men and women, *Transportation Research Record*, 1693, 79–85.

Memmot, F.M. (1963) The substitutability of communications for transportation, *Traffic Engineering*, 33, 20–25.

Menon, A.P.G. and Keong, C.K. (1998) The making of Singapore's electronic road pricing system, in *Proceedings of the International Conference on Transportation in the Next Millennium*, Singapore, Nanyang Technological University.

Metropolitan Washington Council of Governments (2000) COG Sets Regional Telecommuting Goal, http://www.mwcog.org/opa/release_0412.html

Mitchell, H. (1996) The social implications of telework: the UK experience. *World Transport Policy and Practice*, 2, 29–35.

Mokhtarian, P.L. (1988) An empirical evaluation of the travel impacts of teleconferencing, *Transportation Research A*, 22, 283–289.

Mokhtarian, P.L. (1991) Defining telecommuting, *Transportation Research Record*, 1305, 273–281.

Mokhtarian, P.L. (1997) Now that travel can be virtual will congestion virtually disappear?, *Scientific American*, 277, 93.

Mokhtarian, P.L. and Bagley, M.N. (2000) Modeling employee's perceptions and proportional preferences of work locations: the regular workplace and telecommuting alternatives, *Transportation Research Part A*, 34, 223–242.

Mokhtarian, P.L. and Salomon, I. (1994) Modelling the choice of telecommuting: setting the context, *Environment and. Planning A*, 26, 749–766.

Mokhtarian, P.L. and Salomon, I. (1996a) Modeling the choice of telecommuting: 2 a case of the preferred impossible alternative, *Environment and Planning A*, 28, 1859–1876.

Mokhtarian, P.L. and Salomon, I. (1996b) Modeling the choice of telecommuting: 3 identifying the choice set and estimating binary choice models for technology-based alternatives, *Environment and Planning A*, 28, 1877–1894.

Moss, M.L. and Townsend, A.M. (1998) Spatial analysis of the Internet in US cities and states, presented at the *Technological Futures – Urban Futures Conference*, Durham.

National Commission to Ensure Consumer Information and Choice in the Airline Industry (2002) *Report*, Washington, DC, National Commission to Ensure Consumer Information and Choice in the Airline Industry.

National Environmental Policy Institute (2000) *The National Air Quality and Telecommuting Act: Final Report*, Washington, NEPI.

Netherlands Organisation for Applied Scientific Research (1989) *De Invloed van Telecommunicatie op Vervoer; Gevolgen voor Energie en Millieu*, Appeldoorn, TNO.

Nilles, J.M. (1988) Traffic reduction by telecommuting: a status review and selected bibliography, *Transportation Research A*, 22, 301–317.

Nilles, J.M. (1994) *Beyond Telecommuting: A New Paradigm for the Effect of Telecommunications on Travel*, Washington DC, Global Telematics.

Nilles, J.M. (1997) Telework: enabling distributed organizations for its managers, *Information Systems Manager*, 14, 7–14.

Nilles, J.M. and Mokhtarian. P.L. (1998) Will encouraging telecommuting decrease traffic congestion?, *CQ Researcher*, 8, 713.

Nordhaus, W.D. (2002) The progress of computing, Department of Economics, New Haven, Yale University.

Office for National Statistics (2002) *Teleworking in the UK, Labour Market Trends*, London, ONS.

Organisation for Economic Cooperation and Development (1997) *Electronic Commerce: Opportunities and Challenges for Government*, Paris, OECD.

Peet, J. (1999) Shopping and the web, *Economist Survey*, February 26.

Pelletiere, D. and Rodrigo, C. (1999) Does the internet complement or substitute for regional external economies: a proposed framework for analysis and preliminary results, presented to the *Association for Public Analysis and Management Annual Conference*, Washington, DC.

Perret-Gentil, J.-C., Hirsch-Tombet, C., Tomasini, F. and Lay, P. (1992) Videoconférence, Institut für Verkehrrsplanung Transporttechnik, Strassen- und Eisenbahnbau, Zürich, ETH.

Phillips, C. and Mecker, M. (2000) *The B2B Internet Report: Collaborative Commerce*, New York, Morgan Stanley Dean Witter Equity Research.

Piskurich, G.M. (1996) Managing telecommuting work, *Training and Development*, 50, 20–28.

Porter, M.E. (1980) *Competitive Strategy: Techniques for Analyzing Industries and Competitors*, New York, Free Press

Porter, M.E. (1985) *Competitive Advantage: Creating and Sustaining Superior Performance*, New York, Free Press.

Pratt, J.H. (1997) Why aren't more people telecommuting?, *Transportation Research Record*, 1607, 196–203.

Pratt, J.H. (2000) Asking the right questions about telecommuting: avoiding the pitfalls in surveying home based work. *Transportation*, 27, 99–116.

President's Management Council (1996) *President's Management Council National Telecommuting Initiative Action Plan*, Washington, DC, US President's Management Council Interagency Telecommuting Working Group.

Pye, R. (1976) Effects of telecommunications on the location of office employment, *Omega*, 4, 289–300.

Richter, J. (1990) Crossing boundaries between professional and private life, in H. Grossmand and L. Chester (eds) *The Experience and the Meaning of Work in Women's Lives*, Hillsdale, Lawrence Erlbaum.

Romer, P.M. (1990) Endogenous technical change, *Journal of Political Economy*, 98, S71–S102.

Root, A., Schintler, L. and Button, K.J. (2000) Women, travel and the idea of 'sustainable transport', *Transport Reviews*, 20, 369–383.

Rubin, R.E. (2003) *In and Uncertain World: Tough Choices from Wall Street to Washington*, New York, Random House.

Ruhling, N.A. (2000) Our sense of place: home is where the office is, *American Demographics*, June.

Russell, C. (1996) How many home workers?, *American Demographics*, 18, 6.

Salomon, I. (1986) Telecommunications and travel relationships: a review. *Transportation Resources A*, 20, 223–238.

Salomon, I. (2000) Can telecommunications help solve transportation problems? in D. Hensher and K.J. Button (eds), *Handbook of Transport Modelling*, Oxford, Pergamon.

Salomon, I. and Mokhtarian, P.L. (1997) Why don't you telecommute? *Access*. 10, Spring, Davis, University of California Transportation Center.

Salomon, I. and Mokhtarian, P.L. (1998) What happens when mobility-inclined market segments face accessibility-enhancing policies? *Transportation Research D*, 3,129–140.

Salomon, I. and Salomon, M. (1984) Telecommuting the employee's perspective, *Technological Forecast. Social Change*, 25, 15–28.

Salvanathan, E.A. (1991) The demand for transport and communications: applications with Rotterdam and almost Ideal demand systems, paper presented to the *Nineteenth Conference of Economists (Australia)*, University of New South Wales.

Saveri, A. (1995) Mapping the future of the virtual office, *Electronic Engineering Times*, 859, 120–123.

Schafer A. and Victor, D. (2000) The future mobility of the world population, *Transportation Research A*, 34, 171–205

Seth, J.N. and Sisodia, R.S. (1997) A strategic vision of the wireless industry: communications unbound, *International Engineering Consortium*.

Shamir, B. and Salomon, I. (1985) Working-at-home and the quality of work life, *Academy of Management Review*, 10, 455–463.

Shapiro, C. and Varian, H.R. (1998) *Information Rules: A Strategic Guide to the Network Economy*, Cambridge, Mass., Harvard Business School Press.

Shiller, R.J. (2000) *Irrational Exuberance*, Princeton, Princeton University Press.

Shulman, K. and Reiser, J. (1996) Technology, telecommuting: genesis for change, *Managing Office Technology*, 41, 32–34.

Smith, R. (1996) Distance is dead, the world will change: the exponential fall in telecommunication costs will transform our world, probably for the better, *British Medical Journal*, 313, 1572.

Standage, T. (1998) *The Victorian Internet*, New York, Walker.

Stough, R.R. (ed) (2001) *Intelligent Transportation Systems*: Cases *and Policies*, Cheltenham, Edward Elgar.

Sough, R.R., Higano, Y., Button, K.J. and Nijkamp, P (eds) (2003) *Transport and Information Systems*, Cheltenham, Edward Elgar.

Sullivan, M., Mahmassani, H. and Yen, J.R. (1993) Choice model of employee participation in telecommuting under a cost-neutral scenario, *Transportation Research Record*, 1413, 42–48.

Sullivan, S.E. (1999) The changing nature of careers: a review and research agenda, *Journal of Management*, 25, 457–484.

Sun, X., Wilmot, C.G. and Kasturi, T. (1998) Household travel, household characteristics, and land use: an empirical study from the 1994 Portland activity-based travel survey, *Transportation Research Record*, 1617, 10–17.

Sviden, O. (1983) *Automobile Usage in the Future Information Society, Research Report No. 25. The Future of the Automobile Program*, Institute of Technology, Department of Management and Economics, Linkoping University.

Taylor, M.A.P. (2001) Intelligent transport systems, in K.J. Button and D.A. Hensher (eds) *Handbook of Transport Systems and Traffic Control*, Oxford, Pergamon.

Taylor, S.Y. (1999) *Review of Freight Transport Chain Case Studies*, Austroads Project NRSM.9804, Melbourne, ARRB Transport Research.

Telework Analytics International, Inc. (1999) TAI-Teleworking Pros and Cons, http://www.Teleworker.com/pro_con.html.

ter Brugge, R. (1991) Logistical developments in urban distribution and their impact on energy use and the environment, in M. Kroon, R. Smit and J. van Ham (eds) *Freight Transport and the Environment*, Amsterdam, Elsevier.

Transportation Research Board (2004) *Development and Deployment of Standards for Intelligent Transportation Systems: Review of the Federal Program*, Washington, DC, TRB.

Turner, T. and Niemeier. D. (1997) Travel to work and household responsibility: new evidence, *Transportation*, 24, 397–419.

UK Royal Commission on Environmental Pollution (1994) *Eighteenth Report: Transport and the Environment*, Cm. 2674, London, HMSO.

US Bureau of Transportation Statistics (1993) *Transportation Implications of Telecommuting*, http://www.bts.gov/ntl/DOCS/telecommute.html.

US Department of Transportation (1992) *Transportation Implications of Telecommuting*, Washington, DC, USDOT.

US Department of Transportation (1998) Transportation Equity Act for the 21st Century, Wysiwyg://50/http://www.fhwa.dot.gov/tea21/sumover.htm.

US Federal Highway Administration (1998) Transportation-Air Brochure 2B, http://www.fhwa.dot.gov//////environment/air_2a.pdf.

Varian, H.R. (1999) Market structure in the network age, presented to the *Understanding the Digital Economy Conference*, Washington, DC.

Vermunt, A.J.M. (1993) *Ways Towards Provision of Logistical Services*, Tilburg, University of Tilburg (in Dutch).

Vernon, R. (1966) International investment and international trade in the product cycle, *Quarterly Journal of Economics*, 80, 190–207.

Wardrop, J. (1952) Some theoretical aspects of road traffic congestion, *Proceedings of the Institute of Civil Engineers*, 1, 325–378.

Weekly Compilation of Presidential Documents (1994) Memorandum on Expanding Family-Friendly Work Arrangements in the Executive Branch. 30, 1468.

Williams, B. (1996) Trends in employment patterns and policies, *Public Management*, 78, 24–26.

Williamson, O.E. (2000) The new institutional economics: taking stock, looking ahead, *Journal of Economics Literature*, 38, 595–613.

Wise, A. (1971) The impact of electronic communications on metropolitan form, *Ekistics*, 188, 22–31.

Yen, J.–R. (2000) Interpreting employee telecommuting adoption: an economics perspective, *Transportation*, 27, 149–164.

Zook, M.A. (2005). *The Geography of the Internet Industry: Venture Capital, Dot-coms and Local Knowledge*. Oxford, Blackwell Publishers.

INDEX

Abler, R., 155
accessibility, 16-19
Acts
  UK Transport Act (1968), 112
  UK Transport Act (1980), 38
  UK Transport Act (1985), 38
  US Air Cargo Deregulation Act
    (1977), 113
  US Airline Deregulation Act (1978)
    113
  US Americans with Disabilities Act
    (1990), 73, 78
  US Bus Regulatory Reform Act
    (1982), 113
  US Clean Air Act (1990), 73, 78
  US Intelligent Vehicle-Highway Act
    (1991), 141, 152
  US Intermodal Surface
    Transportation Efficiency Act
    (1991), 73, 183
  US Motor Carriers Reform Act
    (1980), 113
  US National Telecommuting and Air
    Quality Act (1999), 74, 88
  US Northeast rail Service Act
    (1981), 113
  US Railroad Revitalization and
    Regulatory Reform Act (1976),
    113
  US Staggers Rail Act, (1980), 113
  US Transportation Equity for the
    21st Century/TEA Restoration Act
    (1998), 74
air transport, 10, 17, 27, 35, 51–3,
  138
  airlines, 10, 11, 27, 29, 43–4,
    51–3, 58, 138

airports, 45, 52
  freight/cargo, 23, 52
Albertson, L.A., 63
American Management Association,
  78
Anderson, W.P., 123
Aoyama, Y., 125
Asian Development Bank, 39
Asian Pacific Economic Community,
  26
Au, W.J., 75
automobiles, 8–9, 14, 45, 72, 77, 82,
  127, 137–54 *passim*, 157
  car ownership, 10, 14, 21-2, 29, 31,
    60
Autor, D.H., 33

back-haul problem, 48
Bagely, M.N., 75, 64
Baldassare, M., 82
bandwagon effect, 100
Banister, D., 2
Barro, R.J., 169
Baum, H., 146
Behr, P., 87
Ben-Akiva, M., 81
Bennison, D.J., 104
Benson, B.G., 142, 148
Bernardino, A., 81
Black, W.R., 66
Blois, K.J., 68, 80
Boghani, A.B., 94
Bonsall, P., 142
Booz Allen and Hamilton, 146
Borenstein, S. 11, 113
Brady, D., 3, 119
Bristow, A.L., 139

Brog, W., 3,
Brundtland Report, 36
Bullen, C., 104
business cycle, 5
Button, K.J., 10, 21, 51, 57, 92, 93,
    94, 96, 100, 105, 128, 162

Cairncross, F., 166
canals, 51
car pooling, 4
Chatterjee, K., 139
Claisse, G., 62, 63
Clark, D., 165
club goods, 24
Cohn, L., 3, 119
commuting, 10, 23, 30, 60–89, 93
    see also, teleworking
computer reservation systems, 14
congestion, 4, 11, 19, 22–4, 35, 55,
    60, 68, 72, 82, 90, 103, 137–54
    passim, 158, 163–5
connectivity, 45–6, 126
cost-effectiveness, 7
costs, 48–9, 53–5, 96–8, 108,
    109–110, 116, 132–4
average, 56
decreasing, 47
fixed, 56, 97
marginal, 50, 56
stranded, 155

Deakin, E., 2
Deeprose, D., 75
demographic trends, 16–40, 63
DHL, 126
dot-com companies, 5
Douglas, S.M., 93
Dupuy, G., 60

e-commerce, 15, 41, 55–8, 112–35,
    138–9
    business-to-business (B-to-B),
        3,14, 112–35
    business-to-consumer, 3,14, 56,
        112–35 *passim*
economic bubbles, 5

Economides, N., 45
economies of scale, 15, 47, 156, 159
    scope, 47–8, 123
    density 47–8, 123
Eisenstein, P.A., 60, 73
Eldid, S., 85
electronic classroom, 90, 105, 114
electronic data interchange, 9, 76,
    114, 131
environment, 3–4, 34–7, 72, 87–8,
    94, 138, 140, 145, 157, 164
    see also, global warming
European Conference of Ministers of
    Transport, 91
European Union, 4, 37, 38, 46, 71
    Commission of the European
        Communities, 4, 114
    Single European Market, 38, 112–3,
        169
externalities, 4, 48–50

Federal Express, 119, 121, 112–13,
    169
Ferguson, E., 72
ferries, 24, 29
forecasting, 10-11
Forester Report, 3
Fukuyama, F., 65, 68, 80

Gardiner, G., 3, 125
Garreau, J., 22, 25, 162
Garrett, A., 145
Garrison, W.L., 2
Gasper, J., 169
gender, 20, 28–32, 69, 84–5
General Agreement on Tariffs and
    Trade, 26
General Agreement on Trade in
    Services, 26
geographical information systems,
    128
Giannopoulos, G.A., 141
Glaesar, E.L., 169
global positioning systems, 113,
    134, 138
global warming, 35

globalization, 14, 26–7, 33, 64–5,
  122, 168, 170
Greenspan, A., 5, 13
Gross, H., 73

Haggerstand, T., 166
Handy, S.L., 61, 75
Harkness, R., 162
Harutoshi, Y., 133
Hensher, D.A., 10, 21
Hewson D., 55
Higano, Y., 164
Hirsch, F., 20, 160
hoteling,65
hub-and-spoke networks, 51–3, 122,
  158
  see also, airlines

Igbaria, M, 70
Ilegenis, V., 33
incident reporting, 9
Industrial Revolution, 1,5–6,12
infrastructure, 12, 17, 35, 45, 51, 68,
  97, 162
  investment appraisal, 53–5
  pricing, 19, 39
institutional economics, 42–4, 66,
  156
intelligent transport systems, 9, 14,
  60, 73, 127–8, 137–54
interconnectivity, 45–6
International Monetary Fund, 115
International Telegraph and Telephone
  Consultative Committee, 110
international trade, 26–7
Internet, 7, 32, 41, 48, 58, 113, 120,
  121–3, 168
inventories, 122–3
ITS America, 178

Jensen, M., 82
Johansen, R., 104
Johansson, B., 162
Jou, R-C., 83
journey-to-work, *see*, commuting
Jovanis, P., 138

Kaldor, N., 159
Katz, M.L., 106
Keong, C.K., 150
Kerwin, K., 119
Kolko, J., 166
Konezny, G.P., 3
Korte, W.B., 70, 75
Kotkin, J., 25, 157
Krugman, P., 169

land-use, 10–11, 13, 35, 60
  see also, urban form
Langhoff, J., 72
Lauder, D., 100, 105
Lehrman, C.K., 93
leisure travel, 27–8, 162
Levine, S.Z., 148
lifestyle, 66–7
Lobel, S.A., 65
logistics, 34, 164
  see also, supply-chain management
  and back-haul problem
Lowe, J.C., 88
Lucas, R.E., 169
Lucking-Reiley, D., 118

Maggi, R., 94, 98, 101
Mahmassani, H.S., 81, 82, 83
Malenstein, J., 149
maritime shipping, 23, 26, 45, 119,
  158
Marshall, A., 41
Mauch, M., 55
McCasland, W.R., 148
McCloskey, D.W., 70
McDonald, M., 141
McFadden, D., 10
McGuckin, N., 84
Mecker, M., 9
Memmot, F.M., 2
Menon, A.P.G., 150
Metcalfe's law, 47, 56
Metropolitan Washington Conference
  of Governors, 87
Minoli, D., 85

Mitchell, H., 80
mobility, 18–19, 24, 28–9
Mokhtarian, P.L., 55, 60, 61, 62, 75, 76, 78, 81, 88, 105
Moss, M.L., 169
Murakani, E., 84
Myrdal, G. 159

National Commission to Ensure Consumer Information and Choice in the Airline Industry, 10
National Environmental Policy Institute, 78, 88
Netherlands Organisation for Applied Scientific Research, 103
network economies, 7, 44–5
networks, 19, 24, 106, 109
   see also hub-and-spoke networks
new economic geography, 155–7
new growth theory, 156, 169–70
new information age, 25, 168
new urban economics, 160
Niemeier. D., 84
Nijkamp, P., 57
Nilles, J.M., 61, 63, 70, 83, 85, 86
Nordhaus, W.D. 7
North American Free Trade Area, 26

Office of National Statistics, 120
Organisation for Economic Cooperation and Development, 26, 37
Peet, J., 3, 120
Pelletiere, D., 169
Perret-Gentil, J-C., 106
Phillips, C., 9
Phillips Curve, 58
pipelines, 23
Piskurich, G.M., 78
Porter, M.E., 33, 85
Pratt, J.H., 75
President's Management Council on Interagency Telecommuting Working Group, 87
principal-agent problem 92
product life-cycle, 33, 101, 107, 118

public transit, 4, 9, 10-11, 14, 17, 23, 24, 29, 47, 72, 83, 103, 161
Pye, R., 104

railways, 5, 17, 22, 23, 24, 45–6, 51, 139–40, 158, 161
   underground, 31
Reagonomics, 38
regulation, 57
Reiser, J., 74
Richter, J., 82
road pricing, 11, 68, 143–4, 150–1, 161
roads, 4, 11, 35, 45, 68, 103, 139, 146–50, 157
   traffic, 11, 17, 22
Rodrigo, C., 169
Romer, P.M., 169
Root, A., 28
route planning, 14, 113
Rowe, F., 62, 63
Rubin, R. 5
Ruhling, N.A., 75
rural areas, 25, 165-6
Russell, C., 72

safety, 60, 139–40, 142–3
Sala-i-Martin, X., 169
Salomon, I., 55, 63, 65, 76, 78, 81, 88, 104
Salomon, M., 65
Saloner, G., 14, 113
Saveri, A., 65, 72, 79
Schafer A., 82
school trips, 18, 30
security, 132–41, 144–5
Seth, J.N., 74
Shamir, B., 65
Shapiro, C., 57, 106
Shibusawa, H., 164
Shiller, R.J., 13,
shopping, 3, 30, 33, 61, 68, 76, 108, 114–115, 119-24, 160, 164
   malls, 19
   see also, e-commerce, business-to-consumer

Shulman, K., 74
sign-posting, 140–2, 144, 149, 152
Sisodia, R.S., 74
Smith, R., 74
Spulber, D.F., 118
Standage, T., 160
standardization, 46–7, 109–10, 151–2
stated preference analysis, 81–2
Stead, D., 2
Stepanek, M., 119
Stough, R.R., 2, 51, 127
subsidies, 50, 68
Sullivan, M., 10,
Sullivan, S.E., 65
Sun, X., 83
supply-chain management, 63, 113,
    117–18, 121–34
    see also, e-commerce
sustainable transport, 36–7
Sviden, O., 64, 94

taxation, 116
taxicabs, 24
Taylor, B.D., 85
Taylor, M.A.P., 145
Taylor, S.Y., 45, 119
telecenters *see*, work center
telecommuting; *see*, teleworking
telephone, 8, 14, 43, 61, 64, 76, 95,
    110, 113
Telework Analytics International Inc.,
    79
teleworking, 4, 10, 14, 24, 33, 55,
    60–89,
    see also, work centers
Telwork Emissions Trading Pilot
    Program, 88
ter Brugge, R., 123
Thatcherism, 38
Townsend, A.M., 169
traffic forecasting, 21–2
traffic signals, 9, 146, 152
Transportation Research Board, 152
travel time budgets, 82, 112
trucking, 17, 19, 45–6, 139
Turner, T., 84

UK Civil Aviation Authority, 38
UK Royal Commission on
    Environmental Pollution, 4
Unwin, K., 165
UPS, 119, 126
urban form, 155–71
    axial cities, 22, 45, 161–2
    concentric cities, 45, 100–1
    edge cities, 25, 163-4
    sprawl, 14
    suburbs, 25, 89, 161–2, 166
urbanization, 20–6, 33
US Bureau of Transportation Statistics,
    17, 18, 21, 23, 39, 62
US Department of Commerce, 9
US Department of Transportation, 61,
    74, 152
US Environmental Protection Agency,
    74
US Federal Highway Administration,
    72
US Federal Trade Commission, 124
US Post Office, 119, 121

value chain, 33–4, 85
value of travel time, 98
Varian, H. R., 57
Verbeke, A., 33
Vermunt, A.J.M., 122
Vernon, R., 169
Vickrey, W., 143
Victor, D., 82
videoconferencing, 61, 64–5, 90–111
von Thünen, J.H., 45, 60

Walters, A.A., 143
Wardrop, J., 51
warehousing, 61, 70, 84, 121-2,
    127–31
    electronic, 14
Westin, L., 62
Williams, B., 74
Williamson, O.E., 42-3
Wise, A., 159
work centers, 55
World Bank, 39

World Travel and Tourism Council, 27
Worldwide Web, 24, 113, 122–4,
     127–32
Wynne. R., 70, 75

X-inefficiency, 133

Yen, J-R., 84

Zook, M.A., 169